MARJORIE O'ROURKE BOYLE has published articles
on religion and intellectual history in such journals as *Vetus
Testamentum, Vigiliae Christianae, Recherches de théologie
ancienne et médiévale,* and *Renaissance Quarterly.*

This book examines how language informs theology in Erasmus'
methodology. Allying historical investigation and philological
research with the discipline of philosophy of religion, Dr Boyle
seeks to restore Erasmus as he was: not a theologian who was
parenthetically a humanist, but a radically humanist theologian.
She undertakes this by analyzing what she terms the 'grammar'
of his method: the linguistic principle which directs his
understanding of the nature and methods of theology. This is
discerned in the *logos,* the word for speech, for method, and for
God's method of speech for the divinization of men in Christ.

The book proceeds from Erasmus' controversial translation of
one biblical word, *logos* as *sermo,* to the fulfilment of his
paradigm in a theological republic. As well as providing an
extensive new analysis of the *Ratio verae theologiae,* it devotes
chapters to the first full examination of the *Apologia de 'In
principio erat sermo'* and to a fresh perspective on that most
popular of colloquies, 'Convivium religiosum.'

This stimulating and original study, illuminating the
contested subject of Erasmus' theology, makes a major
contribution to Erasmus studies and to the intellectual and
religious history of the Renaissance.

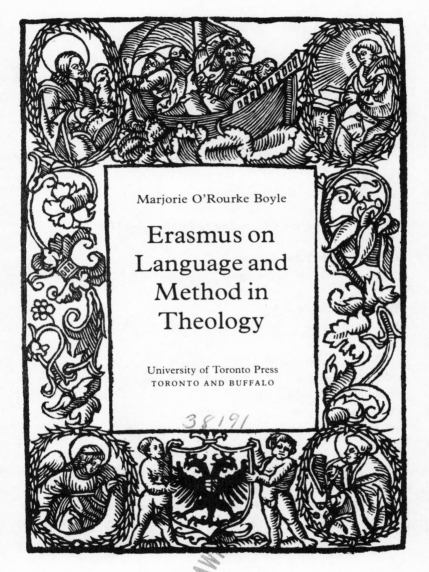

Marjorie O'Rourke Boyle

Erasmus on Language and Method in Theology

University of Toronto Press
TORONTO AND BUFFALO

Library of Congress Cataloging in Publication Data

Boyle, Marjorie O'Rourke, 1943–
Erasmus on language and method in theology.

(Erasmus studies; 2)
Bibliography: p.
Includes index.
1. Erasmus, Desiderius, d. 1536. 2. Religion
and language–History. 3. Theology–Methodology–
History. I. Title. II. Series.
B785.E64B69   201'.4   77-2606
ISBN 0-8020-5363-7

The decorated border on the cover and titlepage is from Erasmus, *De contemptu mundi epistola* (Antwerp: G. Vorstermannum, 1525) courtesy Thomas Fisher Rare Book Library, University of Toronto

This book has been published during the
Sesquicentennial year of the University of Toronto

This book is for the Big Bear

δῆλον γὰρ δὴ ὅτι οἵγε θεοὶ αὐτὰ καλοῦσιν πρὸς ὀρθοτήτα ἅπερ ἔστι φύσει ονόματα.

'For the gods must clearly be supposed to call things by their right and natural names.' Plato

Vides, ut in Christo noventur omnia et rerum vocabula permutentur.

'In Christ everything is created anew, and vocabulary wholly transformed.' Erasmus

❧ Contents ❧

❧ Illustrations ❧

❧ Prologue ❦

THIS BOOK IS A GRAMMAR, an exposition of the parts of speech and the syntax of Erasmus' theological methodology. Grammar here means the study of the principles of a science: its classical sense. Because the principles under investigation are linguistic, the word grammar is doubly suggestive, a figure Erasmus might have liked. The author conceived this book as a heuristic to determine whether an historical text on theological method might be illumined by an exposure of the linguistic concepts which inform it. For if, as philosophy argues contemporaneously, language is not the translation of a prior mental text but the act by which thought is thought, then it is imperative to discover the ordering of method by language.

From this philosophical matrix the book's oblique angle solidly joins with Renaissance studies, confirming Erasmus as a *humanist* theologian. The humanist community of the Renaissance promoted language and method so emphatically, at once so antiquely and so innovatively, that Erasmus of Rotterdam is an obvious historical test of the question: What is the grammar of method in theology? Scholars of Erasmus need not share the author's formal concern to detect the interplay of language and method in theology in order to read this book. It can be digested as intellectual history. But the author does define the book's formal intention more complexly as an experiment *about* method in theology, in the hermeneutical context of philosophy of religion, through the analysis *of* method in theology, in the historical context of Renaissance studies.

A single question rigorously directs the inquiry. How does

Erasmus' understanding of the nature and function of language inform his understanding of the nature and method of theology? It is not a question he broached overtly. An answer must induce what Karl Rahner styles the 'meta-historical connections between the individual lines of thought which appear explicitly.' By re-experiencing the texts, they are traced to their original intellectual event, here exposing that unspoken grammar which informs Erasmus' theological methodology. That grammar is discerned in the paradigmatic *logos*: the word for speech, the word for method, and the word since apostolic times for Christ, who is God's speech and method for the divinization of men. The four chapters of this volume are titled for four cognates of that *logos*: *sermo, oratio, ratio, confabulatio*. The plot progresses from Erasmus' concern for the translation of one biblical word to the fulfilment of his paradigm in a theological republic.

As Erasmus commended his manuscripts to the consensus of learned men of good speech, so I introduce this scholarship, inviting all readers to join the conversation.

❧ Acknowledgements ❦

THE AUTHOR WISHES to express her appreciation to Professor Harry J. McSorley, whose scholarly commitment generously heartened the writing of this book; to Professor James K. McConica, who introduced me to Erasmus and sustained my interest with lively colloquies; to Professor Walter H. Principe, my first graduate theology professor, for reading the first chapter; to Professor John C. Meagher for criticisms of an early draft; to the readers appointed by the University of Toronto Press for their suggestions and support. This book has been published with the help of a grant from the Humanities Research Council of Canada, using funds provided by the Canada Council, and a grant to University of Toronto Press from the Andrew W. Mellon Foundation

ERASMUS ON LANGUAGE AND METHOD IN THEOLOGY

ONE

❧ Sermo ❧

IN THE BEGINNING THERE WAS SPEECH, in that very beginning when God created the world. And everything God made, he made by speaking.

Then in February 1516 an undistinguished theologian, Erasmus of Rotterdam, published a Greek and Latin edition of God's New Testament.[1] Exhausted by a life's labour compressed into months,[2] he awaited the scholarly consensus of theologians. Already heartened by the approval of Leo X, pope and patron of the humanities,[3] his delight increased as congratulatory letters augured the 'way to immortality.'[4] By August he could boast to Johann Reuchlin, 'The New Testament has earned me many friends everywhere.'[5]

Not friends only. Some academic theologians were rankled by his boldness. He had, after all, never completed the course of theological studies at Paris;[6] and his only record of lectures was not a brilliant examination but a jocular note to an equally bored student.[7] Controversy flared into invective, and Erasmus was soon penning defences of his text, of his method, of his exegesis, and of his character.[8]

He admitted that the Novum Instrumentum had been 'hurried through the press rather than edited.'[9] He hoped a revised edition approved by Leo X[10] would make his enemies burst with envy.[11] Erasmus anticipated that it would also provoke accusations that he was dissatisfied with the former edition. Even if that were true, Erasmus rejoined, what crime is there in bettering oneself after the example of Origen, Jerome, and Augustine who also emended their works? He had stated in the first edition that he would correct it if the occasion arose. 'This first edition may be despised,' Erasmus allowed, 'if it were not that I have explained in it a number of passages in which Thomas Aquinas went astray, not to speak of other writers. Let my critics deny this, or refute it, if they can.'[12]

The text of Scripture should be as free from error as possible. Erasmus was convinced of that. His labour would not only correct the mistakes in the extant copies, but prevent future misreadings. And 'if to that controvertial theology, which is almost too prevalent in the schools, is to be added a knowledge of the original sources, it is to this result that our work especially leads.' With confidence that his effort would aid all studies and impede none,[13] Erasmus began his second edition.

No sooner had he determined to revise the Novum Instrumentum than he began to lament his decision. He longed for sleep; he day-dreamed of cloistered retirement in the company of English humanists where he might sing to Christ and the Muses.[14] The ingratitude of some theologians drove him to hate his work.[15] This revision became a 'treadmill' and a 'labyrinth.'[16] It nearly deprived him of eyesight and his very life.[17] But fate had cast his role, Erasmus sighed, and 'we must play out the play.'[18] He begged excuse from invitations and pressed on, in seclusion and under deadline.[19] The progress of good men would be his comfort.[20] He would please posterity or die.[21]

Erasmus was revising the first edition so extensively 'that it will be a different work.'[22] He adopted the plan for the third edition of adages, the Adagiorum Chiliades.[23] He multiplied the corrections of Jerome, added passages, and supplied more authorities in the annotations.[24] In a letter to the apostolic legate, Antonio Pucci, he outlines his method. First, he engaged in a sequence of philological tasks: after collating several copies of the New Testament made by Greek scribes,[25] he produced what he deemed the definitive text. Then he translated this into Latin, being careful 'to preserve as far as was permissible, the integrity of the Latin tongue without injury to the simplicity of the apostolic language.' This translation was juxtaposed to the Greek text, and Erasmus then began his second labour, the commentary. He writes, 'Our next care was to provide that any sentences which had before given trouble to the reader, either by ambiguity or obscurity of language, or by faulty or unsuitable expressions, should be explained and made clear with as little deviation as possible from the words of the original, and none from the sense.' Here he did not invent but relied on the judgement of the ancient authors, Origen, Basil, Chrysostom, Cyril, Jerome, Cyprian, Ambrose, and Augustine. He exposed more than six hundred passages by his own tally. 'We do not tear up the Vulgate,' Erasmus insisted, 'but we point out where it is depraved, giving warning in any case of flagrant error on the part of the translator, and explaining it where the version is involved or obscure.' He did not approve the reading of the Greek scribes in every case, and he indicated where orthodox Latin writers agree or disagree with the Greek text. This variety of readings, he thought, assists the study of Scripture and is no peril to faith.[26]

As the edition neared completion, he indecisively debated a journey to Basel or to Venice. He had to be present at the press to ensure a correct proof. Finally he opted for Germany's overheated inns, highwaymen, and plagues; at least, he supposed, he would escape the heat of the long Italian trip. But the sun was merciless on route to Basel, too, and ten days after his arrival on Ascension Day he contracted a sickness from the city's epidemic. The printing would be delayed. The second edition had 'doubly aged' him.[27] If God had published his Text with ease, surely human scholarship seemed but a faint imitation.

Despite those obstacles, Erasmus persisted in his commitment. The second edition of the New Testament finally issued from Froben's press in March 1519. Erasmus briefly notified his correspondents.[28] An eager admirer hailed it as humanism's passport to the world: 'Our victory depends on this, a prize of so many debates, of such labour, an ovation and a triumph.'[29] But even as his supporters praised him, his enemies rallied.

Erasmus' detractors seized one word to crystallize ecclesiastical opposition, to manoeuvre the civic power of England, to rouse the populace to a stoning mood. That rallying cry which stirred London, Brussels, and Paris was *sermo*. For in his new translation of the Johannine[30] prologue, Erasmus had dared to correct Jerome's rendition, 'In principio erat verbum,' to 'In principio erat sermo.'[31] Because of some 'superstitious dread' he did not take the translator's licence to alter *verbum* in the first edition, 'lest we give opportunity to those who misrepresent any and every occasion.'[32] But friends had persuaded him to be bolder in correcting the Vulgate, and to support his corrections with fuller citations from the Fathers.[33]

The charges which the inflammed scholastics levelled against him were two. The first, exemplified by the sermon of an English bishop, Henry Standish, raving in the churchyard of St Paul's London,[34] was that Erasmus had altered the traditional ecclesiastical reading: 'For when up until now for more than a thousand years the whole Church has read, "In principio erat verbum," now at last, if it pleases the gods on high, a little Greek somebody will teach us that we ought to read, "In principio erat sermo."'[35] The second charge, reported from the sermon of a Carmelite preacher in the Church of St Gudula, Brussels,[36] was that Erasmus 'has not feared to correct the gospel of St. John,' therefore condemning what the evangelist himself wrote.[37] Similar trouble stirred in Paris, as Erasmus learned from the letters of friends.[38]

Angered by their intellectual impudence, and alarmed by their political sedition,[39] Erasmus was pressured into a 'few words' of response. His humanist convictions about the colloquial nature of scholarship equally demanded his reply. The *Apologia refellens quorundam seditiosos clamores apud populum qui velut impium insectabantur quod verterit, In principio erat sermo* issued from Dirk Martens' press at Louvain in a quarto edition near the end of February 1520. An augmented version, almost tripled in length, was printed by Froben in August.[40] The defence included a characteristic grumble that his detractors obviously had not read his annotation of Jn 1:2 in the second edition, where he had already stated his grammatical reasons and the authoritative support of the Fathers.[41] So much ink spilled in controversy when he might be completing his paraphrases of Paul!

The argumentation of the apology is flanked by artful

description of the conspiracy against him, written with outrage that his reputation should be maligned before the ignorant, easily scandalized, populace.[42] Erasmus reproves his opponents for dragging before the common crowd what ought to be debated among scholars. The work was written for the learned, he asserts, in curious contradiction to the intention forwarded in his *Paraclesis* to the 1516 edition. There he had wished that his New Testament be available to commoners so that 'all can be theologians': weavers, farmers, tailors, travellers, masons, prostitutes, pimps, Turks, little women, and (even) the Other Theologians.[43] But suddenly the affair is to be *in scholis*. New lists are drawn of those Christians before whose poor judgement the question is not to be pleaded: weavers, tanners, businessmen, courtiers, and little women.[44] His altered attitude appears to reflect alarm at how easily common man, docile in his ignorance, may be beguiled by the authority of the pulpit rather than persuaded by that of the book. Erasmus reproaches his detractors bitterly and repeatedly for this resort to people's court. If they are not his murderers, then they are as complicit as Paul holding the garments of the rabble that stoned Stephen.[45]

Erasmus feared the bisection of the Christian commonwealth over the cause of good letters. The authority of the holy doctors of the Church wrestled with a wanton conspiracy of churchmen and mob for the helm of Christendom.[46] In a letter from his Louvain retreat dated the first of February 1520, Erasmus discloses to Thomas Wolsey, archbishop of York, the political implications of the *sermo* conflict.[47] And he publicly admits and justifies his resort to Wolsey's power.[48] Spiritual pestilence may be just as fatal as corporeal malady, he warns Wolsey, germinating as it does, not in the stars or in bodily infection, but in love of discord. And the principal sinners in this affair are those who, under the guise of begging,[49] meditate tyranny. One of these, he advises, is among you – a certain preacher who in public assembly shouted that Erasmus had intended to correct the gospel of John by replacing *verbum* with *sermo*. What more foolish declaration could he have made to an ignorant and seditious crowd? he asks. Erasmus seizes the moment to repeat his contention that *sermo* is the better translation. He implores Wolsey to protect the peace of sacred studies, not only in England but throughout the world. Exhort the Roman pontiff to check this licentious attack with his authority, he urges. Christian studies ought to contend by debate, not shouting. The protection of Wolsey's authority for the peace of studies would render great service to the Christian republic, he concludes.[50]

As for curing the intellectual impudence of his challengers, Erasmus marshals two arguments in defence of *sermo*: a bold transformation of the new philology into theological method, and a submissive appeal to Christian tradition. Together they undergird his renaissance of theological letters; the one, by innovating a radical textual method, the other by restoring an ancient hermeneutic, overshadowed by late scholastic[51] preoccupations. Their creative tension would mark him a Janus in the history of theological methodology.

Erasmus tersely advances his grammatical reasons for *sermo*. Sarcastically he informs his critics who scarcely know that John did not compose the gospel in Latin, that the evangelist in fact wrote *logos*, not *verbum*.[52] The Greek noun *logos* is polysemous, he explains, signifying in Latin: *sermo, verbum, oratio, ratio, sapientia,* and *computus*.[53] Erasmus reports that Jerome himself thought that all of these applied to Christ. As for himself, he wonders why Jerome selected *verbum*.[54] The distinctive usage of *sermo* and *verbum* by classical authors substantiates Erasmus' preference for *sermo*.[55] The noun *verbum* signifies a word or a brief saying, such as a proverb or maxim;[56] it is also frequently used to designate a definite part of speech, the verb, *rhēma*.[57] Its restricted application, therefore, does not satisfy the denotation of *logos* as speech rather than word. In order to approximate the meaning of *logos*, Erasmus explains, the noun *verbum* must be pluralized, as in the expressions *verba facere* and *multis verbis mecum egit*.[58] (Surely it would be misleading to translate, 'In principio fecit verba,' occasioning wild confusion about the number of sons the Father engendered!) Erasmus states his grammatical case: Latin authors more correctly, more aptly, and more customarily express *logos* as *sermo* than as *verbum*. Six times he forwards this:

Certainly it cannot be denied that the Greek word *logos* which undisputably the evangelist has used, more correctly and more customarily is expressed by Latin speakers through the noun *sermo* than through *verbum*.[59]

... the Greek noun *logos*, which the evangelist has used, is more correctly expressed by the word *sermo*.[60]

... *sermo* more correctly and more aptly than many nouns expresses the Greek noun than *verbum*.[61]

... since the word *sermo* is more perfect than many nouns, and even pleasanter, since it expresses the Greek noun *logos* more correctly.[62]

... but indeed the word *sermo* more aptly expresses the Greek noun *logos*, which the evangelist has used.[63]

... *sermo* more perfectly explains why the evangelist put *logos*.[64]

The grammar of *logos*, which means speech, and its rhetorical forum establish Erasmus' theological methodology and the subject of this book. For Erasmus, Christian theology (*Theos legein*) must imitate Christ (*ho Logos*). And Erasmus' grammatical analysis of the New Testament presupposes that this *Logos* has subjected himself not only to the laws of flesh, but of grammar also. A sentence in an annotation supplies the clue for investigation. In the note on Jn 1:2 Erasmus explains, 'First, *sermo* more perfectly explains why the evangelist wrote *logos*, because among Latin speakers *verbum* does not express speech as a whole, but one particular saying.'[65] Then follows the theological reason which discredits Jerome's translation, 'But Christ is for this reason called *logos*, because whatsoever the Father speaks, he speaks through the Son.'[66] Because the *Logos* is the copious discourse of the Father, the sufficient revealing oration, *verbum* is inadequate to designate him. Erasmus cleverly shifts the ground of debate from orthodoxy to grammar, and then from grammar to new mediation with the orthodox claim that Christ is God's full revelation. The disclosure and analysis of methodological implications of this translation is our project.

Such grammatical points are 'trifling,' Erasmus admits lightly to his readers, but 'nevertheless, as much as you please, a trifling swing to and fro sets the matter in motion, when otherwise it is in equilibrium.'[67] As every humanist who had been schooled by Erasmus' texts knew, the affair in equilibrium was Christian piety, deadened by scholasticism. Erasmus' supporters would have known that the grammatical points were far from 'trifling,' but rather a propulsion towards humanist theology. And if Erasmus interrupted his editing to defend a single word, and defend it so forcibly, then all had better perceive the conviction shielded by that playful word 'trifle.' For hadn't he explained in correspondence the usefulness of his trifles, approved so enthusiastically by the most serious theologians? And hadn't he confessed his own intellectual pleasure was 'to mix serious topics with my trifles than to show myself a trifler on great topics'[68] as did the scholastics? The schoolmen, he had also observed, think it beneath them to descend to the minute details of grammar. The name of grammarian is no reproach, he rejoined, nor does it credit a theologian not to know grammar. While 'mere knowledge of grammar does not make a theologian; still less does ignorance of it; and certainly some scholarship conduces to a knowledge of theology, while the want of it impedes such knowledge.'[69]

In both the *Annotationum in Evangelium Joannis* and the *Apologia de 'In principio erat sermo'*, the grammatical defence is presented first. But in the *Apologia* it is weighted by protracted appeal to the authority of orthodox doctors who also interpreted Christ as *sermo*. This shift in emphasis was necessitated, no doubt, by allegations of heresy. These forced Erasmus to align himself more assertively with the tradition of the Church by refuting the charge of novelty.[70] Any brandishing of his skill as a philologist would only have angered the scholastics more, incomprehending and hostile as they already were to the cause of good letters. Better to score in this forensic contest by quoting Thomas Aquinas in their faces.

Erasmus repeats that there is 'no difference' between *sermo* and *verbum*.[71] This cannot be sudden denial of his demonstration of the lexical differences between the two words. What he means is that there is no difference for orthodoxy whether one expresses Christ as *sermo* or *verbum*, since the Fathers use them interchangeably. The Church has not pronounced. Therefore, the issue is not orthodoxy as the scholastics suppose, but grammar in the service of eloquence: the correct and appropriate word.

Since the Church has not pronounced, the translation is not a matter for consensus, but one which allows variety. In the annotation of Jn 1:2 Erasmus had stated, 'My design lies in this: where variety is greater, more benefit proceeds.'[72] In his textbook on composition, *De duplici copia verborum ac rerum*, Erasmus had already instructed his schoolboy readers in the art of varying language by synonymy. Copious language is a 'divine excellence.' 'There is nothing more admirable or more splendid than a speech with a rich *copia* of thoughts and words overflowing in a golden stream,' he had instructed. Nature itself rejoices in variety. Men more eagerly examine what is polished new by the art of copiousness. Without the variety of Proteus, the whole profit of speech is lost upon a bored audience.[73] Why then, we may infer, should the Church, the community of divine oratory, weary men with homologous language? Copiousness is a sign of an eloquent Church. So Erasmus must have reasoned.

Synonymy is the first and simplest method of *copia*.[74] Surely the Fathers displayed wisdom in commanding a variety of Latin synonyms for *logos*. Because God is designated *pater* does not exclude for Erasmus his being called *parens*, or *genitor*, or *sator*. The designation of the Second Person as *filius* does not eliminate *natus*, *proles*, *germen*, or *progenies*.[75] A set of variables may properly substitute for one another. But however semantically alike two words may be, they must differ in some respect so that *omnes mortales*, for example, may not be substituted indiscriminately for *omnes homines*. Some words may be more becoming, more exalted, more polished, more humorous, more emphatic, more sonorous, more suitable for composition than others. Therefore, Erasmus instructs, 'discrimination should be exercised by one who is going to speak, so that from all, he chooses the best words.'[76]

Verbum and *sermo* may both be orthodox, for the Church has not designated any Latin translation of *logos* singularly correct, but *sermo* is the choicer word. This is the intention of Erasmus' defence, although it may have been wasted on the scholastics, trained in silly mediaeval grammars like the *Catholicon* and *Mammotrectus* which he loathed.[77] This argument that *sermo* is a copious alternative does not conflict with the argument that *sermo* is more correct than *verbum*. The two relate to different issues: the first to the ecclesiastical legitimacy of alternate translation, the second to the grammatical correctness of a particular translation. Variety by synonymy is Erasmus' response to the challenge of orthodoxy, a justification both theological and rhetorical against the scandal that he had dared to dispute the Vulgate. The apology for the superiority of *sermo* addresses a different question: once the principle of variety has been established, how best to render the text. That is the grammarian's lot.

Erasmus enlarges these arguments with two others. Surely, he persuades, the gender of *sermo* (m), which agrees with Christ, commends itself more than the neuter noun *verbum*.[78] He adds the rhetorical consideration that *sermo* is a softer sound than *verbum*.[79] These composite arguments sufficiently justify his translation, he states, without any appeal whatever to Christian tradition, 'even if nowhere until this time has the Son of God been called *sermo*.'[80] His defence of the right to translate is emphatic: 'I think that this was without a doubt free for me to do.[81] This declaration is modestly intended, however. His decision to correct both Jerome's translation and his own translation of 1516 does not negate his respect for the Church's authority. *Sermo* is not in his judgement a doctrinal issue, but a grammatical one. It is the province of translators, not of bishops. Yet Erasmus is cautious to conciliate his translation with the popular authority which the Vulgate had accreted from sustained usage. Particularly he needed to circumvent the opinion of those university theologians who declared the Vulgate inviolable, sanctioned by protracted reading in council and liturgy.[82] Five times in his apology and at the beginning of his annotations on the gospel of John also he reiterates that he only intended the translation for private reading in chambers.[83] He disclaims any intention to rival the publicly read version of the text.[84] His translation remains without official status, although he reminds his readers that it has the full approval of the supreme pontiff.[85] While it is naive to assume that Erasmus entertained no hopes that his edition would supplant Jerome's – his humanist reform aimed to produce purer texts to the Church – still he respected consensus.[86] 'It is not my right, nor that of others like me, to overthrow what has been received by public use.'[87] His own pronouncement of his edition's superiority could never make it so for the Church. He would wait for just recognition.

Happily Erasmus found ample theological support for his independent grammatical judgement. He parades a precedence of texts – biblical, patristic, and mediaeval – to the embarrassment of scholasticism and the glory of good letters. In Erasmus' apology for *sermo* the arguments from classical grammar and from theological literature converge. The appeal to grammar is not to a normative semantics, logically legislated by dialecticians in search of pure meaning, but to the usage of Latin-speaking men, what Latin authors wrote. Grammar is a form of tradition. The appeal may extend retrospectively to antique civilization, but nevertheless that civilization refreshed the conversation of Renaissance men with a dialogue established in texts. In Petrach's sentiment, 'They live and dwell together with us in conversation.'[88] As early as 1511 Erasmus had written in *De ratione studii* that linguistic skill was not to be acquired by learning normative grammar, but 'by intimate colloquy with men speaking in a restrained manner and by the assiduous reading of eloquent authors.'[89] Erasmus' recourse to the translation *sermo* in the Fathers is not to revealed doctrine, but to their own grammatical usage, their distinctive transformation of the vernacular into speech about God: theology.

The patristic texts are not merely offered as witness to the tradition of *sermo*. Erasmus underscores his challengers' ignorance of this treasury of the Fathers.[90] The humanist triumphs not only by his acute knowledge of Greek and Latin grammar, but also by his superior command of texts, the texts of Christian tradition. Erasmus simply has more texts than his opponents, a polemical weapon characteristic of his method in theology. His challengers have but one text. At least a statement of Augustine's is the only authority the preacher Standish summons, while the Carmelite friar is foolish enough to suppose that the evangelist himself wrote the Latin word *verbum*.[91]

This feeble appeal to one text, a caricature of scholastic method,

Erasmus disarms neatly. Standish had reminded his congregation that, although Augustine demonstrated that the Greek word *logos* signifies in Latin both *verbum* and *ratio*, the noun *verbum* better pleased the holy doctor for designating the Second Person in the disputed passage. The little Greek mimics have not understood Augustine's reasons, Standish alleged, and yet they have dared to contaminate Scripture with *sermo*.[92] In his retort Erasmus does not trouble to discuss Augustine's theological arguments, but merely points out that Augustine deals with *verbum* and *ratio*, not *verbum* and *sermo*. Therefore, he concludes, the text 'applies not at all to me, since I interchange *sermo* with *verbum*, not *ratio*; and thus I prefer *sermo*, as I do not reject *verbum*.'[93] Erasmus may be indebted for this defence to his lawyer and humanist friend, Thomas More, who advocated the same argument to Standish at a court banquet. When Standish stubbornly declared himself content with Augustine's choice, and uninterested in other authorities, More concurred about the unsuitability of *ratio* for the *Logos*. 'But what does that have to do with *sermo*?' More queried deftly, 'because Erasmus has not translated, "In principio erat ratio," but "In principio erat sermo." '[94]

Not only does Erasmus the humanist command more texts than the scholastics, but also he consults the best patristic editions, some of which he himself has learnedly composed.[95] Textual purity becomes a cardinal issue of the emerging humanism in theology. Thus in forwarding his first witness for the defence of *sermo*, Cyprian, Erasmus anticipates his detractors' counter-attack that he forged the passage when he edited Cyprian's works.[96] Erasmus suggests that to allay suspicion his contenders consult the ancient manuscript codices as well as other editions of Cyprian.[97] Cautiously he adds his awareness that in several codices *verbum* has been written for *sermo* in the relevant passages. This certainly was the fault of the copyist who relied on memory, he decides. He argues that unless *sermo* is read consistently, the demonstration will not correspond to the promise of its title, 'That Christ is indeed the *sermo* of the Father.' And the titles are not later additions, but mixed with the argumentation in the old codices; moreover, Cyprian himself acknowledges the titles elsewhere. Finally, Erasmus deduces, 'Cyprian either read, "In principio erat sermo," or thought there was no difference at all, in sum, between *verbum* and *sermo*.'[98]

This establishment of the authenticity of the text, a philological procedure which the scholastics resisted adopting, serves as an exemplar of method. Erasmus assumes the role of pedagogue to his detractors, not only by asserting a superior knowledge of Christian tradition, but more especially by demonstrating how a theologian ought to proceed. For the historical impact of waning scholasticism and emerging humanism was methodological, and only subsequently involved doctrinal dispute. Even a treatise like this *Apologia* for *sermo*, which is not professed to be methodological, should not be read as mere defence of a translation. Erasmus is always holding school. The apology for *sermo* demonstrates the mastery through grammar of the texts that comprise Christian tradition. That this is deliberate pedagogy is evident from Erasmus' juxtaposed caricature of scholastic method: one poor text and a silly syllogism.

Beginning with Cyprian, then, Erasmus proceeds windily to establish that Christ is called *sermo* in the canonical books; in daily Church usage; and in the writings of orthodox doctors, both ancient and more recent. This litany of approbation is sung several times.[99] The demonstration that Christ is called *sermo* in the canonical books coincides with the demonstration from the Fathers since they alone testify to the existence of no longer extant translations of the New Testament. The eloquent martyr Cyprian writes, 'In principio fuit sermo, et sermo erat apud Deum, et Deus erat sermo.'[100] Erasmus triumphs, 'Behold! they have the very passage about which they set in motion such tragedy; they have an author so ancient, by all standards so approved by the most acceptable men, that no man may contemn him.'[101] For measure Erasmus submits three more psalm verses and a passage from the book of Revelation, in all of which Cyprian thinks that the noun *sermo* refers to Christ.[102] Like Erasmus, modern scholars consider Cyprian a capital source of the Old Latin Bible, not only because of his antiquity, but also because he cites almost one-ninth of the New Testament.[103]

If this testimony should not satisfy the opposition, Erasmus advises them to consult Tertullian whose witness is unquestionably impartial. Referring to the disputed verse, Tertullian stated that the custom of the Latin people was to read, 'In principio erat sermo,' although he himself preferred *ratio* to *sermo*.[104] He also wrote 'quia et sermo caro factus' and applied one of the *sermo* psalms to Christ.[105] Erasmus next quotes the very Augustine upon whom Standish leans. Explaining Jn 17:18 'Thy *sermo* is truth,' Augustine mentions that the Greek gospel has *logos*, which word also occurs in Jn 1:1. While the Greek always has *logos*, he continues, the Latin codices vary between *verbum* and *sermo*. While some versions have 'In principio erat verbum' and 'Verbum tuum veritas est,' others have 'In principio erat sermo' and 'Sermo tuus veritas est.' But without discrimination, Augustine decides, this is God's Word, his only-begotten.[106] This is the witness of Augustine. Erasmus concludes that there were approved manuscripts with *sermo* in the Johannine prologue, and that his correction of the Vulgate is therefore consistent with the ancient faith.[107] Other passages in which Augustine applies *sermo* to Christ in the gospel of John, in the psalms, and in the Pauline corpus corrobrate this.[108] So do the writings of the ancient doctors Hilary,[109] Ambrose,[110] Jerome,[111] Lactantius,[112] and Prudentius,[113] he argues, as do those of the mediaeval scholastics Anselm[114] and Remigius.[115]

In case his challengers should be tempted to dismiss patristic witnesses because of their antiquity,[116] Erasmus presents the invincible ones, Aquinas, Hugh of St Cher, Nicolas of Lyra, Anselm of Laon, Anselm of Canterbury, and Remigius. First, Thomas: interpreting Heb 4:12, 'For the *sermo* of God is living and active,' he refers *sermo* to the Son of God. Erasmus cites his very words so the schoolmen cannot escape: 'Considered in itself, that word seems to present a difficulty, but if we consider another translation, the meaning is plainer. For where we have *sermo*, in Greek it is *logos*, which is the same as *verbum*; whence *sermo*, i.e. *verbum*.'[117] If Thomas appealed to the Greek text for clarification, Erasmus' contemporaries had long forgotten the ways of their angelic doctor; they would not have known Greek from Latin even if they had the manuscripts to consult. Erasmus also forwards other Thomistic interpretations which clarify that *sermo* and *verbum* may refer interchangeably to Christ.[118]

Nicolas of Lyra agrees,[119] Hugh of St Cher concurs,[120] the interlinear Gloss interprets the same verse of Christ.[121] But weightiest of all is the testimony of the ordinary Gloss, 'which has the most authority by the common consensus of theologians.'[122] Commenting on Heb 4:12 and on Wis 16:12, its author interprets the word *sermo* as the Son of God.[123] Neither can Anselm of Canterbury's testimony be dismissed, Erasmus decides. Explaining the disputed verse Jn 1:1, he not only terms the Son of God *sermo*, but also *dictio* and *loquutio*.[124] He corroborates Augustine's interpretation of Jn 17:18 as well.[125] Remigius, too, identifies *sermo* as Christ in his exegesis of Heb 4:12.[126] Nor does Erasmus doubt that, if he had the time, he could unearth 'innumerable examples' by which the mediaeval doctors called Christ the *sermo* of the Father.[127]

Not only are his opponents deaf to these orthodox writers, they are deaf at daily choir.[128] Erasmus' appeal to ancient manuscripts is capped by his appeal to the living text; that is, Scripture daily recited and received by the Church. 'Thus today the Church sings' completes 'thus have ancient orthodox men spoken.'[129] The noun *sermo* is repeated of Christ in daily office and recited in the schools, 'so that the word may be seen very frequently,'[130] he reminds his readers. As proof Erasmus summons mediaeval commentary on Wis 16:12 and 18:15. Thomas Aquinas accepts Augustine's interpretation of the omnipotent *sermo* of God (Wis 18:15) as Christ;[131] so do Nicolas of Lyra,[132] Hugh of St Cher,[133] and the author of the interlinear Gloss.[134] That *sermo* in Wis 16:12 also applies to Christ is stated by Hugh of St Cher[135] and the interlinear Gloss.[136] If I am condemned for blasphemy, Erasmus judges, then 'either before me, or with me, it is necessary that they damn so many extraordinary princes of the Church, Cyprian, Ambrose, Jerome, Augustine, Hilary, Prudentius, Lactantius, and with these, Thomas, Lyra, Hugh, the ordinary Gloss, *yes indeed the whole Church.*'[137]

This catalogue of the tradition serves also as background for Erasmus' refutation of a scholastic syllogism which had been constructed against his translation *sermo*. The intelligibility of this section of the *Apologia de 'In principio erat sermo'* is strained, however, by the haste of its composition. Citations run together pell-mell, and almost elliptical commentary forces the reader to supply the lacunae in his argument. Erasmus knew he wrote too hastily; 'I am by nature extemporaneous and exceedingly lazy about editing,' he confessed.[138] This fault must have irritated his scholastic readers, accustomed to reasoned architectonics.

Erasmus lampoons the Scotist[139] who attempts to refute his translation, not with grammar or text, but with a silly syllogism. Erasmus reports it:

> *Verbum* is a tacit concept
> but if Christ is rightly called *sermo*,
> it follows that *sermo* is also a tacit concept,

which he wished to make appear outrageously absurd, ' "since *sermo*," as he says, "is a concept expressed vocally." '[140] 'This,' Erasmus draws the reader aside, 'is the syllogism of an exceptional theologian, among the first, not only according to many others, but also in his own judgement.... What if,' Erasmus speculates, 'they who undertake by sophistic arguments to teach that Christ is correctly called *verbum*, incorrectly *sermo*, prove nothing other than that so many exceptional princes of the Church blasphemed?'[141] To the argument that Christ is incorrectly called *sermo* because he is correctly called *verbum*, Erasmus inquires whether it follows that Christ is falsely called 'light' or 'truth' because he is truly called 'word.'[142]

He reminds his adversary of the inadequacy of human language, which leads dull man to reflection on God. 'No human nouns express divine affairs in a proper sense,' he instructs. Expressing a theory of proportion, he writes, 'Several things are attributed to single things as if proper, which however are not proper to the true thing; but nevertheless, those are predicated more aptly concerning others according to the human mind's power of comprehension. We do it as often as it is necessary that we make full use of human words.' He schools the Scotist that the Son of God is neither a tacit concept nor a vocal expression. What the philosopher understands as a tacit concept of the soul is the Son abiding in the Father and one with him in essence. What the philosopher considers the sense of the soul as revealed by speech (*sermo*) is the Son always born from the Father and distinguished from him by property of person.[143] For Erasmus, then, the terms express different aspects of the Son, but not different realities. His argument with Augustine, in whose camp he evidently places the Scotist, clarifies this.

Erasmus proceeds to disprove the major term of the syllogism by demonstrating grammatically that *verbum* does not signify a tacit concept. He disagrees with Augustine's distinction between the internal *verbum* and the *verbum* which sounds externally. And he disagrees with Augustine's opinion that only the internal *verbum* was eternal, and that this became an external *verbum*, or sounding word, when the *Logos* assumed human nature.[144] Erasmus' correction of Augustine reflects Jerome's position on the unity of the eternal *sermo* and the assumed Man: 'Not that the assumed man is one [person] and the *sermo* who assumed is another, but that one and the same [person] according to a variety of causes is declared now humble, now sublime.'[145] 'Nothing forbids,' Erasmus writes, 'that the same word be uttered from the mind of the Father in various ways; he is uttered when he is begotten, the truest word, since most like the Father. He has been uttered when through that [word] the Father established the universe and by his word secured the heavens. But most solidly, and in the manner most familiar to us, he was uttered when assuming a human body, he spoke to us in human fashion.'[146] Erasmus then offers passages from Augustine which suggest this very truth.[147]

Erasmus omits for his reader, however, the fact upon which the full intelligibility of his demonstration depends; namely, that Augustine thought that the term *verbum* more properly belongs to the internal word, of which the *verbum* sounding aloud is only the sign. 'For that which is produced by the mouth of the flesh is the sound of the word, and is itself also called the word, because that inner word assumed it in order that it might appear outwardly.' So wrote Augustine. For Augustine the human analogue of the divine word is not the word sounding aloud, nor even its silent forethought. It is, rather, the 'word of a living being endowed by reason ... the word of the image of God, not born of God but made by God; this word cannot be uttered in sound nor thought in the likeness of sound, such as must be done with the word of any language; it precedes all the signs by which it is signified, and is begotten by the knowledge which remains in the mind when this same knowledge is spoken inwardly, just as it is.'[148] *Verbum* is the offspring of that knowledge then from which the thought is truly formed and at last expressed in speech. This somewhat Platonic understanding of language which Augustine sanctioned for theological speculation is the theory underlying the Scotistic syllogism which Erasmus attacks.

Erasmus regards the process of semantic transference to be the opposite of Augustine's attribution. *Verbum* is properly the spoken word: '*verbum* is better called what sounds than what is conceived by the soul.'[149] Further, what the soul conceives (the 'tacit concept' of the syllogism) cannot be called *verbum* by attribution unless it is vocalized. Erasmus quotes Durand of Saint Pourçain in support. 'It must be noted that *verbum mentis* does not have the meaning of *verbum* except insofar as it assumes the concept to be manifested.'[150] The soul's concept is only termed *verbum* because what the voice expresses is a sign of its mental condition; thinking is speaking to oneself, after a fashion. And if this condition may be called *verbum mentis*, Erasmus argues, then it also may be termed *sermo mentis*.[151]

Greek lexicology sanctions this transference, Erasmus continues, because *logos* still means *ratio*; and *logismos*, *cogitatio*; and *logizomai* *cogito* or *reputo*. But, he adds, the meaning of *sermo* approximates the denotation of *logos* as *ratio* better than *verbum* does. *Sermo* is derived etymologically from *serare* (to sow, beget), whence *disserare* (to speak). *Verbum*, grammarians think, originated semantically in the vibration of air, as in the sound from *boare* (to cry aloud, roar).[152] Erasmus catches 'Augustine' testifying against himself by accepting the etymology of *verbum* as the vibration of the air or the ear.[153] By implication then, the etymology of *verbum* does not include the thought which the word signifies, but only designates the rude physiological vibration. The major premise of the syllogism is refuted by grammar. *Verbum* is not a tacit concept, as the Scotist asserted, but like *sermo* a vocal expression. *Sermo* may apply therefore to the Son of God. If one wishes to refer to the tacit concept, the term *sermo mentis* is even preferable to *verbum mentis* because it approximates *ratio*.

And so, Erasmus concludes the argument of his apology, 'there is nothing which does not work for my behalf.'[154] He had striven to be inoffensive towards all, admonishing, complying, and pacifying both his learned and unlearned adversaries.[155] Had not Jerome forcefully mocked the Africans for overthrowing a bishop who recited to the populace an unusual translation of his?[156] Erasmus claims the same right to self-defence. Insisting that he has not altered the gospel any more than a man exchanging garments,[157] he now waited for his enemies to acknowledge the cause of good letters for the progress of Christian men.

The modern scholar, in command of a treasury of philological research, can only approve Erasmus' choice of *sermo* rather than *verbum* for the translation of the Johannine prologue. *Logos* means speech: a continuous statement, narrative, oration; verbal expression or utterance; a particular utterance or saying; expression, utterance, speech regarded formally. Both the New Testament and patristic literature in Greek preserve these meanings. Even in the classical lexicon, where other meanings were in ascendency, *logos* signified a phrase, complex term, sentence, or complete statement, in opposition to a discrete word (*verbum*). It was a continuous statement such as a fable, legend, story, or speech delivered in court or assembly. Rarely meaning a single word, *logos* could never signify grammatically a vocable (*epos, lexis, onoma, rhēma*).[158]

As Erasmus acknowledges, *oratio* is the Latin counterpart of this denotation of *logos*.[159] But its incongruity of gender prevents him from attributing that feminine noun to Christ,[160] and so Erasmus resorts to *sermo*. Of this Latin equivalent of *logos*, Varro had written: '*Sermo* "conversation," I think, is from *series* "succession" ... for *sermo* "conversation" cannot be where one man is alone, but where his speech (*oratio*) is joined with another.'[161] *Sermo* signifies a literary conversation, discourse, disputation, or discussion that is more informal and unpretending than *oratio*. *Sermo* signifies ordinary speech, speaking, talking, and the language of conversation, as opposed to *contentio*. Literarily it is used of satiric verses in a conversational style, as in Horace. *Sermo* is also common talk, synonymous with report or rumour, and extends in that meaning to slander and calumny.[162] During the fourth century *sermo* became the Christian term for preaching, including catechesis and exegesis.[163] Erasmus admits that the sense of familiar colloquy which *sermo* bears does not represent the force of *logos* as oratorical discourse.[164] But evidently this drawback did not outweigh the sexual disadvantage of *oratio*. At least he could be content with knowing that *sermo* means the speech of a nation, an application of no mean importance for a Renaissance humanist. And the colloquial sense of *sermo* included Christ's discursive partners in a fellowship that *oratio* did not explicate.

Erasmus' appropriation of *sermo* emphasized the speaking activity of the *Logos* as the Father's revelation to the forum of creation. While the restrictive format of annotation did not permit Erasmus to stray beyond grammatical justification and patristic quotation, he disclosed *sermo* with fully theological conviction in his *Paraphrasis in evangelium Joannis* of 1523. He revives that once familiar motif of men huddled in shadows waiting for the glorious revelation in Christ of the God of mysteries, which suffused Johannine letters and braced Greek patristic literature from Ignatius of Antioch to Origen.[165] Erasmus introduces the prologue to his lay audience with a discourse on the impenetrability of God to human reason, capped with the gospel announcement: 'No one knows the Father except the Son and any one to whom the Son chooses to reveal him.' Not to scrutinize divine mysteries, but to hold fast to this certain revelation preserved in Scripture, is the definition of Christian philosophy, writes Erasmus.[166] Thus the compulsion of faith finds its perfect intellectual complement for him in the humanist programme of textual edition and commentary, because the revelation of God, hence the meaning of man, is to be discerned singularly in this pronouncement, this *sermo*.

Without a glancing reference to Anselm's ontological argument, Erasmus states that sacred letters proclaim God as 'that highest mind, than which nothing can be thought either greater or better.' 'Thus,' he continues, 'they call his only Son, his speech (*sermo*).' The Son is not the Father, but reflects him in a kind of likeness, a likeness between generator and generated which perfectly surpasses human similitude. But what, Erasmus poses, expresses the concealed image of the mind more fully and more evidently than uncounterfeited speech? 'For speech (*oratio*) is truly the mirror of the spirit, which cannot be discerned with corporeal eyes.' Erasmus forwards the argument which every rhetor since Isocrates had promoted: If a man wishes to make his will known to others, he has no surer nor quicker recourse than speech fetched from the recesses of his mind. Through the receptive ears of the listener, by some occult energy, the spirit of the speaker is transferred into the spirit of the hearer. 'Nor is any other thing among mortal men more efficacious for stirring every affection of spirits than speech (*oratio*),'[167] Erasmus decides.

Now Christ is called the Son (*filius*), Erasmus explains, because although eternally one with God he may be distinguished by property of person. 'He is called the Speech (*sermo*),' additionally, 'because through him God, who in his own nature cannot be comprehended by any reasoning, wished to become known to us.' Through this eternally promulgated *sermo* God established the universal staging of the world, populating it with angelic intelligences and with the human race, a mean between spirit and beast. As omnipotent Lord he wished to publish his commands, and so he spoke creation into existence. Creatures would read his message in the admirable text of creation, and thus God by this strategem would 'insinuate himself into our affections.' In time God spoke again to man more solidly and familiarly in his Son Jesus Christ, twice born, now from the Virgin Mary, true man from true man.[168]

Erasmus cautions his reader that this speech transcends the human experience of discourse, and he buttresses his caution with reminders about the eternity and incorporality of divine *sermo* which echo patristic citations he had included in the *Apologia de 'In principio erat sermo.'*[169] There he had quoted the speculations of Hilary, 'Ambrose,' Jerome, Anselm, and Remigius on the application of *sermo* to Christ. This *sermo* eternally springs from the eternal mind of the Father, and as divine eloquence differs from the organic vocalization of human speech. It is a voluntary operation, a virtue of God's nature, 'the providence of the thoughts of God from the intention of the heart.' And echoing the poetic personification of Yahweh's *dābār* which extends into the oral traditions of the Hebrew people, *sermo* is the principle through which God created everything.[170] In the paraphrase on John, Erasmus catalogues heresies about the nature of this *sermo* and his relationship with the Father, painstakingly stating and repeating variously the orthodox doctrine of the eternal generation of the Son.[171] His paraphrase on Jn 1:1–3 then circles back to that luminary revelation which dispels the tenebrous peril of man. 'What therefore the sun is to material things, this divine speech (*sermo*) who is Jesus Christ is to mortal minds, which through sin having fallen down in a swoon into death's deepest shades, he zealously sought to aid by his ineffable charity.' For men used to live in ignorance, Erasmus adds, but now they have the light of eternal truth.[172]

What ancient christology has competed for more scholarly attention than the *logos*-doctrine? It needs no exposition here. To articulate their faith in Christ as God's revelation, *ho Logos*, the versatile Fathers borrowed from the Hebrew theology of *dābār*, from the inventive Philo, from the Stoic philosophers, and of course from the inspired New Testament. But although Erasmus was well schooled in the plastic *logos*-doctrine of antiquity, his own interpretation indicates no precise antecedent. By the year 1505 he claimed to have read most of Origen, whom he judged a quarry of original ideas and a master of the principles of theological science.[173] Yet Origen's celebrated theory subordinates the interpretation of *logos* as speech and designates *logos* as reason. It is 'that which removes in us every irrational part and constitutes us truly capable of reason.'[174] Modern scholarship asserts that Origen 'rarely conceives the relation of the Father and the Son on the model of the relationship between the understanding and its verbal expression,'[175] exactly the model which Erasmus thought so vital. The recent opinion of some Erasmus scholars that he is influenced by the Alexandrian *logos*-theology, especially Origen's,[176] ought to be abandoned then. In only two texts, both in the commentary on John's gospel, does Origen exegete the title *logos* as speech, and then only as a condescension to earlier tradition: 'Now it is possible,' he writes, 'that the Son may also be the *Logos* because he reveals the secrets of his Father, who is intellect in a fashion analogous to the Son called speech. For just as in us speech is the messenger of the intentions of the intellect, in like manner the speech of God, because he knows the Father whom no creature can approach without a guide, reveals him whom he knows, the Father.'[177] This argument approximates Erasmus', but it is not characteristic of Origen; it is Origen merely reciting the opinion of his predecessors.

Erasmus' specification of the *Logos* as the revealing discourse of the Father is more related to Johannine literature and to the theology of the second-century Fathers than to the later celebrated theories of Origen or Athanasius.[178] Ignatius of Antioch wrote, for example, that God is disclosed through his Son who is his speech sprung from silence,[179] and Justin Martyr claimed that the Son is titled speech because he transmits to men the message of the Father.[180] What distinguishes Erasmus' apology for *sermo*, the definition of the *Logos* as the *total* oration of the Father, suggests but one seminal text, however. In his polemic *Contra haereses*, which Erasmus edited in 1526, Irenaeus teaches that 'this Father of our Lord Jesus Christ, through his word which is his Son, through him reveals and publicises everything which he reveals.'[181] Except for the discrepancy *verbum*, which the Latin translation of the no-longer extant Greek manuscript offers, the argument coincides with Erasmus'. His apology for *sermo* is thus aligned with pristine theology, with the doctrine of Irenaeus whom posterity has venerated as the first Christian theologian. Erasmus restores the verse Jn 1:1 *ad fontes*.

The face of Christ which Erasmus delineates in his writings is as protean as the apostolic witness of the New Testament which accommodated divine revelation to human myopia: now this profile, now that. But its prominent features can be drawn into a litany which resounds the ancient chant of faith in the revelation of God:

> *Christos ho aggelos*
> *Christos ho didaskalos*
> *Christos to prosopon*
> *Christos ho logos*

Christ the envoy, Christ the teacher, Christ the visage, Christ the discourse. He is the revelation of the hidden God. In his paraphrase on that *comma Joanneum* (1 Jn 5:7) which provoked such inflated controversy, Erasmus defines succinctly the Persons of the Trinity in their economic roles. 'The Father is the author (*auctor*), the Son is the courier (*nuntius*), the Spirit is the prompter (*suggestor*).'[182] A Trinity of humanists all: writing, publishing, advising. Those modern Christians who lament that Eramus has exchanged the redeemer Jesus for a pale pedagogue[183] might reflect on the evangelical proclamation of Christ as the teacher of wisdom and bearer of good news: *to euaggelion Iēsou Christou*. Ancient Christian iconography depicted Jesus, not crucified, but book in hand, a master of disciples; and the early figures of him in bas-relief were copies of statues of classical orators.[184] Erasmus' textual portraiture of Christ is not one falsely adapted to humanist interest in pedagogy; rather, he adopted pedagogy as the excellent vocation because it was the role which God himself had assumed, teaching in flesh and voice the lessons of wisdom. A courier from on high, not an angel but a man, is God's own Speech figured into human discourse. Christ declaims oratorically in the forum of creation, teaching, delighting, and persuading Everyman to know the perfect mind of the Father fully and evidently in uncounterfeited Speech.

This interpretation diverged from the Vulgate's *verbum*, the single word grammatically abstracted from the context of discourse and audience. The justice of Erasmus' critical analysis of *verbum* may be verified by consulting modern lexicons. *Verbum* means one word; to gain the sense of speech (*logos*) it must be pluralized, as in *verba facere* and other idiomatic expressions. In the singular form its meaning may be extended to a *sententia*, but this usage is ante-classical; the widest range of speech which *verbum* properly embraces is a proverb. In grammatical parlance *verbum* is also a verb. The Greek counterpart of *verbum* is not *logos*, but *lexis*,[185] precisely a vocable that *logos* can never signify grammatically.[186] Erasmus studied well.

Jerome wrote no commentary on John which might explain that choice of *verbum* which Erasmus thought so astonishing. Nor does his homily on the prologue discuss this semantic issue.[187] By researching Latin patristic literature predating his redaction of the Vulgate, one discovers that the most ancient sources report *sermo*. Both Tertullian and Cyprian employ *sermo* in every direct citation of these opening verses of the prologue.[188] There is also the valuable witness of Tertullian that this was the *customary* reading.[189] If one accepts the modern theory of dual sources, North African and European, for the Old Latin Bible,[190] then Tertullian and Cyprian may only witness conclusively to the former tradition. No European patristic writings in Latin contemporaneous with Tertullian survive. *Sermo* remains the earliest extant translation of *logos* in Jn 1:1 and the reading in common circulation.

The first instance of *verbum* in the Johannine prologue appears to occur in the trinitarian tract of Novatian, a contemporary of Cyprian. Twice he records *verbum*, but once *sermo*.[191] Hilary cites the opening verses of the prologue nine times, and in each case the word is *verbum*.[192] By the fourth century *verbum* has gained universal preference in the West. Eusebius Vercellensis' treatise on the Trinity reports *verbum* in every quotation of the prologue.[193] His witness is relevant not only because he may have transmitted the oldest European version of the gospels, preserved in the codex Vercellensis (*a*),[194] but also because he prefixes his quotation with 'as it is written.'[195] Isaac Judaeus, writing his exposition on the catholic faith at about the same time, also quotes *verbum* in the Johannine prologue, prefixed with 'thus it is said.'[196] Zeno Veronensis reports *verbum*;[197] so does Maximus.[198] The prestigious Ambrose quotes *verbum* in eighteen different citations of the prologue, twice prefixed with 'I read' and 'he read.'[199] Meanwhile, the African author Lactantius quotes *verbum* as the translation for *logos* in Jn 1:1 in the context of his own demonstration that *logos* means *sermo* or *ratio*.[200] Arnobius preserves no fragment of the text,[201] while Marius Victorinus persists in preserving the Greek noun *logos* throughout his Latin hymns on the Trinity.[202]

As Erasmus demonstrated, Jerome's contemporary, Augustine, knew of two manuscript traditions, one which transcribed 'In principio erat sermo' and the other, 'In principio erat verbum.'[203] Was Augustine, a native of north Africa, privileged to codices of that regional tradition which Jerome never examined? Perhaps

Jerome was ignorant of the alternate translation *sermo*. Without transmitting an explanation, he chose *verbum*. He could not have anticipated that his translation would strike popularity and eventually win at Trent over contending vulgates, including Erasmus' editions. When the conciliar fathers authorized Jerome's translation, they also instructed that alterations be made.[204] The re-introduction of *sermo* to the Johannine prologue was not among the emendations. And so the Latin Church has read 'In principio erat verbum' since.

In defence of his edition Erasmus reminded his challengers that the ancient Church had maintained faith without the Vulgate. To the charge of his faltering friend Maarten Bartholomeuszoon van Dorp that the Vulgate had been adopted for ancient conciliar decrees and therefore must be preserved, Erasmus retorted, 'You write like one of our ordinary divines, who habitually attribute anything that has slipped somehow into current usage to the authority of the church. Pray produce me one synod in which this version has been approved.'[205] But pressure would force him in the fourth edition of 1527 to reprint the Vulgate adjacent to the text of his own translation.[206] Erasmus' hope that *verbum* would be supplanted has only been realized with an ironic suppression of *sermo* also. The emergence of vernacular translations during the Reformation and in the Catholic Church since Second Vatican Council has virtually eliminated the public or private reading of either Latin text.

Whether the translation of *verbum* for *logos* originated in lexical chance, or whether it gained for theologians some polemical advantage, is impossible to establish and difficult to assess. Belief in the sufficiency of Christ's mediation in the divine economy was reflected in trinitarian definitions of the distinction of the Son from the Father. There appears in Latin theology (and this is my speculation on a rationale for *verbum*) a confusion of the doctrine of revelation (*logos, sermo*) with the doctrine of the only-begotten (*monogenēs, unigenitus*) so that one Son has been conceptualized as one Word. Tertullian was the first to claim that the Persons of the Trinity are numerically distinct, although inseparable, and thus 'capable of being counted.'[207] But it was Augustine who, in exegeting Jn 1:1, equated one Son with one Word.[208] He essayed to disclose to the inquiring mind of the believer a Son who was the unique, singular generation of the Father. Preoccupied with distinguishing God's Persons against the modalistic claims of Sabellius and others, Augustine's argument lapsed into a theological reckoning of three-in-one; the problematic he had inherited, of course, from his adversaries. Whereas Augustine might have argued cogently and grammatically that the one Son was one Oration, the Son became for him one Word, the singular and undivided utterance of the Father. An interpreter has even read in Augustine's conversion an attachment to the single Word in deliberate repudiation of his career as a rhetor, a salesman of many words.[209] Although his seminal treatise *De trinitate* engendered a brilliant psychology of divine relationships, it never developed a phenomenology of the Son as copious discourse (*logos*), the full oration of the Father. Despite his own modesty about his speculations, his partial perspective on the mystery was wholly adopted and it limited speculation for centuries.

Anselm of Canterbury, who fathered scholastic method, was still explaining in the eleventh century that 'this expression [of the Spirit God] does not consist of more words than one, but is one Word.' The unity and indivisibility of the supreme Spirit dictate that his expression must be consubstantial with his nature. 'For, if it is so consubstantial with the supreme nature that they are not two spirits, but one; assuredly, just as the latter is supremely simple, so is the former. It therefore does not consist of more words than one, but is one Word, through which all things were created.'[210] Anselm did not recognize the inconsistency[211] in terming the divine *logos*, *locutio*, and then claiming that this consisted of one, single *verbum*. Thomas Aquinas canonized the confusion by arguing that because God understands himself and all creation by one act, only one Word is begotten. Aquinas' doctrine of *verbum* does express relationship and includes the Son as the Father's revelatory conversation with all creatures.[212] His term *verbum* cannot do so, however.

Patristic and mediaeval faith in the sufficiency of Christ was formulated also in the theory of the *verbum abbreviatum*. Frequently occurring in apologetic writings directed against the 'perfidy' of the .

Jews, is the argument that Jesus is an abridged word. The many words of the Hebrew authors have yielded to the one Word, Christ, in whom the entire Scripture uniquely converges. Theologians appealed to the verse, 'An abbreviated word God spoke upon the earth.' This term *verbum abbreviatum* equally denoted the immense Second Person who became concentrated in the Virgin's womb.[213] Here was another example of how theological concern to emphasize the singularity of Jesus exploited *verbum*, word, to the diminishment of the doctrine of *sermo*, conversation.

Verbum: this semantic indiscretion of the early Latin Church, undetected for centuries, is Erasmus' contention with the Vulgate translation of Jn 1:1 and its scholastic defenders. If the choice of *verbum* was not intended originally to support the christological and trinitarian speculations sketched above, it served those ends eventually. Labouring in the example of Lorenzo Valla, Erasmus believed passionately that only the appropriately correct word could flower into true theology; semantic error must necessarily generate theological error. Thus while he refrained from pronouncing *verbum* unorthodox, Erasmus was nevertheless convinced that this translation of *logos* eclipsed the ancient faith in a Christ who is the Father's eloquent discourse to men, leaving only a corona of truth visible to the trained eye. *Verbum* or *sermo*? The implications for theological method are substantial, for Erasmus held the *Logos* as the paradigm of human language, whose most eloquent expression was true theological discourse. A range of modern literature, too comprehensive to survey, underscores the vital relationship of model and method in the humanities and sciences. This fact did not escape Renaissance man either, least of all Erasmus. The archetypal word must be rendered faithfully, or the human enterprise fails. If theology is the verbal imitation of the divine *Logos*, then it matters profoundly to know whether this paradigm is one single word or a complete oration.

Erasmus did not deny that there was only one personal Son of the Father. But he did conceive of the Son as an eloquent speech, rather than as a single word. Augustine, Anselm, and Aquinas might have objected that *sermo*, a composite of many words, jeopardized faith in the simplicity of the Father's utterance. Either one could choose *verbum* for this trinitarian reason, safeguarding the simplicity of the Father's generative act, and distend grammar to serve theology. Or one could employ the grammatically precise *sermo*, faithfully rendering the biblical text, but restrict its theological application. Which compromise was better? Was Erasmus even aware of the theological dilemma? His apologies for *sermo* only record that he opted for the second alternative. He might have retorted that the unity of the Second Person would not have been compromised by *sermo* any more than the unity of an oration is compromised by its composition from many words. He might have added characteristically that theological language only approximates God's reality. The fact is that he promoted Scripture as the text to which Christian theology must correspond, and he expended his life in ensuring the precision of that text. 'The theologian derives his name from divine oracles, not from human opinions,'[214] he judged. Apologetic arithmetic was speculation. To argue whether there might be five words in God rather than one would be like imagining the *Logos* incarnate in a beetle rather than inhominized. Erasmus lampoons this silliness often and cautions reverence before the mystery of God.[215] What man may know of God is already disclosed in Scripture and in the Church's daily reading of her text. 'It is sufficient for us to believe, to hold, and to adore what has been written.'[216] Not to scrutinize divine mysteries but to scrutinize the text is the theologian's task.[217] And that text says *logos* not *lexis*.

TWO

⚙ Oratio ⚙

ALTHOUGH ERASMUS ALTERED *verbum* TO *sermo*, he would have preferred *oratio*, for 'nothing renders the emphasis of the Greek noun more aptly than *oratio*,'[1] had not the gender of that noun been incongruent with Christ.[2] Yet he does not trouble to exchange the equally feminine *via, veritas, vita* of Jn 14:16, for example, for masculine synonyms.[3] His attention to Jn 1:1 emphasizes its paradigmatic status. Erasmus' fastidiousness, which does not allow him to identify Christ as the feminine *oratio*, involves a neoterism, however. It establishes an agreement between signifier and signified which violates classical grammar. There is no sanction for his argument in the early latinists, nor in Niccolò Perotti whom he recommended as the finest contemporary grammarian.[4]

Varro had proscribed such confusion of natural and grammatical gender: 'In like fashion, we say, a man is called *Perpenna*, like *Alfena*, with a feminine form; and on the other hand *paries* "housewall" is like *abies* "fir tree" in form, although the former word is used as a masculine, the latter as a feminine, and both are naturally neuter. Therefore those which we use as masculines are not those which denote a male being, but those before which we employ *hic* and *hi*, and those are feminines with reference to which we can say *haec* or *hae*.'[5] Accepting Varro, most grammarians perfunctorily listed the genders, varying in number from three to seven, without speculation on origin. Any amplification consisted of rules for classifying gender according to nominative case ending.[6]

Diomedes, whom Erasmus considered the best of the old

latinists,[7] supposed, however, that a noun's gender conveyed to the listener the sex of the animal it denoted.[8] Priscian thought that the masculine and feminine genders reflected the plan of nature. In support he cited Varro's etymology of *genus* (gender) from *genero* (generate).[9] Marius Servius Honoratus,[10] Pompeius,[11] and Consentius adopted the observation. In his *Ars, de duabus partibus orationis nomine et verbo* Consentius divides grammatical gender into the natural and artificial, claiming that the natural genders reflect the division of the sexes in animal life. Then he offers what appears to be the first philosophical thesis of the origin of natural grammatical gender. The nouns themselves are not properly masculine or feminine, he explains; they reflect the sex of the bodies they represent. 'For nouns do not generate, but bodies, of which they are the names.'[12] In the eighth century Tatwin repeats this passage almost verbatim,[13] and the bond between grammatical gender and natural sex is cemented for mediaeval grammar. Should the angels be termed Cherub, Cherubim, Cherubin? muses the influential Alexander de Villa-Dei whose *Doctrinale* was the standard first-year grammar in the universities.[14] In his modist *Grammatica speculativa* Thomas of Erfurt attributes stereotyped sexual traits to grammatical gender: masculine nouns are active, feminine nouns are passive.[15] Siger de Courtrai, also a modist, asserts confidently that grammatical gender is derived from the process of procreation in which the male of the species possesses active power and the female is passive.[16]

Erasmus' scrupulosity about the gender of the Latin synonym for *logos* originates in this mediaeval embroidery on the loom of language. A noun reflects the thing it represents; and its gender, the sex of that thing. His rejection of the translation *oratio*, although he recognized it to be the accurate synonym for *logos*, suggests a concern for propriety.[17] Erasmus later will pen a dialogue (*Ciceronianus, siue de optimo dicendi*) on the propriety of Christian eloquence, playing the Ciceronians as a foil. The selection of a theological vocabulary, he will argue, must be measured appropriately by attention to the subject and audience of the discourse. It need not reproduce classical nomenclature.[18] What does propriety require for the translation of the *Logos* in the

Johannine prologue? Arnobius, for one, had argued against pagan anthropomorphism that the Christian attribution of masculine gender to God did not designate sex; it expressed the usage of everyday speech.[19] Erasmus might have reasoned, however, that the *Logos* was not neutral, but personal. That person was disclosed historically in the man Jesus of Nazareth. Was it proper to term God's Son *verbum* (n) or *oratio* (f)? Judged by that mediaeval rule of gender, neither of these nouns would be aligned with the Christ whom they were meant to signify. If linguistic integrity was essential, so was the canon of decorum. Grammar yielded to the advice of rhetoric, and *logos* became *sermo*.

This discrimination of the apt word for the communication of reality was to be enhanced by correct pronunciation and proper orthography.[20] Erasmus' programme was an inclusive one in which the oral sounding and the visual transcription of speech were to reproduce reality sensuously, as did the grammatical choice intellectually. His reform of pronunciation recalls the resonance of the forum and the classical canons for persuading the minds of the listeners through their ears. The orator was to regulate the tone of his voice and choose his words judiciously in order to effect a euphonious combination of sounds, appropriate to the subject and circumstance of the discourse.[21] Cicero advised 'the pleasing elegance of a sonorous and smooth vocabulary' and 'combinations of words that avoid rough collisions of consonants and gaping juxtapositions of vowels.'[22] Erasmus' rhetorical argument that the noun *sermo* sounds soft or smooth, whereas *verbum* is harsh,[23] is not parenthetical then. The sibilant and labial consonants of *sermo* persuade the ear to Christian faith more gently than do the fricative and plosive consonants of *verbum*. This aural impact of speech was to be complemented by its visual transcription. The first edition of the Novum Instrumentum, plagued with typographical errors, was more than an eyesore to Erasmus. A careless amanuensis and pied type had conspired not just to spoil the appearance of the folios, but also to confound the very comprehension of things. Erasmus galloped to Basel and endured the epidemic with conviction. He had to be present at Froben's press to ensure a correct proof. He had to see with his own eyes that movable type which imaged eternal truth.

The act of naming invests scholarship with gravity for Erasmus. He does not exploit Adam's naming of the paradisal animals as the primal expression of human hegemony; that biblical sanction for the act of naming was to be revived later by the curiosity of eighteenth-century men in the origin of language. A good part of erudition he thought, nevertheless, was to know the vocabulary of things.[24] The scholastics were betraying their ignorance by confusing fish for gem, trousers for cabbage, and thus frustrating the truth of Scripture. 'What does it profit you,' Erasmus jibes, 'to have arranged a syllogism in *Celarent* or *Baroco*, disputing about a crocodile, if you do not know what genus of tree or animal a crocodile may be?'[25] Erasmus lamented the neglect and disrepute of grammar among the scholastics. They think it beneath themselves to descend to the minute details of grammar, he had observed.[26] In the monasteries scarcely three months is devoted to letters, and then the theological candidate is whisked on to sophistry and dialectic. The schoolmen flatter every profession with an academic badge of dignity, 'but a grammarian is nothing other than a grammarian, just as a shoemaker is nothing other than a shoemaker.'[27] Indeed, if the theologians who had attacked his substitution of *sermo* for *verbum* had troubled to examine even mediaeval grammars, they would have discovered that *sermo* was a common translation of *logos* in etymologies of words with a *logos*-stem (including *etymologia*).[28]

Erasmus' pedagogical reform of theology would strain to re-establish the panoply of knowledge which had marked the ancient *grammaticus*. The theologian ought to be learned in arts which might assist with the interpretation of the divine text. He ought to peruse Theophrastos' *De plantis, ventis, ac gemmis*; Seneca's *Naturales quaestiones*; Nicander's *De noxiis bestiis*. Especially he ought to learn from the humanities the names of things which occur in the sacred texts because 'not rarely from the very peculiar nature of the thing depends the comprehension of the mystery.'[29] The theologian ought not to shirk the plodding task of grammar. In minute details which appear frivolous there is more than a little usefulness.[30] 'Things of no special worth in themselves may perchance be recommended by the genius of eloquent men, as the little light derived from a star may be increased by bringing in a lantern.'[31] It is better to mix serious thoughts with trifling subjects than to trifle with subjects of importance was Erasmus' advice.[32] The implication was that, as in the gospel parable of the pounds, the steward faithful in little things would be rewarded with many.

Erasmus defended his Novum Instrumentum against the charge of humanist Guillaume Budé that it loitered in grammatical subtleties by conceding Budé's opinion. He estimated his own genius and pleasure as 'born for small details.' 'I find everything of mine trifling,' he replied in correspondence, 'and often wonder in my own mind what there can be that some people praise so highly.' Rather he deserved praise, he thought, for acknowledging his intellectual limitations and for selecting tasks suited to his poor talents, when he might have pretended magnificence. Erasmus declared himself concerned with the utility, not the splendour, of scholarship, and he pledged himself not to despise the meanest task which might promote honest study. And, he reminded Budé, 'these trivialities, such as they are, are welcomed by the most authoritative theologians, and they say they have derived a flood of light from them.'[33]

The name grammarian is no reproach, Erasmus assured his public. For a theologian not to know grammar is no accolade. While 'mere knowledge of grammar does not make a theologian; still less does ignorance of it; and certainly some scholarship conduces to a knowledge of theology, while the want of it impedes such knowledge.'[34] Erasmus indicated the splendid example of Valla, who while burdened with the epithet 'grammarian,' illuminated the New Testament.[35]

When a commentator discusses a form of expression, does he act the grammarian or the theologian? Erasmus asks. Emphatically he decides, 'Indeed this whole business of translating the Holy Scriptures is manifestly a grammarian's function. Nor indeed is it absurd if in certain spheres Jethro has greater competence than Moses. But I do not really believe that Theology herself, the queen of all the sciences, will be offended if some share is claimed in her and due deference is shown to her by her humble attendant Grammar; for, though Grammar is of less consequence in some men's eyes, no help is more indispensable than hers.' Answering the insistence of some theologians that interpretation depends upon the influence of the Holy Spirit, and not upon the laws of grammar, Erasmus repeats Jerome's distinction between the gifts of prophecy and interpretation. In prophecy, the Spirit foretells the future; in interpretation, discourse is understood and translated by an erudite command of language. 'Again', he poses rhetorically, 'what point would there be in advice from Jerome himself on the proper method of translating the Scriptures if the power to do so is bestowed by divine inspiration?' The errors which exegetes and scribes have committed must not be imputed to the Holy Spirit. Just as human ignorance or carelessness caused textual perversions, so they ought to be corrected by an equally human diligence.[36] The sagacious theologian will graciously accept the assistance of grammar to explicate the sense of the biblical text.

Especially the theologian ought to gather from the humanities a knowledge of the names of things which occur in Scripture. As Erasmus observed, 'Not rarely from the very peculiar nature of the thing depends the comprehension of the mystery.' The name is the index of the reality. In his early treatise *De ratione studii*, Erasmus had noted that knowledge is double: of things and of words.[37] Unlike the dialecticians of Plato's republic, pressing to know reality itself without words,[38] the pupil of the Christian commonwealth was to apprentice himself to language.[39] Did not truth proceed from God's mouth? was not Christ himself a divine language? Erasmus did not commend those who scrambled to learn truths but neglected their artful expression. 'For things,' he philosophized, 'are only intelligible to us through vocal signs; he who is unversed in the signification of speech is blind also in the discernment of things; necessarily he hallucinates, he is delirious.' Those men who pretend to behold reality bare, declaring that they ignore its language, are the very ones who quibble most sophistically about verbal particles, Erasmus noted.[40] For Erasmus this claim characterizes the schoolmen, who choke on the words they seek to transcend.

The programme of reform was clear. A pupil ought to learn the best of both kinds of knowledge, words and things, and that from the best sources. In the study of the trivium, grammar must precede logic; a mastery of Greek and Latin establishes the better foundation for the pursuit of truth.[41] The ability to speak, Erasmus notes, is easily acquired by practice. Parents and nurses bear the responsibility for the first instruction in speaking clearly and accurately. It is through neglect of this early training in speech that the discipline of theology has become corrupt or extinct. The child schooled at his mother's knee, and reinforced by suitable tutors, servants, and playmates in refined conversation, is the clay from which the great theologian is moulded. The plastic mind and tongue of the child may easily acquire facility in the sacred languages necessary for true theology to flourish.[42] Erasmus could indicate successful case histories of men, like Rodolphus Agricola, who began studying Hebrew in middle age. He could profer his own foray into Hebrew, which had inspired John Colet to learn Greek 'though I am almost an old man.'[43] He could encourage the theological candidate to pursue such example, at whatever age, rather than to rely second-hand on sordid dictionaries.[44] But the ideal education of the theologian, he stressed, began at infancy with training in dignified speech. No age was too immature for learning to speak for this composed a man's nature, as did a bitch training her puppies to fawn or to chase a hare.[45] The acquisition of the biblical languages consisted entirely of memory and imitation, and, as Erasmus commented, children not only imitate easily by natural instinct, their memories are tenacious. What syntax the elderly man learns today, he can scarcely recall two days later.[46]

For this first education to humanity, 'a certain native pleasure of imitating, whose vestige we see in starlings and parrots, attracts the babes.'[47] The exercise of speech springs from the animal instinct of imitation with which nature has endowed the infant.[48] The imitative progress from prattling to intelligible discourse is, then, the first ratiocination of animal instinct, the first expression of human nature. What distinguishes man from beast is reason (*ratio*), as every literate man in sixteenth-century Europe knew, if not from philosophical convention, then from the popular *Enchiridion militis Christiani*.[49] Erasmus' literary attempt to nurture a brutal soldier into a manly Christian focuses on this tenet. Virtue's method is to know oneself and to act according to the dictates of reason, not the instincts of animality. Erasmus reminds his reader, enslaved like a dumb brute to his appetites, of this vital distinction.[50]

It is speech, Erasmus had said, which first manifests the triumph of humanity over animality. Erasmus equates the philosophical term *ratio* with the Pauline expressions 'spirit,' 'inner man,' and 'law of mind.'[51] Good speech exhibits the ascendency of spirit. Jesus' own disciples called his discourse 'words of life' because it sprang from his soul, in communion with God who was restoring man to immortality.[52] Just as Jesus spoke from this interior communion with God, so the Christian's language should reflect the spiritual integrity of the inner man. As Socrates commanded, 'Speak, that I may see you.'[53] As the gospel teaches, 'from the abundance of the heart a man speaks.' If God dwells within a man, he will speak a living language.[54] If a man speaks this living language, he reveals the God who dwells within him, like Christ orating the Father.

In contrast to the living language which the interior spirit prompts, there is the corrupt speech of the body. Such speech deflects the revelation of human nature and its divine origin. The instinctual animality of man is the 'flesh,' 'body,' 'outward man,' or the 'law of bodily members,' again in Pauline terms.[55] Obscene or malicious language indicates the dominance of brutality. 'The heart is a tomb and the throat and mouth comprise the opening to it,' Erasmus imagines. 'Suppose you hear some fellow using language that is lewd, arrogant, scurrilous, shameless, foul – railing with rabid invective at his neighbor. Do not think for a minute that that man's soul is living: a stinking corpse lies in the sepulchre of his heart, giving off a stench that infects anyone close by.'[56]

Language is the index of reason, and therefore of moral character, which reason directs. It measures humanity. Like Isocrates, Erasmus too considered speech the mark of an understanding man, a reflection of character, an outward image of the inward virtue of the soul.[57] The Creator had conferred speech on man so that through this medium he might become self-aware of his human nature and comprehend the spiritual intentions of other men.[58] This creation of man in God's image, with the power of revelation through speech, imitates the eternal generation of the *Logos* as the image and discourse of the Father. The temporal incarnation of the

Logos is, in turn, analogous to the revelatory power of human discourse. 'For that reason,' Erasmus explains, 'the Son of God, who came upon earth so that through him we might know the mind of God, wished to be called the Father's conversation (*Sermo Patris*).'[59] The gift of speech mediated man to man; the gift of Speech mediated man to God. The recreated consort of divine and human societies in Christ is a dual mirror in which God and man catch the vestiges of one another. Christ, as discursive revelation, is a two-way glass in which man glimpses the Father's light and sees reflected his own nature, destined for divinization. In Christ the Father beholds the perfect image of himself, and traces the outline of man, being ever-transformed by grace from shadow to light. God commands man, 'Speak, that I may see you.'

When a man speaks well, God may admire the mirrored image of his own oration, Christ. The divine *Logos* is the archetype of human discourse. God as the supreme artist impresses his likeness in the image of his Son, a perfect resemblance, who then in absolute simplicity and truth allows 'no jarring note at all to mar the resemblance between the archetype of the divine spirit and the likeness of it described in his words.'[60] There is no mendacity in this *sermo* of the Father which copies his eternal mind in perfect truth.[61] This very archetype is also impressed in the human spirit, 'in which we assuredly express our resemblance to the nature of God, upon which the supreme artist inscribed with his finger the eternal law of righteousness from the archetype of his own mind, that is, according to his own spirit. By this we are cemented to God and made one with him.'[62]

The same divine *ratio* and its expression in *oratio* which describes the relationship of the Son to the Father is copied analogously in the relationship of the sons to the Father. The Father's generation of the Son is complemented in creation by the human mind: 'What in divine affairs is the Father generating from himself the Son, is in us the mind, the seat of thought and speech (*sermo*).' The Son's being born is complemented by human discourse: 'What in that case is the Son being born from the Father is in us speech (*oratio*) issuing from the spirit.'[63] This is the doctrine which Erasmus professes in a treatise on language, *Lingua, sive de usu et abusu*. As he has also argued in his paraphrase on the Johannine prologue, uncounterfeited speech reflects the spirit perfectly. It was because the Father wished to make his mind known that he spoke its true image, his Son.[64] As often as a man speaks truly then, it must be inferred, he expresses his resemblance to God in a bond of filiation. He repeats in the temporal order of creation the Son being eternally spoken by the Father. As often as a man speaks without deceit he aligns his expression with its spiritual source and so imitates by fulfilling nature's own law the divine *Logos* who perfectly reveals his origin, the Father who speaks him. Good language is the imitation of Christ.

By the mid-fifteen twenties Erasmus has telescoped the convention that speech exhibits the rationality which marks human nature. In the *Dialogus de recta latini graecique sermonis pronunciatione,* the biblical Bear and Lion note that man shares his form with statues and his spirit with beasts. But the learned Lion is persuaded by reading Galen that 'man is distinguished from other animals, which we call speechless, not by reason (*ratio*) but by speech (*oratio*).'[65] No doubt Lion had learned his Galen from the Latin translation which the great Erasmus had so thoughtfully just published for the edification of men.[66] Erasmus must have judged Europe to be sparsely peopled. So many men prefer to express their animality rather than their humanity, he observed, that the continent more resembles a menagerie than a commonwealth. Lion reports, 'I see that very many speak not with human voice, but bark with the dogs, whinny with the horses, grunt with the pigs, moo with the cows, yelp with the foxes, shrill with the crickets, groan with the camels, trumpet with the elephants, gnash with the wild boars, roar with the panthers, growl with the bears, bray with the asses, bleat with the sheep, honk with the geese, chatter with the woodpeckers, caw with the crows, croak with the ravens, rustle with the storks, whistle with the swans; indeed they resemble any kind of animal whatever rather than speak in a human manner.'[67]

A scholar who observes the criticism which the earlier humanist Konrad Celtis directs at the schoolmen, that they 'cackle like geese and confound the ears like mooing cows,' supposes that this is the 'mere "huff and puff" of humanist lupinity,' an illustration of the humanist temperament 'which tells us little of the issues' which prompted such 'outpourings of eloquence.'[68] On the contrary, this animal imagery displays the very issue of the humanist attack on the scholastics. Erasmus' criticism of the barbarism of scholastic language is a fundamental judgement on the inhumanity of its speakers. To low with the cattle or chatter like magpies is to confound the order of creation. Yet the only book on Erasmus' position towards scholastic method ignores the language question.[69] Another theologian claims that the humanist charge that scholastic style lacked harmony and elegance was diversionary, a 'pretext' for a more essential attack on the ignorance of scholastic method.[70] This is not the case. Erasmus' charge capsulized the total indictment. To accuse the scholastics of barbarous language was not merely to criticize their rhetorical inelegance. Because humanist doctrine proclaims speech as the essential expression of human nature, any indictment of language implies an allegation of rational and moral corruption. 'Speak, that I may see you.' Barbarous language is a condemning manifestation of inhumanity, the sign of reason and spirit gone awry. It marks the failure to imitate Christ's generation and so for Erasmus cannot be termed Christian or be suited for theological discourse.

If speech distinguishes man from beast, then the bestiality of scholastic language is an indefensible indictment. By ridiculing the parroting speech of the schoolmen,[71] Erasmus suggests that their intellectual growth is stunted in animal mimicry. Their discourse is babyish. Two favoured epithets of his for the schoolmen, particularly for his enemies, are 'they stammer' and 'they bark.'[72] Every time Erasmus publishes, the schoolmen yelp. They are raucous, unintelligible animals, excluded from the fellowship of holy and eloquent men. Their 'barking' betrays their instinctual animality, untutored in humanity. In his exegesis of the adage *Canina facundia* Erasmus reflects on its classical denotation of those who slander the study of eloquence by dog-like brawls. Saint Jerome, Erasmus recalls, labelled his detractors 'dogs' for this reason. Such men belonged to the class of philosophers who either on account of a sordid life or because of their bite lived by soliciting like dogs.[73] Erasmus himself was often bitten by such mendicant philosophers and he called these modern cynics, barking dogs. Sometimes he judged his

critics more lupine than canine: wolves caught by the ear that one
could neither overpower nor release, fawning in his presence but
back-biting.[74]

In the 'Epithalamium Petri Aegidii' the Muses journeying to the
wedding are questioned:

> ALYPIUS: Where do you go in such array and with such joy? Not
> paying a call on the University of Louvain, are you?
> MUSES: Don't mention *that* if you please.
> ALYPIUS: Why?
> MUSES: What have we to do with that place where so many swine
> grunt, asses bray, camels bleat, daws scream, magpies chatter?[75]

Or, could any reader of the colloquies forget the vision of Reuchlin
sweeping into heavenly apotheosis, pursued by Dominicans?

> BRASSICANUS. Far behind, he said, some birds followed, black-
> feathered save that with wings spread they displayed yellowish
> plumage (more yellowish than white). In color and in cry they might
> have passed for magpies, except that each one was the size of sixteen
> magpies; they were as big as vultures, with crests, hooked beaks, and
> talons, and puffed-up bellies. Had there been only three of them,
> they might have been taken for harpies.[76]

Reuchlin dismisses the screaming birds with the sign of the cross.
'Be off, you accursed pests, to where you belong. You ought to be
working mischiefs on mortals; your madness has no jurisdiction
over me now that I am enrolled among the immortals.' Reuchlin is
hailed as a colleague by holy Jerome, who appears as a dignified
elder, not feathered like the Dominican theologians, but robed in a
crystalline gown which is decorated with dazzling tongues of fire to
signify the three sacred languages.[77]

More leniently Erasmus admits the schoolmen to the human
race, not as adults, however, but as babies who stammer in animal
imitation. Thomas Aquinas might have retorted that for theological
discourse stammering is the only possibility.[78] Erasmus would have
conceded that some human imitation of divine eloquence is
stammering: God babbles to our infancy and we babble back. The
wisdom of God may accommodate itself to men by childish

stammering, Erasmus explains, just as a solicitous mother suits her speech to a babe's inadequacy. 'But naturally,' he continues his instruction, 'you should hasten to mature ... Wisdom stoops to your incompetence; but you, conversely, should mount upward to her sublimity. To be always the infant is unnatural.'[79] Are not theologians to be men, grown to full stature in Christ?

The oratorical failure of the scholars who bored Erasmus in the lecture hall was failure through neglect and contempt of language and not failure through frailty. A man must strive for theological eloquence to complement his humanity, surpassing baby-talk. He acquires this eloquence through the imitation of the paradigmatic oration, Christ the Son, God's own persuasion. From zoo to republic, from nursery to forum, is the direction of Erasmus' reform of society through language. Every scholar who has pursued Erasmus' humanism recognizes his insistence on imitation of the authors as the educational programme. Through the copying and embellishment of the best-speaking men, what Latin authors wrote, the mediaeval schoolboys would revive civilization. They would progress beyond mimicry to that mature imitation, emulation, which marks the eloquent man. Erasmus' confidence in the method of imitation shared the enthusiasm of all humanists for this classical ideal, even if he did not sanction its extravagances or scruples. While the flourishing of imitation in the Renaissance, as the Renaissance, needs no rehearsal, its relation to theological language deserves some attention.

What is theological imitation for Erasmus? how is the Father's creative oration which is his Son to be reproduced humanly? Theologians are not to suppose that they gain immortality by the reproduction of words. Erasmus scores the theological discourse of the self-styled Ciceronians as infantile. Pretentious men ape the language and style of Cicero just as toddlers ape the speech patterns of mentors. 'Monkeys' is the shared epithet of babes and Ciceronians.[80] In infants such animal mimicry is a natural instinct; in adults, a retardation. Erasmus lavishes his satiric wit on linguistic nonsense, mocking those contemporaries who have exchanged Christian heaven for the Olympus of Jupiter Optimus Maximus. Although he was attentive to correct usage, Erasmus did not share the sort of scruples that the scholastics who condemned his New Testament edition because of *sermo* displayed, or the Ciceronians who damned an entire volume, however elegant, on account of one non-Ciceronian particle.[81] Despite his fastidious dedication to the demands of grammar, he did not consider language ritualistically, as if the correct word magically evoked the desired reality. The subtle and seraphic doctors, haggling over what words must be pronounced of Christ, were scandalous. 'As though,' Erasmus rejoined, 'one is dealing with some wayward spirit who is evoked to your own destruction if prescribed words are not carefully followed and not, instead, with the most merciful Saviour.'[82]

Since it is the *Logos* who serves as paradigm of human discourse, Erasmus' view of the attribution of words to Christ must be normative for his linguistic theory. Who is Christ but 'the most merciful Saviour' and not a god to be conjured by words? If Christ was the restorer of human nature, as Erasmus confesses,[83] then he was also the renovator of its essential manifestation: speech. Erasmus teaches that 'in Christ everything is created anew, and vocabulary wholly transformed.'[84] Because in the Christian economy previously unperceived reality is disclosed, and known reality assumes fresh significance, the words which denote these are either wholly new or newly adapted from common vocabulary. Christ mediates man to God, graciously saving the inadequacy of human language, translating *oratio* into *Oratio*. Just as in Galilee he once accommodated his oratory to the inadequacy of human comprehension,[85] so he now accommodates our speech to his own wisdom. Man's vocation is to 'hasten to mature,'[86] because he is destined for communion with God.[87] 'Wisdom stoops to your incompetence; but you, conversely, should mount upward to her sublimity.'

The classical thesis that the orator was a saviour (*sōtēr*) of citizens[88] might appeal to any humanist who desired to transmute the imitation of antique eloquence into the imitation of Christ. If Christ was the 'most holy Saviour' of language, then the Christian orator might by imitation save the commonwealth also. The Creator had conferred on man the gift of speech as 'the principal reconciler of human relationships.'[89] Just as Christ, oratory incarnate, had divinely reconciled man to God, so the Christian orator might through similar persuasion reconcile man to man. The humanist mediation of grace copied the divine economy by which God had disclosed his mind to man through speech. Imitation fulfilled the human order of men making themselves known to one another through speech, nature to nature. 'Speech has been chiefly given us by God,' Erasmus testified, 'so that man might live together with man more agreeably.'[90] By gathering men together in sympathy, the orator would imitate the saving recapitulation of reality in Christ's lordship. He would heal the fracture in the body of Christendom.

This curative power of *logos* was a legacy from the ancients. Greek philosophers appealed to the goddess *Peithō*, personifying the psychological and social efficacy of language, as the cathartic agent to cure spiritual maladies: from Homer's witness to the therapy of prayer, the magic charm, and the cheering speech to Plato's theory of the *kalos logos* which integrates psychic life. For Aristotle too verbal catharsis operated medicinally.[91] Wise in this culture, Erasmus repeats to the reader of his *In evangelium Lucae paraphrasis* the Greek adage: 'Conversation (*sermo*) is the medicine of the burdened soul.'[92] Tapping the biblical and patristic theme of Jesus as the soul's physician and medicine, Erasmus amalgamates faith's testimony to the healing *Logos* with the classical doctrine of logotherapy. It was because the Father observed the human plight of disease and wished no man to perish that he published his conversation (*sermo*), a heavenly medicine for the liberation of all men from spiritual illness. As this physician, Jesus aroused the dead by his conversation (*sermo*) and by his conversation routed severe and chronic diseases. But Erasmus rejects superstitious credence in magic spells. Jesus 'was not a magic spell (*sermo magicus*), but the omnipotent conversation (*omnipotens sermo*) of the all-powerful Father.' A true panacea, he dispelled diseases by his discourse as was promised in prophetic literature. 'The living speech (*sermo*) of the Father is Christ ... Only the Father's conversation (*sermo*) was efficacious for saving sick men, not only men who were more lightly ill, but also those mortally ill.' When he ascended into heaven, Erasmus continues, Jesus bequeathed to the apostles his pharmaceutical, the gospel. This efficacious drug must be swallowed into the stomach and disseminated through the veins into the entire anatomy, for it is the singular prescription of eternal life.[93]

As editor and exegete of the New Testament, Erasmus was himself a kind of pharmacist, dispensing the oratorical medicine of Christ. The urgent business of Erasmus was to save: to recall his contemporaries to a sense of lost humanity and to induce receptivity to wisdom and grace: renaissance. Erasmus' programme to restore creation through oratory, in imitation of Christ who had restored it as oration, was not implemented by heroic gesture, but by scholarly attention to detail in the service of uncommon eloquence. Grammar was to foster this germination and maturation of humanity reborn. The correct word is the word well-spoken; the word well-spoken springs from living spirit; the spirit is most revived by eloquence. In this circularity of language and life, grammar is human tradition, never abstract norm. The choice of vocabulary must be measured by the context which generates discourse, namely, the historical situation of a society, and by the context of the entire oration. One might suspect, judging from Erasmus' insistence on restoring the most correct classical translation for *logos*, that he would demand a conversion of all Christian vocabulary to the Roman rule. This is not the case. True eloquence is not the conservation of antique nomenclature, as though the sixteenth century were not a new revolution of history's wheel. 'Wherever I turn I see things changed, I stand on another stage, I see another theatre, yes, another world. What shall I do? I, a Christian, must speak to Christians about the Christian religion. In order that I may speak fittingly, shall I imagine that I am living in the age of Cicero and speaking in a crowded senate in the presence of the senators on the Tarpeian rock?'[94]

Erasmus' question was rhetorical. The theologian, proclaiming the gospel in the marketplace, needed to cultivate a sense of propriety which would direct his language. Certain terms, like *Spiritus Sanctus*, could not be translated to their classical correlative without corrupting their Christian meaning. In a satiric translation of doctrine Erasmus demonstrates the scandal and ridiculousness of equating Christian truths with their pagan ancestors. Take this sentence, invites Erasmus:

> Jesus Christ, the Word, and Son of the eternal Father, according to the prophets came into the world and was made man; of his own will he suffered death and redeemed his Church.

This is how a Ciceronian would render it, he suggests:

> The interpreter and son of the most excellent and mighty Jove, preserver and king, in accordance with the response of the soothsayer, flew down from Olympus to earth, and assuming the shape of man, sacrificed himself voluntarily to the shades below for the safety of the Republic and thus freed the state.[95]

Such Ciceronian vocabulary obscures the sacred meaning. 'Never in Cicero did we see "Jesus Christ," the "Word of God," "Holy Ghost," "Trinity," ' or other essential terms, catalogues Erasmus. Are we to replace the term *ecclesia* by *civitas*, *apostolus* by *legatus*, *baptismus* by *tinctura*, and the *synodus generalis* by *S.P.Q resp. Christiana*? When Erasmus writes that it is better to adopt the expressions of Thomas Aquinas and Duns Scotus than to pervert the creed to Ciceronian Latin,[96] the reader knows how serious the discrepancy between pagan vocabulary and the Christian lexicon can be. Had not Christ wholly transformed vocabulary? The theologian needed the wisdom to know what words ought not to be changed, and what words like movable feasts ought to be rescued from their decline into barbarism and restored to their pristine form. In his own editions of the New Testament Erasmus had provided such a model, altering many words, but leaving many more intact. Erasmus' choice of *sermo*, rather than *verbum* or *oratio*, was but one detailed implementation of a code of theological propriety which he argued in his *Ciceronianus*. And *sermo* is not a Ciceronian rendition, for he thinks that a devotee would translate Jerome's *verbum* by *interpres*.[97]

One must not suppose that Erasmus' statements on naming constitute his entire or even principal posture on the nature of human language. Names comprise but one of eight parts of speech: nouns. Nouns may be significative within a sentence for Erasmus,

C

but a sentence is not formed by the concatenation of discrete words. This practice of concatenation, which Erasmus terms *battologia*,[98] is a perversion of rhetorical composition. The schoolmen pile words to the heavens, erecting a tower of Babel.[99] The Ciceronians sew patches onto the garments of speech.[100] Early in their schooling, Erasmus advised Servatius Rogerus against writing by accretion: 'not in your old style, taking little snippets of second-hand wisdom, or even (which is worse) collecting phrases indiscriminately from Bernard here and Claudian there and fitting them, or rather sewing them clumsily on, to your own observations, exactly like a crow decking itself out in peacock's feathers. That is not literary composition but mere scissors-and-paste.'[101] He tersely attests his own commitment to the primacy of syntax over semantics in the dedicatory epistle to some translations: 'I have followed the old rule of Tully, that a translator's business is to weigh sentences and not words.'[102] If it cannot be claimed that Erasmus anticipated Chomsky's transformational grammar, one may still be assured that in his substitution of *sermo* for *verbum* he weighed more than the word. What mattered was to disclose the meaning of the *Logos* in Jn 1:1 in the context of that proclamation which only a reading of the entire gospel could secure. Erasmus scored theologians who hoisted interpretations on fragments of the text; like the ancestral Fathers he insisted on the context of a complete reading.[103]

The art of imitation for Erasmus is more than copying words. It is the adoption of the example of eloquent men: imitation rather than simulation. The best imitation is emulation, surpassing the style of the master by cultivating one's own native beauty in harmony with the persons and conditions of contemporary life.[104] The speaker must reflect the individuality of his own mind as in a natural mirror; any mimicry of another man's gifts will distort the reflection, as if the person were masquerading.[105] Latinity must be measured by human judgement or it will fail to manifest spirit in a new world. The best models for the theologian to imitate are the apostle Paul and the eloquent Fathers of antiquity. They lived the humanist ideal of pious learning and learned piety. The justice of Cyprian's translation of *sermo*, for example, is witnessed not only by classical grammar but also by his sanctity. Men who lived appropriately could be relied on as textbooks of theological eloquence, for they copied Christ.

Even the Fathers, however, should not be imitated indiscriminately; only insofar as they copied Christ might they be emulated.[106] Even the Fathers were men, not gods; as Erasmus often reminds his readers, they could be mistaken.[107] What they promoted as a linguistically appropriate expression of faith might not be so apt for Erasmus' age. Faith matures, customs change, language itself metamorphoses.[108] The declamations of ancient wisdom, even the words of Scripture, must be accommodated by the mature expression of contemporary men of eloquence. What is intelligible? what is appropriate? what is persuasive? Few modern scholars have commented on Erasmus' philosophy of language; those who have claim for him a theory of the strict equivalence of word and reality.[109] This is not just. Through his conversational beasts in *De recta pronunciatione* Erasmus states that it is unnecessary to represent vocally the entire object. 'It is sufficient for some similitude to appear.' Otherwise Lion should be better called *reo* than *leo*.[110] Language is not magical arbitration of reality for Erasmus. Only by wrestling Proteus with every linguistic skill, properly ordered, does man bind meaning. Even then it slips the knot.

The rhetorical method of imitation recalls a classical theory that language itself copies a better model of reality.[111] Erasmus repeats a linguistic commonplace in his assertion that 'words are but the paltry, crude, and inadequate containers of vast mysteries.'[112] Words sheathe meanings as clothing covers and ornaments the human body. 'What clothing is to our body, diction is to the expression of our notions.'[113] But must we assume that these meanings which diction clothes are non-verbal for Erasmus? Although his modern translators have interpreted the term *res* of the division *res et verba* in the entirely Platonic sense of 'ideas' or 'thoughts,'[114] this assumption may not be justified. *Res* can simply mean 'things,' 'facts,' or 'truths,' the approved translations in the classical lexicon.[115] One may not easily impute an ideational epistemology to Erasmus. There is evidence of resort to that classical convention by which language is the communication of prior thought, but there is evidence also of the modern thesis that language is the act in which thought is thought. In the *Apologia de 'In principo erat sermo'* Erasmus does not subscribe to Augustine's theory that the primordial speech is thought, of which the oral articulation is but a reflection. He advocates the reverse analogy: thinking is like talking to oneself;[116] not, talking is like thinking aloud. And in the *De recta pronunciatione* his Lion announces that it is not thought, but speech, which constitutes human nature. Erasmus also recognizes significant forms of speech which are not imitations of pre-verbal 'ideas' or 'thoughts,' but rather imitations of other language. Figurative language, which not only comprises most of Scripture, but also provides its interpretation, is such a case. It translates a simpler form of language. When Erasmus urges the exegete to 'add the wrap of allegory,'[117] he is advising the interpreter to clothe, not naked idea, but naked language. Erasmus also understood his annotations on the New Testament, which were grammatical rather than ornamental, as a garment for the naked text.[118] Both rhetorical figure and grammatical fact can be language laminated on language.

Some language imitates other language. Do the barest human utterances ultimately imitate things, thoughts, or God's primordial language? A scholarly answer must be tentative. Erasmus' texts explicating discourse as an imitation of speech generated from the Father are more theologically correct if read to suggest a non-ideational yet paradigmatic concept. The Father spoke his oration so that he might disclose his mind, Erasmus had said. Such a statement might be argued philosophically as indication that thought is prior to speech for Erasmus, that he holds to the Platonic convention. But that is untenable for orthodox theology since there is no temporal separation of Father and Son, nor any subordination of the Son to the Father. Erasmus' claims for speech as the revelation of the Father's mind are embedded in affirmations of his knowledge of the orthodox doctrine of the eternal generation of the Son and his unity with the Father.[119] The Father is the speaker and he enjoys perfect unity with his speech. The objection that his speech is not self-generating but springs from the Father does not demand that the divine paradigm of human discourse be considered ideational, at least not from a theological perspective. Mind and speech are eternally one in God. The *Logos* is simultaneously the thought (*ratio*) and the discourse (*oratio*), or better phrased, he is the Father's eternally thought speech. If this divine activity is the model for human oratory, then one may assume rather than doubt that for Erasmus the human process of speaking imitates proportionally this same unity of thought and expression. Whatever philosophical posture might be inferred from Erasmus' theology of the act of speaking in God, his intention is clear. And it is a moral intention. This perfect mirror of the Father's mind which is his speech provides man's model. A man is to align his speech with his spirit as the perfect expression of that inner nature created through the *Logos*, and so to imitate divinity in humanity. Participating by imitation in God's creative act, he becomes a little creator on earth.

Erasmus abstracted himself usually from debates about intellectual operations, the *modi significandi* which had converted theological faculties into schools of speculative grammar. Had not those *modi* sufficiently tormented his childhood?[120] Instead he chose to accept language as a human fact, the certain index of divine vocation, and to promote its power to transform society. His prolix tract *Lingua* considers the 'use and abuse' of language in society rather than theories of language.[121] His preoccupation with speech as the cultural act shares the perspective of classical rhetors, charged with fostering the civilizing agency of language. Isocrates revered speech as the source of most human blessings, allowing man to escape the kingdom of wild beasts.[122] 'This is the one endowment of our nature which singles us out from all living creatures and ... by using this advantage we have risen above them in all other respects as well.'[123] The guide to action in all affairs, speech has enabled men to conduct civilized lives, found cities, establish laws, and invent arts.[124] Cicero lauded the power of rhetoric to gather scattered humanity and to lead it towards civilization from a brutish life in the wilderness. Speech conferred the power to establish laws and civic rights. 'Who therefore would not rightly admire this faculty, and deem it his duty to exert himself to the utmost in this field, that by doing so he may surpass men themselves in that particular respect wherein chiefly men are superior to animals?'[125] Quintilian repeated these conventions and further extolled oratory as the 'fairest gift of god to man, without which all things are stricken dumb and robbed alike of present glory and the immortal record of posterity.'[126] Erasmus' portent, Lorenzo Valla, revived the spirit of these panegyrics for late Christendom. He proclaimed Latin as truly divine nourishment for the soul, educing liberal arts, law, wisdom, and civilization from barbarity. As Rome had once asserted civil supremacy, not only through military skill, but also through the propagation and diffusion of the Latin language, so might sixteenth-century man subdue the earth with tongue and pen. In the custody of barbarians and conquering hordes, Latin still conserved, holy and religious, its sacramental power to signify reality and effect the transformation of men.[127]

Erasmus the humanist shared antiquity's confidence in the civilizing agency of mature human language. If law declined into decadent legalism, if the arts languished for want of invention, then that primal expression of humanity, speech, must have perished. Valla's principle was succinct: If Latin flourishes, studies and disciplines flourish; if they perish, men perish.[128] Erasmus testified to his just perception. Theologians had reverted to the brutish life of the wilds, erecting towers of Babel on the brambles of disputation, whereas, their Fathers had once established the city of God on the fruitful foundations of eloquence.[129] The touchstone of human failure was for Erasmus the factitious dispersion of men. If Cicero had observed the power of eloquence to gather scattered peoples, Erasmus observed the force of barbarism to dispel fraternity. The divisive effect of scholastic argument, which sent the commonwealth 'scurrying in all directions,'[130] is well documented in Erasmus' writings.

Schoolish logic imposed on the New Testament fails to generate discourse which exhibits spiritual maturity and promotes thereby the commonwealth. There is striking coincidence between Erasmus' condemnation of the scholastics and the allegation which classical orators levelled against the false rhetoricians: they dismiss the crowd for home less better men.[131] The infallible sign of the failure of scholasticism is its centrifugal force, its dispersion of the human community into factions. Once the bond of spirit is loosened, concord dissolves. The schoolmen, who have expelled themselves from the garden of the authors which imitates the paradisiac conversation of God and man, revert to a beastly life in the wilds among the sterile thorns of disputation.

Oratory and logic: both words are derived from *logos*. Both are forms of speech. Observe, invites Erasmus, their social force. Oratory persuades men sympathetically, directing their lives to faith and concord.[132] Dialectic traps the intellect in snarls of argumentation. Which is proper to theological method when 'in this kind of philosophy, located as it is more truly in the disposition of the mind than in syllogisms, life means more than debate, inspiration is preferable to erudition, transformation is a more important matter than intellectual comprehension'?[133] The tenor of Erasmus' criticism of the curriculum which he endured at Paris complicates an evaluation of his comprehension of the purpose of scholastic logic. To secure reform of the unviersities the humanists sometimes resorted to propaganda, belittling the academic establishment. Erasmus pens the stock phrases vigorously. His observations also ventilate personal animosity. He portrays himself as the precocious child of the Muses, yawning among dullards in the lecture hall, and trudging off to his infected room at dusk with an equally infected spirit.[134] After the initial outrage to his religious and aesthetic sensibilities, the coarse exercise of logical trivia only lulled him into boredom. His later criticisms evidence resentment for the creative energy dissipated at the Collège de Montaigu.

The comprehensive analysis of Erasmus' critique of logic must be the lot of scholars more learned in the shifting modes of the late mediaeval trivium.[135] The humanists were not without their own logic, best exemplified in the *De inventione dialectica* of Agricola,[136] of whom Erasmus approved and who displaced Peter of Spain as the mentor of young dialecticians. What Erasmus opposed in the curriculum was the proliferation of a logic which swallowed up the functions traditionally alloted to grammar and rhetoric. Modist and nominalist logic, which bred contentious schools populating too many chairs of theology, claimed to be grammatical in orientation. This new *sermocinalis scientia* became the discipline for discerning meaning. What had this frigid quibbling about the modes of signification to do with human conversation in the commonwealth? And how dare the theologians imagine that their new science imitated the eloquence of God's *sermo*?

In his celebrated treatise on theological method Erasmus terms scholastic disputations *logomachias*, just as Paul had scored the vain philosophical debates of the apostolic community.[137] But there is a patristic application of this epithet, one which Erasmus knew, disclosing the profound theological implication of verbal wrangling or linguistic vacuity. *Logomachein* is to 'contend against the *Logos*.'[138] No syllogism to argue whether the *Logos* might have become incarnate in a beetle rather than inhominized could be a looking-glass of God and man. The renaissance of true theology required a proper ordering of the trivium, a Ciceronian subordination of logic to rhetoric and grammar. Erasmus did not intend to abolish scholasticism, or so he claimed.[139] The Scotists might continue to niggle, if only they would yield the principal orientation of theology to the literate interpretation of Scripture. That text and the human spirit were the two traces of the *Logos* in the world. By mediating divine inspiration and human scholarship, the Christian would tap divine order and human purpose.

Erasmus proposes no elaborate theory of religious language as distinct from ordinary, artistic, or technical discourse. It is human language ordained to a sacred purpose. He avoids adopting Aquinas' doctrine of analogy, although he does consider attribution to be proportional. As he asserted in his *Apologia de 'In principio erat sermo,'* 'No human nouns express divine affairs in a proper sense.' According to the mind's power of comprehension, some words are predicated more aptly of God than others, even if they are not proper to his true nature. And despite the inadequacy of language, it does draw man to reflect upon God.[140] Erasmus never fails to strain human energy in the pursuit of that eloquence which reflects not only the glory of God which is Christ, but the glory of man in Christ. If one must venerate mystery in silence, then he may do so only as a final resort. Erasmus was quick to remind his readers that if Paul was assumed mystically into heaven, he still sent Timothy to fetch his manuscripts when he returned to earth.[141]

Unless like the disciples in the upper room one could expect the Pentecostal gift of tongues, then the theologian had better apply his mind to the learning of grammar.[142]

That labour of scholarship, that human plot of language, was the fairest imitation of God's creation of all things through his own oration: 'All things were made through him, and without him was not anything made that was made.'[143] The exhaustion of nightly labours, the stench of the press, the disappointment of rebuke to his scholarship – Erasmus bitterly complained of these. But was not this the humanist method of imitation, the human way of reflecting God's creative image, ushering civilization from chaos by speech? Christian oratory was the perfect expression of humanity divinized. Erasmus' programme to renew theology by the imitation of Christ in more lucid, faithful, and eloquent discourse is grounded in this essential conviction of his about the analogy of human and divine orders, converging in the *Logos*. In the *Apologia* to the Novum Instrumentum, Erasmus estimated that God 'hates proud eloquence, I allow; but much more, the supercilious and arrogant inability to speak.'[144] Not to speak was the primordial sin of defiance against creation, now recreated in Christ. And so Erasmus determined to struggle for the education of lapsed humanity, in that chiaroscuro landscape of late Christendom, where every darkness edged on light.

THREE

❧ Ratio ❧

GOOD LETTERS WOULD RENDER MEN HUMAN; theology would
crown them gods.[1] To that second edition of the New Testament
which altered *verbum* to *sermo*, Erasmus prefaced a remarkable
treatise. If the *Paraclesis* of 1516 was the 'trumpet blast' of his
theological renaissance,[2] then the *Ratio* of 1518 was its full
orchestration. The insistence of friends that he develop the earlier
Methodus occasioned its composition, he confides;[3] these may have
been the same friends who prompted the controversial revision
sermo. The *Ratio*, however, stirred no immediate contention: no
enraged sermons, no appeals to London or Rome, no seditious mob
grappling for Erasmus' throat. It influenced theological scholarship
for five centuries, after *sermo* had long been forgotten, even by
curators of antique terms.

Dirk Martens, whose press would issue the apology for *sermo*,
published in November 1518 the first edition of the *Ratio*.[4] The
edition, dedicated to Albert of Brandenburg,[5] was inscribed with
the printer's device of a sheet-anchor. The mark was one of three
which identified Martens' press; Erasmus adapted symbolically,
appending the lines: 'Lest the force of the tempests bear you away: a
sheet-anchor. You ought to fix your mind on it; it's about to be cast
out to you.' And the adages, which serve as parenthetical
justification:

> In wine, truth.
> Often one suffers shipwreck in waves of wine.[6]

The emblematic *gera agkura* or *sacra ancora* which surfaces in

Erasmus' religious writings is not a 'sacred anchor' as some translators suppose,[7] but a sheet-anchor,[8] which every sailor knows as the large anchor employed in emergency. Erasmus is casting out safety to a floundering republic. The anchor truly is 'sacred' because in his pun it is Scripture. Amid such a variety of human opinions, he advises the abbot Paul Volz in a letter allied with the *Ratio*, the sure recourse must be the 'reliable sheet-anchor of the gospel teaching.'[9] Again in the very text of the *Ratio* he signals the 'sheet-anchor of evangelical doctrine.'[10]

Once again Erasmus had appealed to the symbolism of Christian antiquity, for the most primitive emblem of its faith was not the cross, as many assume, or even the icthyograph, but the anchor. Perhaps inspired by Heb 6:19, the anchor appears on the earliest Christian funerary monuments to mark hope in God's promise of immortality in Jesus.[11] This Erasmian emblem of Scripture, the anchor of true theology, is, in a humanist analogy of divine and human eloquence, the sign of his book's publication also. In those harried months when Erasmus had struggled with the revision of the New Testament edition, he had likened his scholarship to a maritime adventure. Erasmus, the wave-tossed voyager, praying for the breath of Christ upon the gale. Erasmus, glimpsing the distant harbour and safe anchorage for his book.[12] Now he had cast upon the troubled waters of Christendom a handbook for theologians; this he hoped would incite that rebirth of civilization through Christian oratory which he had designed as his pedagogical vocation. His claim of navigational skill is understated. In the introduction to the *Ratio* he compares himself as a methodologist to those sailors, whose own ship having dashed upon the cliffs, nevertheless swim away naked more aware of the perils of the sea.[13] Quintilian's suggestive portrait of the venerable orator, now retired but counselling young men in his house, seems more appropriate: 'And he as their father in the art will mould them to all excellence, and like some old pilot will teach them of the shores whereby their ships must sail, of the harbours where they may shelter, and the signs of the weather, and will expound to them what they shall do when the breeze is fair or the tempest blows.' For like this weathered orator Erasmus had authored his *Ratio* 'inclined not only

Fig. 1 The Sheet-Anchor of Evangelical Teaching. Frontispiece to the first edition of the *Ratio*, 1518. (Courtesy University Library of Amsterdam)

by the common duty of humanity, but by a certain passion for the task.'[14]

The *Ratio* did not appear abruptly, but was developed and published in continuity with the Erasmian programme expounded in the prefaces to the first edition of the New Testament.[15] That 1516 publication had been accompanied by an *Apologia*; by an exhortation to the universal reading of Scripture, *Paraclesis*; and by the *Methodus*, the skeleton of the later *Ratio*. In the *Apologia* Erasmus claims only to supply other theologians what fortune has denied them; namely, a thorough learning of the scriptural languages. He emphasizes the necessity of restoring the depraved text of Jerome's Vulgate, and outlines a philological approach. As textual restorer Erasmus imagines himself the very servant of the Holy Spirit who, while abiding with the Church, still relinquishes to men a portion of the work. His scholarship will serve to render Scripture not more elegant but more eloquent: more lucid and faithful to the apostolic discourse.[16]

The second preface, *Paraclesis*, is the manifesto of the philosophical republic of Christ. Acting as town-crier Erasmus heralds a Christian society constituted by Scripture. The common citizenship of baptism, he declares, admits all men to the theological profession. The philosophy of Christ, proclaimed in the transforming biblical text, is more simple and satisfying than human philosophies. Erasmus urges all Christians to seize this patrimony, too long appropriated by monkish schoolmen. Scripture accommodates all classes of men without discrimination of age or sex. And what else is this philosophy, Erasmus asks, than what Christ himself names it, a 'renaissance?'[17]

A final preface, *Methodus*, guided the aspirant theologian towards recovering this authentic primacy of Scripture. That treatise was preserved and amplified in the *Ratio* of 1518. During Erasmus' lifetime nine different presses would issue the work.[18] This successful text outlined Erasmus' programme for the education of the theologian in method: a man knowledgeable in the secular arts, a man well-versed in the biblical languages especially, who would revive Christian civilization by tapping its pristine springs. Too diffuse a work to invite structural analysis, a tabulation of its content does not represent the *Ratio* well either. Readers may easily note emphasis on the exegesis of texts in the original languages rather than in translation, the appeal to the Fathers as distinguished progenitors of method, the service of secular disciplines to theology, the catalogue of hermeneutical rules. What distinguishes the *Ratio* immediately is the emphatic restoration of biblical exegesis as normative theology. The prolix catalogue of biblical pericopes which composes the bulk of the treatise announces a renaissance of true method, countering human speculation which filled decadent scholastic commentaries on scholastic commentaries in an involution of spirit. Like every theological work of distinction which advances the articulation of Christian faith, the *Ratio* is better appreciated evaluatively for its achievement than descriptively by content. From a matrix of ancient and contemporary convictions, Erasmus engendered a methodology of theology as scholarship in the modern critical sense, a new complement to traditional modes of theology as wisdom or science. Concentration on the text of Scripture, which had distinguished the finest expressions of patristic and mediaeval theology, was asserted now with an intensity which new humanist methods allowed and which has since captivated the allegiance of theologians, extending even to the modern obsession with hermeneutics.

But it is more brilliantly that Erasmus merges the intellectual demand of humanism for exegesis of the authentic, primal text (*prisca theologia*) with faith's single-sighted vision of Christ, the divine oration, the copious revelation of God and man in whom every partial truth is reconciled. For the mediation of the contemporary demands of the intellect with the traditional claims of faith, the *Ratio* deserves an appreciative and attentive reading. The particular reading here will be an analytical discernment of the grammar which informs his methodology. How does that intellectual and religious conviction of the *Logos*, grounding reality and enfleshed in Everyman's good speech, direct Erasmus' under-standing of true theology and the way to achieve it? How may one parse the syntax of his methodology to expose the animating spirit of the creative *Logos*, through whom every human word is spoken and every human act is practised? What is the grammar of method?

To begin in Erasmian style with an investigation of those words which may yield the apprehension of realities, one should compile and define the vocabulary of method. Without relating the serpentine history of technical terms for method, it must be said that Erasmus' titular words, *ratio*, *methodus*, and *compendium* are synonyms for method.[19] The original appellation of the treatise, *Methodus*, is a mediaeval latinization of Plato's *methodos*[20] perhaps devised by Boethius for translating Aristotle's TOPOI.[21] The term is not classical. Cicero, who coined much Latin philosophical terminology, apparently used *via et ratio* for the Greek *methodos*, and most Latins followed his paraphrase. Quintilian added *breve compendium*, or at least Renaissance philologists claimed that he did.[22]

Another scholar who has investigated the history of the term calculates that, although *methodus* appears in mediaeval translations of Greek philosophy, it never gained currency as a technical term for 'method.' Thomas Aquinas, he argues, explained Aristotle's *methodos* in the customary lexicon of classical Latin: *ars, ratio via*.[23] One should remember, however, that Aquinas was neither the most influential nor the most widely read among mediaeval scholars; his *Summa Theologiae* was reserved by the monks of his order and those obscure few who persevered sixteen years in a university divinity course. *Methodus*, despite the contrary claim, was certainly a mediaeval technical term for method. It stands boldly in that most quoted of all scholastic definitions, in perhaps the most influential and universally examined treatise of the age,[24] the *Summulae logicales* of Peter of Spain. This is one scholastic text that even Erasmus admits having read.[25] The opening sentence of this definitive textbook claims: 'Dialectic is the art of arts and the science of sciences, possessing the method for the principles of all methods (*methodorum*).'[26] *Methodi ratio* is also the opening phrase of Thomas of Erfurt's commanding *Tractatus de modis significandi sive grammatica speculativa*, already noted as a disseminator of confusion about gender and sex.[27] Was there anyone in Europe, from the schoolboy sweating through the 'little logicals' to the master of theology pondering speculative grammar, who did *not* know the term *methodus*?

Erasmus, that elegant humanist forever scolding the barbaric scholastics, thus adopts their own neologism. The Italian purists eschewed the word. Erasmus' contemporary Mario Nizzoli listed *methodus* in the appendix to his Ciceronian lexicon among the 'barbarous and non-Ciceronian' words.[28] In his expanded version of the treatise, Erasmus compromises with Ciceronian latinity and alters the title from *Methodus* to *Ratio seu methodus compendio perveniendi ad veram theologiam*. His use of *methodus*, innovative for a humanist, inspired a spate of sixteenth-century pedagogical works boasting the word in title.[29] Within the text of the treatise the word occurs only three times, however, and in conjunction always with either *ratio* or *via*.[30] Why *methodus*? Erasmus' selection of the word was an irony. It challenged the dialecticians on their own terms. His was the method of *true* theology.

Ratio, the first word of the new title, was the noun Augustine had allegedly rejected in favour of *verbum* for the translation of the Johannine prologue.[31] *Ratio* corresponds to the primary denotation of *logos* in the classical lexicon: reckoning, account, calculation, computation. It also signifies the mental faculty which is the basis for this computation; namely, judgement, understanding, reason.[32] As a theological term *ratio* translated the *logos endiathetos* whom some Fathers recognized as Christ summing up reality as God's immanent reason. *Ratio* also represents the Greek *methodos* and its cognates: course, conduct, procedure, mode, manner, method, fashion, plan; a theory, doctrine, or system based on reason.[33] Many of these synonyms appear throughout the text of Erasmus' *Ratio* in an obliquely methodological sense, especially *modum*.[34] Thus the term *ratio* comprises both method in the modern sense of technique and the rational order or understanding which grounds it.

Erasmus obeys the classical rules for explicating a discipline. The first task of any methodologist was to state whether the subject was simple or multiform.[35] Erasmus, for whom theology was the teaching of Christ exclusively,[36] explains that true oratory is simple and nothing is truer or simpler than Christ.[37] Erasmus directs this treatise on the method of theology, not to arrogant Scotists stillborn in their dialectical art, but to untutored commoners, to intellectual characters of inferior disposition. He is concerned to assure the tyro that method is easy, extremely easy to master. The purpose of the *Ratio*, he modestly says, is to simplify for the untutored man what Augustine in his *De doctrina christiana* and Pseudo-Dionysius the

Areopagite in *De divinis nominibus* and other works had expressed so much more elegantly for erudite scholars.[38]

In reply to the anticipated ridicule of his readers that he indicates a path that he never travelled, or only travelled sterilely, Erasmus imagines himself a Mercurial statue. From their perspective atop pillars, those ancient figures advanced the traveller with their index finger to a destination where they themselves would never arrive. He proposes to show his candidate, affectionately addressed in the familiar form, the way (*via*): 'Not a minimal part of the task,' he advises, 'is to recognize the path for approaching the task. And he hastens enough who nowhere deviates from the path.'[39] The metaphor of the road which ornaments the opening paragraphs of the *Ratio*[40] recalls Renaissance etymologies of *methodos: meta* (into the middle of / in pursuit of) and *hodos* (the path).[41] The sacred journey or pilgrimage of Christian life had already been well mapped in the *Enchiridion*. Erasmus was now indicating in the *Ratio*, not the troop-road of spiritual warfare, but the path of theological learning. In seizing the metaphor of the road he contends by allusion with Peter of Spain's notorious claim for dialectic 'possessing the road to the principles of all methods.' The schoolmen also designated their coteries as *viae*; philosophical realists like Aquinas comprised the *via antiqua*, and nominalists like William of Occam, the *via moderna*.[42] Erasmus reassigns the term *via antiqua* to the ancient Fathers and indiscriminately terms all varieties of scholasticism the *via moderna*.[43] In the *Ratio* he urges the theological candidate down the path of 'true theology,' the well-travelled road of antiquity.

As early as the publication of the first edition he had confided to a friend that he wanted 'to construct a road for other persons of higher aims, so that they might be less impeded by pools and stumbling-blocks in carrying home those fair and glorious treasures.'[44] Erasmus' method is no meandering footpath, but a shortcut, a *compendium* as the title proclaims.[45] In self-description he writes, 'He who indicates the shortcut, that man assists the student with a double benefit: first, that more seasonably he may arrive where he tends; and then, that by less labour and expense he may attain what he pursues.'[46] This notion of method as a shortcut or compendium appears not to be classical either, although it was attributed in mediaeval commentaries to the Greeks. But the brevity of life, Erasmus often reminds his readers, compelled one not to linger; one ought to proceed quickly to the essentials.[47]

The schoolmen professed their own *ratio compendiaria*: logic.[48] Erasmus spurns the compendium of dialectic and applauds the compendious rhetoric of the Fathers. Against scholasticism, which claimed to be a shortcut and yet produced 'so many obscure volumes ... huge commentaries of interpreters at odds with one another,'[49] he argues the example of John Chrysostom. This eloquent theologian 'frees himself from all question by a compendium.' To the query about *hupostasis* Chrysostom thinks it sufficient to profess that in the person of Christ the divine nature was cemented by some ineffable bond to a corporeal and human soul, composing the same *hupostasis*, although the natures remain distinct. 'How moreover this may be,' he then warns, 'do not inquire; the fact is that God himself knew.'[50] To the query about the nativity of Christ, Chrysostom simply exclaims, 'What the omnipotent Spirit of God did is not incredible.'[51] Thus by a compendium he professes the faith, without quantification.

Erasmus, hailed as a promoter of copious discourse, appreciated the virtue of Attic brevity too. In the epilogue of the *De copia* he instructs the art of brevity: abstain from prefaces and appeals to emotion; set forth the subject simply and cursorily; use only the chief arguments and those compactly; avoid those figures which amplify or ornament speech. The ideal is not brevity alone, but brevity ordered by propriety, elegance, and simplicity. 'Let the lover of brevity see to it that he not do only this, i.e., say few things, but let him say the best possible things in the fewest words. And he who is pleased by that Homeric expression, *few indeed*, let him take pleasure in this also, which immediately follows, very acutely.' In proposing a compendium of true theology, then, Erasmus directs the candidate to those few things essential to the discipline. Once the student has grasped these essentials, he will be able to emulate either exuberance or moderation of style, as the occasion demands.[52]

The theologian, expected to deal with the shifting circumstances of Christian experience and its expression, needed in Erasmus' judgement a succinct handbook such as the *Ratio* from whose narrow base he could foray. If the candidate required a model of copious and brief styles both, he could imitate Erasmus himself. While his copious theological style has been acknowledged universally, a certain ignorance of rhetoric has caused some modern commentators to misconstrue his complementary style of conciseness as reductionism or scepticism.[53] Erasmus' sometimes economical language is no hesitance in or failure of faith, but a rhetorical device to deal with those mysteries[54] which in his estimation properly required brevity rather than amplification. Questioned about the hypostatic union, Erasmus would prefer a compendious reply such as Chrysostom's. Questioned about the peace of Christ's Church, Erasmus would discourse abundantly in an assembly of publications. The rhetorical canon of propriety, applied to theology, sometimes dictates a compendious method, sometimes a copious method. A compendium of true theology such as the *Ratio*, Erasmus was sure, would be useful in orienting the candidate towards judicious decision. Erasmus, like other humanists, was captured by the unorthodox notion that an art ought to exhibit rules which would clearly tend towards the pursuit of some useful end.[55] The schoolmen, he observed from his seat in the lecture-hall, were failing not only the criterion of eloquence, but also the criterion of utility. He would set theology back on a short and useful path.[56]

Before divulging any techniques, however, Erasmus counsels the aspirant theologian to that piety which promotes theology. Godly discourse can only spring from spirit, that flowering of human nature which overcomes the animal instinct of body. Until a man crushes cupidity, he can only bark with the dogs and grunt with the pigs in a factitious and futile mimicry of theological eloquence. The Erasmian campaign for the integrity of theology is barricaded with pleas for the integrity of the theologian. These reflect his humanist conviction of the essential bond between character and speech. Any reader may gather his own *florilegium* of texts entreating piety, so profusely do they stud his writings. This is not the nostalgic sentimentality of a rhetorician, wearied with a polluted Church and

longing for pristine, apostolic simplicity. This is not the scorch-
ing reform of a Pelagian who requires a purified Church to beckon
the Spirit's grace. This is the human plea of the same Erasmus
who courted Folly and knew she must have her liege; who puzzled
over the ambiguity of Silenus and the mutability of Proteus, yet
knew they were Christ's own traits. Erasmus exhorted integrity,
but in the end he counselled tolerance.[57] Would that the folly of
men more resemble Christ's folly, and ambiguity tend towards
concord!

If Erasmus had wished, he could have mounted the pulpits of
Europe. He was no preacher, however, but a teacher of teachers.
The printing press could straddle the continent more effectively
than any sermon, and it served him well. How would humanism in
theology mutually renew the piety which it required for its very
expression? It would tap the pure, clear founts, overgrown with the
thorny disputes of scholasticism. A piously learned examination of
Scripture would release a golden stream of eloquence where only
muddied rivulets of schoolish debate had trickled.[58] And this
gushing fountain of Christ's oratory would refresh the spirits of
men, reviving human nature in a great renaissance.

Piety, for Erasmus, canopies the manifold of virtues. Erasmus
does not mean by piety its popular connotation of devotion, as in
telling beads, but rather an interior disposition. Piety expresses for
him that adopted sonship which is the Christian's proper relation
with God. Pious Aeneas was the man of classical filiation, attentive
to family and fatherland, reverent before the gods.[59] Abraham,
binding Isaac to the pyre, acknowledged by the sacrifice of his spirit
an analogy between Isaac's sonship to him and his own piety before
Yahweh.[60] In the new covenant man is adopted into the very
sonship of Christ, making him a new creature. This is Christian
rebirth. '*Renascimur!*' exults Erasmus.[61]

Piety as the filial disposition of the Christian is complementary to
humanist method, which aims to restore men to themselves through
language. Both piety and method share a common source in Christ,
in my reading of Erasmus' grammar. The same Christ who confers
sonship on man, bidding him by grace to express this filiation in
true religion, is the *Logos* who confers intelligibility on man,

bidding him to express with grace his understanding in true eloquence. Piety and humanism, religion and eloquence, mutually serve and interpret. 'Let thy heart,' Erasmus urges his tyro with a stunning metaphor, be the 'library of Christ himself.'[62] Piety prepares the humanist theologian by stirring that purity of heart and docility necessary for interpreting Scripture. The *Paraclesis* had already encouraged: 'The journey is simple, and it is ready for anyone. Only bring a pious and open mind, possessed above all with a pure and simple faith. Only be docile, and you have advanced far in this philosophy.'[63] In the *Ratio* Erasmus summons the neophyte to a spiritual lustration, a cleansing from every vice and cupidity. As in a placid stream or a mirror wiped clean, the tranquil soul will reflect the image of eternal truth. Even the pagan mystery cults demanded purgation, Erasmus reminds his student.[64] And Hippocrates, the classical exemplar of the man who acquires art through the comprehension of criteria rather than through chance or routine practice,[65] exacted moral integrity from his disciples.[66] 'How much more just is it that we approach toward the school of this divine wisdom or the truer temple with the most purged souls?' Moses ran to the burning bush on Sinai, but was not admitted to divine colloquy until he had shed his shoes. Was not this the symbolic casting off of burdensome earthly desires from the spirit?[67]

If the theologian approaches divine conversation purely, then God will speak to him more truly and efficaciously through Scripture than he did to Moses in fire. Prepare your heart, Erasmus advises the candidate, so that you may be called by the prophetic word *Theodidaktos*, taught of God. 'Let the simple and dovelike eye of faith be present, which does not distinguish except heavenly things. Let the highest ardor for learning approach.' As you near the sacred threshold of theology, he continues, banish pride and arrogance. The door of the queen's palace stands open in access, with august inner chambers, to the humble heart alone. Banish all hunger for glory; banish obstinacy, the parent of quarrels. And when you ascend, you will kiss and adore the holy altars of religion, as if some numen pervaded everything. In the shrines of the divine Spirit you must stoop forward to kiss what is given to see; whatever remains secret, you must adore with simple faith and venerate from afar. Veil impious curiosity, as Moses shrouded his face on Sinai.[68]

If there was an impious curiosity, then there was in Erasmus' judgement also a pious curiosity,[69] one directed towards the scrutiny of texts. The cultivation of this curiosity and its guidance by methodological principles is the plan of the *Ratio*, for as he had said, there were certain mysteries which a theologian 'must stoop forward to kiss.' How to proceed then? In his earlier *Enchiridion* he had advised the Christian exegete of Scripture that 'one ought not to follow conjectures of his own mind but acquire a method (*ratio*), and, so to speak, a kind of skill (*ars*), something a certain Dionysius gives us in his book called Concerning the Names of God and Saint Augustine in his work entitled Christian Doctrine.'[70] A modest version of the same instruction, useful once the candidate had prepared spiritually in private, was precisely what he intended his own *Ratio* to provide.

From his earliest *obiter dicta* about method to the deliberately fashioned *Ratio*, Erasmus' focus is emphatically pedagogical. In correspondence, for example, he had advised young Pieter Gillis to moderate his studies by *ratio*: Arrange your library and papers, he wrote; do not be distracted, but tenaciously read one author to his conclusion, noting his worthwhile sayings; schedule your life with determined tasks for each hour; do not crowd projects without completing what you have begun; keep a diary to aid your memory.[71] With such a sensible plan no wonder Gillis later attracted the Muses to attend his wedding rather than pay call on the theologians of Louvain. Method: what the poet learns from infancy, drinking in Latin with his mother's milk and wisdom spoken over the spinning wheel.[72] Method: what every schoolboy uses like a craftsman who obeys 'certain rules of his trade that make it possible for him to produce a given quantity of work, not only more accurately and quickly but also more easily.'[73] Method: what the teacher employs to direct his disciples towards civil and sacred eloquence. This is the modern and now common sense of method: technique. Erasmus' passionate concern for the reform of pedagogy occasioned in 1511 a small book, *De ratione studii*. It outlines the correct method of acquiring linguistic skill through reading, grammar, and composition.[74] His theological *Ratio*, too, is for the schoolboy, the candidate lingering on the threshold of sacred learning.[75] Erasmus shares the enthusiastic conviction of all humanist pedagogues that education makes the man.[76] In 1518 he was still persuaded by his own effusive rhetoric that 'all can be theologians': weavers, farmers, tailors, travellers, masons, prostitutes, pimps, Turks, and little women.[77] Free from any premonition of mob scenes in three European capitals, he opens school. If his readers should scoff that he exemplifies the proverb, 'the blind leading the blind,' Erasmus invites them to continue reading nevertheless.[78] He might have added Plato's admonition that to pretend to master an art *without* analysed method is to be the real blind man.[79]

THE SCOPE OF THEOLOGY

If the theologian is to be acute in the discernment of reality, he must enter the path to knowledge with a grammar book in hand. 'Words first'[80] is the Erasmian catchword. 'For things,' he had explained, 'are only intelligible to us through vocal signs; he who is unversed in the signification of speech is blind also in the discernment of things; necessarily he hallucinates, he is delirious.'[81] Learning Greek, Latin, and Hebrew is the theologian's first concern, for the mysteries of Scripture are couched in those alphabets.[82] Erasmus encourages the faltering candidate in the *Ratio* with case histories of men who in middle age mastered them,[83] and adds that even Augustine does not exact a miracle of eloquence from the theologian. A clean and elegant style, a moderate ability for discerning the grammar of the texts suffice.[84] But the theologian may not neglect the discipline of language. Erasmus underscores the obvious: 'No man understands what he reads without a knowledge of languages.'[85] His insistence that the candidate master language as the first method of true theology is unastonishing. How else would he mature to express that humanity which is destined for communion with God? And what else is theology but godly eloquence?

The theologian is in the Erasmian scheme a holy orator declaiming in the forum of the commonwealth. He sees divine things through human words. Language is like perspective, that brilliant technique of Renaissance art for fleshing flat surface, through which the theologian discerns the configurations of reality, the vestiges of *logos* in the world. But, unlike other men who peer at things through words, the theologian fixes his eye on those archetypal words which are the ultimate revelation of things: Christ, *oratio*, that full disclosure of the Father's mind which is perfect knowledge. Everyman may recapitulate in the human order the generation of the Son, if only he expresses his true mind in good speech. The theologian repeats the divine act in the most explicit and exemplary way, however, because he engages in the deliberate imitation of Speech by the human paraphrase of divine oratory. The analogy of divine and human eloquence, oblique in other circumstances, is manifest in true theology. This is, in my reading, the rationale of the *Ratio*, the grammar of Erasmus' method. By focusing singly on Speech, the theologian learns how to read that image inscribed by the Author's finger on the human spirit. By imitating Christ oratorically he acquires godly eloquence and enhances humanity which was created from the beginning through that oration. Each method (*ratio*) which Erasmus advocates is finally grounded in that divine method of speech, the *Logos* (*ratio-oratio*) by which the Father revealed himself to men. The learning of the sacred languages becomes the capital method towards the learning of Language. Through the assimilation of divine grammar, the human comprehension of reality is achieved.

Each discipline, Erasmus explains in the *Ratio*, has its own sighting. The rhetor looks towards speaking copiously and splendidly; the dialectician towards inferring sagaciously and ensnaring his adversary. The theologian has one focus only: that he may speak metamorphically, transfiguring humanity into the very doctrine of Christ. 'This is your first and only goal; perform this vow, this one thing: that you be changed, that you be seized, that you weep at and be transformed into those teachings which you learn.' The programme is the Christian transmutation of oratory into flesh, word into act. Again Erasmus instructs, 'The special goal of theologians is to expound Scripture wisely; to render its doctrine according to faith, not frivolous questions; to discourse about piety gravely and efficaciously; to wring out tears, to inflame spirits to heavenly things.'[86]

If the theologian is to attain the ancient wisdom by which one perceives not only the goal of his learning but also the method towards it, then he needs, Erasmus is convinced, 'certain sights to which he may confer what he reads.' Especially he needs to focus on the one immovable sighting which centres reality at its intelligibilizing axis: the *Logos*, Christ.[87] This vision of the ultimate reality of God made speech will ensure the realization of the immediate sighting of the rhetorical theologian, the transformation of men.

If it is true enough that each discipline has its own view of reality, it is also plain from scanning history that theologians adopt varying perspectives from different stances on the panorama of revelation. Aquinas, for example, had synoptic eyes which swept the spectacle of creation, integrating the finest details of God's tracery into a harmonious vision and baring the luminous penetration of mystery into all things. Luther's eye was singly focused, tenaciously fixed on God's unique salvation in Jesus. What a theologian adopts both as the focus and the perspective of his art defines his charism and measures his fidelity to the gospel and its tradition. Erasmus terms this sighting the *scopus* and declares that in true theology it is Christ.

This term, which one philologist notes as 'a very favourite word in the Erasmian vocabulary,'[88] codifies the grammar of theological method. Interpreters translate it as 'aim,' 'goal,' or 'target,'[89] in an oversight of its ingenious signification in Erasmus' theological methodology. The Latin lexicon lists two nouns, *scopos* as a 'mark' or 'aim' and *scopus* as a 'goal' or 'target,' offering the same phrase of Suetonius as substantiation for both; the second version is noted as doubtful.[90] To translate Erasmus' *scopus* as the 'goal' of true theology is not incorrect, but it is to shutter the liberal disclosure of meaning, as in translating *logos* by *verbum* rather than *sermo*. *Scopus* is not the technical term for the goal of an art or science. Both philosophers and theologians translated the Greek *telos* by *finis*, *terminus*, or later *obiectum formale*.[91]

The latinization *scopus* occurs as early as the second century after Christ in Tertullian's commentary on Phil 3:14. Erasmus records this.[92] The only other theological use prior to Erasmus upon which this reader has chanced is the version *scopos* in the *Omnes inquit artes* of Florens Radewijns, successor to Gerard Groote at Deventer: 'And likewise the end (*finis*) indeed of our path is the kingdom of God. But what the *scopos* might be ought to be sought diligently ... The end indeed of our profession, as we have said, is the heavenly kingdom; but our resolution, the design or *scopos* [of our life] is the purity of heart without which it is impossible that anyone whosoever may arrive at that end.'[93] It is tempting to imagine adolescent Erasmus browsing among the volumes of the Deventer library, and that *scopos* was a religious term particular to the schooling there. But the sentiments which provide the context of Radewijn's *scopos* are common coinage; to establish any dependence would be tendentious. The word had some currency among the humanists also. Marsilio Ficino uses it once in his translation of Pseudo-Dionysius,[94] and Budé favours it.[95] There is also Martin Luther's reference in the *Ecclesiastes Salomonis cum annotationibus*: 'Therefore our first task will be to hold to the certain *scopus* of the book, what it seeks and by what means it looks.'[96] But this appears only after the term is already well established in Erasmus' own writings.

The word first occurs in Erasmus' vocabulary, it appears, in his initial letter, composed in 1499, to the sea-faring poet, Publio Fausto Andrelini. 'Is our Scopus, suddenly converted from a poet to a soldier, handling dread arms instead of books?'[97] In this sentence *scopus* has the Greek sense of a 'lookout-man' or 'scout.'[98] Erasmus next attends to *scopus* in compiling classical adages. *Scopum attingere* is 'to obtain a promise or by prophecy to pursue the very thing.' He cites the usage of Lucian. He notes related forms of the proverb; namely, *non attingere scopum* and *aberrare a scopo*. Diogenes and Pindar supply examples, as does Gregory Nazianzen.[99] Examples of this proverbial usage of *scopus* as a 'mark' or 'goal' will occur later, in the *Ciceronianus* for example.[100]

It is in the *Enchiridion*, however, that the noun acquires significance as a theological term. The context is emphatically ocular. The rule of the Christian knight is 'set Christ before you as the only *scopus* of your whole life and direct all your efforts, all your activities, all your leisure, all your business in his direction.' This injunction, in which Christ becomes a prefixed sign, is followed by the advice to 'let your eye be clear' and 'look at Christ alone.' Barren and harmful deeds, Erasmus warns, result from a 'misdirected eye' which 'looks elsewhere than at Christ.' 'What end do you have in view?' Erasmus inquires of his reader. If you fast only for pious display, then 'your vision is corrupted.' If you fast because you fear sickness, 'your vision is faulty.' If you do anything for yourself and not for Christ, 'you have strayed from the sign which a Christian ought everywhere to have set before him (*a signo ... praefixum*).' But if you decline to fast, and instead eat in order to sustain a prayerful life, then 'you have attained the mark (*scopum attigisti*).' Erasmus contrasts the Christian who sights Christ alone with the fellow who 'eyes' St Christopher or 'gazes at' images of Job. He assures the reader that by scrutinizing his efforts in the light of this rule, to sight Christ as the *scopus* of life, 'you will not stray from the path at any time.' 'Do not let the eyes of your heart stray in any way from Christ, your exemplar. Following the lead of truth you will not go astray; walking in his radiance you will not stumble in darkness.'[101] In the *Ratio* it is true theology which serves this pilgrim by taking Christ as the *scopus* of the discipline. By the year when Erasmus composes the *Ciceronianus* the Christian commonwealth is so fractured by wars of religion that Christ becomes not the distinguishing *scopus* of theology alone, but the '*scopus* of all erudition and eloquence.'[102]

The Greek origin of the latinization illuminates Erasmus' appellation of Christ as *scopus*. In the classical lexicon the verb *skopeō* means 'behold' or 'contemplate,' referring to a particular object rather than to those universals which *theōreō* connotes; *skopē* is a lookout or a watchtower on a hilltop. *Skopos*, the antecedent of *scopus*, may signify an overseer, lookout-man, spy, and scout; or it may signify that particular mark or object upon which he fixes his eye. This latter sense of *skopos* as a 'sighting' appears both in Homer and in Plato.[103] Metaphorically *skopos* extends to 'aim' or 'end,' and Cicero employs this trope, preserving the Greek, in '*skopos* ... nihil praebere.'[104]

The Septuagint includes *skopos* in seven verses.[105] The word occurs only once in the New Testament, in Phil 3:14: *kata skopon diōkō eis to brabeion tēs anō klēseōs tou Theou en Christō Iēsou*. In

Erasmus' own annotation of this verse he tersely comments, '*kata skopon*, that is, following after a *scopus* or a prefixed sign.'[106] He chides Jerome for having interpreted the verse 'not so badly, as obscurely.' Jerome had considered *skopos* to be a 'sign pierced by arrows,' i.e., a target, the destination of the spirit. Augustine read for *kata skopon* 'following after the intention'; Cyprian read 'I pursue the rule'; and Tertullian, merely latinizing the Greek, 'following after the *scopus* I pursue the palm.'[107] As a synonym for *scopus*, then, Erasmus offers *signum praefixum* rather than *meta*[108] or *finis*. Whereas Jerome uses *praefixum* in the minor sense of 'pierced or transfixed by something,' suggesting a target, Erasmus means the primary sense of 'fixed or fastened before, set up in front.'[109]

Signum praefixum not only serves as Erasmus' synonym for *scopus* in the annotation; it also represents the Greek noun *skopos* in his translation of the Pauline verse, 'Juxta praefixum signum insequor ad palmam supernae vocationis Dei per Christum Jesum.'[110] Erasmus' commentary on the epistle seeks to interpret Paul's use of *skopos*,[111] and does not exclude, of course, applications of the word which Erasmus might make independently. But it does provide in *signum praefixum* an explicit synonym for *scopus* in a theological context. In the *Ratio* Erasmus interchanges *scopum praefixerat* for *signum praefixerat* when he writes of Paul's undertaking an apostolic function.[112] The 'sign fastened before' is a good equivalent to the Homeric and Platonic *skopos* as the particular sighting upon which the observant scout fixes his eye.

Patristic usage preserves the meaning of *skopos* as a lookout-man and develops the classical notion of an *epi-skopos* to signify a bishop, the man who oversees the Church. The Greek Fathers also extend *skopos* metaphorically as an end, aim, or object.[113] There is evidence too of the use of *skopos* to mean model or exemplar.[114] But it is Athanasius, championing orthodoxy in the fourth century, who baptizes the word. He charges the Arians that they would not have shipwrecked the faith, if only they had clung fast to the *skopos ekklēsiastikos* as the anchor of faith.[115] Here is a curious conjunction of Erasmus' emblematic anchor and his sighting. The patristic Greek lexicon assigns this *skopos ekklēsiastikos* of Athanasius a distinctive meaning: 'the purport, meaning, significance of tradition.[116] One ecclesiastical historian claims that Athansius' *skopos ekklēsiastikos* is the 'Church's peculiar and traditionally handed down grasp of the purport of revelation.'[117] No rationale is offered for this denotation, although it does reflect John Henry Newman's interpretation of Athanasius' 'ecclesiastical scope' as the *regula fidei.*[118]

The navigational context of Athanasius' usage, which reappears in Erasmus' *Ratio*, suggests to me rather that the *skopos ekklēsiastikos* is an angle of vision, a navigational sighting such as a star-fix which the Church shoots towards the cosmos. Whatever Athanasius may have intended, this is precisely the figurative context which Erasmus adopts to exploit his methodological *scopus* of true theology. Whether Erasmus applied the text of Athanasius, or whether they drew independently from a commonplace, can only be conjecture. The KATA AREIANŌN LOGOS PROS ranks as Athanasius' most important work. Although such polemical tracts were not so popular during the Middle Ages and the Renaissance, Erasmus did read it. Indeed he published Athanasius' commentaries on the Pauline epistles in 1518, the year of the *Ratio*, and in the following year an edition of his *Opera omnia.*[119] This circumstantial evidence suggests that the new nautical turn which he gives *scopus* in the *Ratio* may have been inspired by a reading of that venerable bishop who sought to rescue an imperiled Church, much as Erasmus was now casting on its rough seas an emergency anchor. If Athanasius did not define his *skopos*, Erasmus was explicit. The *scopus* of true theology is Christ.

Erasmus' emphatic connection of the human eye with its *scopus* reflects the literal Greek denotation of *skopos* as a 'sighting.' Do not drop your eye from its sighting, Erasmus warns his theological candidate. The nautical imagery further suggests that he imagines the *scopus*, at least in the *Ratio*, as an astronomical sighting through a navigational instrument. He likens himself as a methodologist to those sailors who, their ship having dashed upon the cliffs (*scopulus*), swim away naked, more aware of the perils of the sea.[120] What does Erasmus consider those rocks upon which a student of theology would perish other than sirenic dialectic?[121] And what else would Erasmus help his tyro do than avoid shipwreck on the *scopulus* by navigating by the *scopus*? He warns his candidate early in the *Ratio* not to sight Cynosura lest he drift aimlessly on uncharted waters.[122] Cynosura was the Greek's name for the constellation Ursa Minor, and ever since Thales suggested in 600 BC that the Greeks adopt the Phoenician method of navigation, sailors had voyaged in the northern seas at night by Cynosura.[123] A navigator's first task was to locate the celestial pole, the lodestar in Cynosura's tail, by sighting the guards beta and gamma. He calculated the height of the pole star by shooting with a cross-staff, aiming at the star just as a cross-bowman aimed at a mark. The nautical expressions 'shooting a star' and 'taking a star-fix' which are still current today,[124] suggest very much the *signum praefixum* which Erasmus equated with *scopus*.

If the *scopus* of theology is a 'sighting,' or more astronomically a 'fix,' as the evidence indicates, then it is a precise and restricted view, just the opposite of what modern methodology means by the 'scope' of a discipline, or modern criticism by the 'scope' of a text. In employing the cross-staff and the sea-astrolabe the sixteenth-century navigator sighted a single mark – not a panoramic view – through pin holes. *Scopus* was also to provide the root for those other precise scientific sighters, the telescope, the microscope, and the periscope. If Luther's use of *scopus* in referring to the text of Ecclesiastes is related to Erasmus', then the nineteenth-century Germans who exploited his term in hermeneutics,[125] diverged from Luther's sense of the word. The 'scope' of theology and of its text, the Bible, has since passed from a restrictive to an inclusive meaning, from what Thomists would call the 'formal object' to the 'material object.' For Erasmus the scope of theology is still particular: it is Christ. By referring everything to Christ, the theologian will achieve his more immediate goal of transforming the republic.

Like Luther, Erasmus has a singly focused eye, but it is also one which, like Aquinas, allows him to explore generously the diffusion of Christ to the peripheries of human vision, as recorded, for example, in classical literature. But now the storm warnings are up: Christendom in peril of shipwreck. In Erasmus' rutter the only sure navigation for the ship of the Church is to focus on Christ and to

Fig. 2 Sighting the Pole Star with a Cross-Staff
Pedro de Medina, *Arte de navigar*. Valladolid, 1545

cast the sheet-anchor of Scripture in this emergency. The ancient
Christian metaphor of 'Peter's bark' (*navis ecclesiae*)[126] was to
preoccupy Erasmus with more urgency in the few years which
bridged the publication of the *Ratio*, his own emergency-measure,
and the emergence of his polemics against the shipwreck of
Reformation. In 1522, for example, he extended the metaphor in an
impassioned preface 'to the pious reader' which accompanied his
paraphrases for laymen on the first gospel. Recalling the evangelical
texts of Jesus and his disciples in tempests at sea, Erasmus portrays

the contemporary Church as a ship buffeted by the winds of ambition, avarice, and cupidity, and innundated by war. In such peril it ought to repeat with Peter's faith the cry, 'Lord, save us lest we perish.' And Christ will once again quiet the tempest.[127]

In his paraphrase on the same gospel Erasmus reminds his reader that the mind's eye ought to be directed with sharp vision to its true *scopus* which alone yields happiness.[128] The true astrotheologian does not gawk at pagan deities frozen into constellations like Cynosura. He fixes on Christ alone. Only this determined focus will restore Christendom through the method of true theology. Erasmus' warning in the *Ratio* that the theologian not navigate by Cynosura, but focus rather on Christ, seems also a slap at the extravagances of late mediaeval piety. Devout sailors imagined the pole star to be the Virgin Mary, guiding them steadily to their heavenly port.[129] The cult of Mary as the northern star was popularized in the hymn 'Ave Maris Stella.'[130] It was drummed into every schoolboy's ear through the one thousand one hundred and fifty-five hiccuping verses of John of Garland's *Stella Maris*.[131] As an adult Erasmus could still groan in remembrance of John of Garland's voguish school texts.[132] Erasmus' colloquy on shipwreck disparages the cult. In 'Naufragium' the sailor Adolph recounts the experience of a catastrophic voyage to an amazed landlubber.[133] In exchange for the hymns and vows and lamentations of the shipwrecked crew, Mary offers only a salty bath and five survivors from fifty-eight.[134] Determined to provide the theological candidate with a rutter by which he can securely navigate the ship, Erasmus enjoins him to take Christ alone as his celestial guide-star and Scripture as his sure anchor.

METHOD DIAGRAMMED

But language is more an oral-aural phenomenon than a visual experience, at least before its universal dissemination in print. How does 'sighting' Christ with a clear and docile eye yield the theologian that eloquent tongue which is the human imitation of the *Logos*? The theologian who knew his rhetoric would not have been troubled by the mixed metaphor of Erasmus' grammar. For Quintilian had instructed the student orator that vivid conceptions called

D

phantasms (*phantasiai*) 'must be kept clearly before our eyes and admitted to our hearts: for it is feeling and force of imagination that makes us eloquent.'[135] Civil rhetoric intended to persuade the citizenry to virtuous judgement and action by stirring emotion, even to tears. The aim of Erasmus' rhetorical theology is similarly 'to wring out tears, to inflame spirits to heavenly things.'[136] By adopting Quintilian's precept of imagination the theologian could enflesh his language. By focusing on Christ at the centre of the cosmic forum, he would command the inspiration for persuasive speech.

'There are certain experiences which the Greeks call *phantasiai*, and the Romans *visions*, whereby things absent are presented to our imagination with such extreme vividness that they seem actually to be before our very eyes. It is the man who is really sensitive to such impressions who will have the greatest power of the emotions.'[137] Such images which yielded eloquence must not only be gazed at, but also admitted to the heart, as Quintilian wrote. Similarly Erasmus urges the tyro not only to sight Christ but to transform himself into the very doctrine which he learns.[138] For of what use is food for the mind, he asks, until it becomes visceral?[139] Indeed the only eye which can view Christ is the 'eye of faith,' the 'eye of the heart.'[140] This eye which discerns Christ is an interior organ; interior disposition makes the theologian an eyeful reader. To become a theologian, a discourser on God, one need only develop that 'simple and dovelike eye of faith, which perceives nothing but heavenly things.'[141]

What is this phantasm of Christ upon which the theologian takes his sighting? Erasmus deplored the profitable trade in icons which ornamented every peasant's hut. Christians eagerly venerate the tunic of Christ in reliquary, or even his supposed footsteps, he observed. The lavish gems and gold on their favourite statues. 'But why do we not venerate instead the living and breathing image of him in these books? ... Why not rather, mark with gold and gems ... these writings which bring Christ to us so much more effectively than any paltry image?'[142] The theological sighting is not mere vision, but vision rendered intelligible through language. It is the text. It is that text in which Christ spoke as *sermo* the Father's holy mind: Scripture. The religious pedagogy of mediaeval centuries, which relied on visual image, is succeeded by the humanist doctrine of the published text. In literature 'Christ lives for us even at this time, breathes and speaks, I should say almost more effectively than when he dwelt among men.'[143] The image, Erasmus explains, 'represents only the form of the body – if indeed it represents anything of him – but these writings bring you the living image of his holy mind and the speaking, dying, rising Christ himself, and thus they render him so fully present that you would see less if you gazed upon him with your very eyes.'[144]

This assertion, the striking coda of the *Paraclesis*, is echoed in the *Ratio* when Erasmus claims that sixteenth-century man reading the Bible beholds God more effectively than did Moses on Sinai in the burning bush.[145] The reproduction of Christ's image in Scripture is truer than what human eyes see, the *Enchiridion* had taught.[146] Thus the humanist persuasion that an eloquent text orates reality expands in Erasmus to a lively faith in the real presence of Christ as text. As one scholar states, in Erasmus' theological method it is 'the text of revelation which provides the fundamental principle of organisation.'[147] This text is the divine *sermo*, who is Christ, preserved for the eyeful reading of Everyman. Scripture is the phantasm. If the theologian is to effect in his listeners that sense of vivid presence which propels human emotion towards act, then he must focus on the picture alphabetized: Christ the text. Eyeing that image will loosen his tongue. He will discover a colloquial partner greater than Petrarch's beloved ancients; he will hear and converse with Discourse itself. An Erasmian colloquy delineates this well. A Carthusian monk instructs a soldier that Scripture provides 'conversationalists far more witty and charming than the ordinary run of boon companions ... You see this book of the Gospels?' he continues, 'In it one talks with me who long ago, as an eloquent companion of the two disciples on the road to Emmaus, caused them to forget the hardship of their journey but made their hearts burn most fervently in their wonder at his enchanting speech.'[148] By perceiving the text and by assimilating it into his heart's eye, the theologian will be possessed by that phantasm which guarantees true eloquence, because it is the true image of the mind of him who authors all things.

Erasmus provides his tyro in the *Ratio* with a diagram, a simple mnemonic device to aid the student in apprehending this focal Christ and the configuration of reality which surrounds him. Graphically it is neither so elaborate as William Caxton's chessboard[149] nor as Nicholas of Cusa's anatomy of state.[150] Erasmus deplored pedagogical machines so intricate that they hindered rather than alleviated learning. He singled out for attack all 'mnemonic puzzles contrived for making money or for ostentation more than usefulness.'[151] But he thought that simple ocular impressions aided the student's memory. He advocated geographical charts, genealogical trees, tables of syntax, emblematic rings and cups, doors and windows inscribed with maxims, all of which might contribute to knowledge. Trivial in themselves, they would have a cumulative value.[152]

As Erasmus instructs his student with the diagrammatic allegory, the Christian commonwealth is a sphere of three concentric circles radiating outward from Christ.[153] Christ is the *scopus*, the sighting, who must remain intact. 'Do not remove Christ from his own central position,'[154] Erasmus admonishes. In the first circle, nearest to the centre, Erasmus locates the priestly estate which succeeds Christ, adhering to him and following wherever he goes: priests, abbots, bishops, cardinals, and popes. Proximate to this sacerdotal procession is the circle of the secular princes who serve Christ in their own fashion with arms and the law. The third, most solid circle is allotted to common man.[155] With this device Erasmus supplies the student a mnemonic model of Christ as the central focus of true theology and all men tending, each class by its own methods, towards a transformation of life which will relate men more closely to Christ.

This diagrammatic allegory shares some distinctive traits of the genre of estates literature. In its mediaeval and Renaissance form this genre is characterized by an ennumeration of the estates of the world; by lament over the particular failures of each estate; by a philosophy of dependent harmony among the estates; and finally, by a remedy, often religious, for the defects of the estates.[156] Unlike

the finely detailed portrait of the classes who troop after Folly in the
MŌRIAS EGKŌMION (Praise of Folly), this mnemonic device is
pared to the three general estates of the culture: church, civil
government, and common life. Erasmus catalogues the respon-
sibilities of the priestly and princely classes, stressing those of his
own estate, a tendency of the genre.[157] Priests are to 'offer
acceptable sacrifices to God, nourish the people with the food of
evangelical discourse (sermo), colloquy with God in undefiled
prayer, and, whether they intercede for the safety of the flock or
meditate at home in secret studies, render the people better.'
Princes are to maintain civil order, serving divine justice and public
peace. Whereas the priestly estate mirrors Christ in a glass, the
princely estate reflects him in iron. Erasmus also ennumerates the
vices to which these classes are prone: priests to love of pleasures,
zeal for money, ambition, avidity for life; princes to exercising
power in their own interests, to inciting war and civil strife.
Erasmus here omits the duties of common man, but he blames him
for his pliability to the persuasions of evil leadership, a vulnerability
occasioned by ignorance.[158] This device of complaint on the
degeneration of the age recalls to the reader a more perfect
civilization in which the estates each served its duty and kept
faith.[159] Erasmus desires a renaissance of that civilization. He
preaches that the common sacrament of baptism demands co-
operation in Christ;[160] each estate has its divinely sanctioned
purpose for the good of the commonwealth.

Erasmus' noted letter to Volz, penned in the same year as the
publication of the Ratio, proposes a more elaborate version of this
diagrammatic allegory. In that correspondence the organic
metaphor of the human body is superimposed upon the geometric
model of concentric circles. Christ is the head. The priestly class
composes the eyes. The noblemen form the arms. And common
man is the genitals, legs, and feet of the body.[161] The analogy
between the body politic and the human body was again a familiar
device of estates literature.[162] When the theologian takes a clear
sighting on Christ he will gain the vision to accommodate the
members of Christ's body, each in its special needs. The sure
remedy for the dissension fracturing the body of Christendom is a

return to evangelical teaching. By concentrating 'faith's clear and docile eye' upon Christ at the centre of the commonwealth, its concord will be restored. This is the conviction which supports Erasmus' presentation.

This diagrammatic allegory of Christ as the central sighting in a sphere of concentric circles which also form his body may serve well as a heuristic for discerning the grammar of Erasmus' method in theology. Western culture has borrowed mainly from the ocular science of plane geometry to diagram its logic of speaking. Epistemology relies almost exclusively on visual metaphor (understanding as 'seeing') and on measurement (meaning as 'definition,' i.e. drawing limits, or as 'explanation,' i.e. laying out flat).[163] The theologian, too, has resorted to Euclid for measuring his concept of religious language. Both Thomas's doctrine of analogy[164] and Tillich's theory of symbolism[165] are, for example, conceived on spatial depth models. Meaning is referential in that the sense of the word 'God' and talk predicated of him is derived from relationship to a referent *beyond* the language. Meaning, dependent upon the ontological reality which the words denote and / or evoke, lies *behind* the words. Religious language is a system of paradigms reflecting the structure of existence, not by direct anthropomorphism or by mythology, but nevertheless 'somehow' (Thomas' *quodamodo*). The dualism of the depth model is manifested, as another scholar observes, in that specific words rather than others have validity to reveal and construct the divine level.[166] The depth-dimensionality of these cardinal theories is placed in relief by contrast with a theory of extensional meaning, such as Wolfhart Pannenberg's argument that meaning lies at the *end* of history.[167] John Hick's linguistic theory of eschatological verification[168] approximates a horizontally linear model.

This abbreviation of the geometry of religious discourse suggests why Erasmus' concentric model may disclose not only the symbolic logic of the macro-microcosm which constitutes his vision of reality, but also his grammar of method in theology. Northrop Frye has observed concisely that the 'link between rhetoric and logic is a "doodle" or associative diagram, the expression of the conceptual by the spatial ... Very often a "structure" or "system" of thought can be reduced to a diagrammatic pattern – in fact both words are to some extent synonyms of diagram.'[169] One may appeal also to Ernst Cassirer's claim that the intellectual orientation of the cosmos, including the form of logico-mathematical definition, sprang from the spatial orientation of the mythical beginnings. 'The simple spatial terms,' he philosophizes, 'thus became a kind of original intellectual expression. The objective world became intelligible to language to the degree in which language was able, as it were, to translate it *back in terms of space*.'[170] Finally there is Walter Ong's guarantee that 'at the time of the Renaissance, nothing is more evident than the role which spatially oriented conceptualizations began to play in the notion of knowledge itself.'[171] By exegeting Erasmus' diagrammatic allegory, his picture alphabetized, we may secure a more penetrating appreciation of the rationale of his *Ratio*, the grammar of method.

In Erasmus' visual conception of theology's scope, Christ is both located at the centre geometrically and identified as the head organically. An ideal model for reproducing the allegory spatially is an armillary sphere with its concentric bands rotating around a central axis.[172] The ring dial invented by Gemma Frisius, professor of mathematics and medicine at Louvain and a contemporary of Erasmus,[173] is also instructive as it has only three bands. Erasmus states his conception of the commonwealth as spherical in shape.[174] How Christ can simultaneously be the 'centre' and the 'head' of this conceptual globe resolves cleverly with some knowledge of Renaissance navigation.

In the regiment of the pole star the northern point of the mariner's compass, or the tail of Cynosura, was metaphorically dubbed the 'head.' Renaissance astronomical drawings depict the body of a man splayed out over the celestial globe, with his head at the pole star, his hands touching the eastern and western compass points, and his feet in the southern quarter or antipodes. Leonardo da Vinci's well-known sketch of Microcosmus is illustrative. In Pedro de Medina's cardinal *Liber de cosmographia*, considered the first literature of navigation, the cosmographer instructs the pilot:

PILOT. Why is it that when we take the altitude of the north star, we call 'head' the part above, and 'foot' the part below? How is it that there are head and foot in the sky?

COSMOGRAPHER. Let me explain that there are four parts of the sky, east, west, south, and north. Those four parts we compare to the body of a man. We call the east, although most noble, the left arm; and the west, the right arm; the north is called head and the south foot.[175]

Recalling that the theologian's model of the commonwealth is a celestial globe or armillary sphere, one may comprehend how the 'head' is also the 'centre.' The 'head' is the northern compass point or lodestar. This star is not cosmologically discrete but an arctic (*arktos* = bear) pole which forms the northern axis of the sky, passing through the centre of the earth and binding the universe together. This is my reading of the *Ratio*'s rationale: the recapitulation (heading) of all things in Christ at the axis of intelligibility. The brilliance of Erasmus' symbolism begins to emerge. The philosophy of Christ is indeed 'heavenly,' but penetrating earth. From his central position at the axis of reality, Christ will teach the theologian how to read the secret alphabet engraved in the human spirit and in the biblical text, those mirrors of his own colloquial Self.

The complexity of Erasmus' grammar diagrammed, which locates Christ variously at the centre and on the northern circumference at the head of the cosmic body, is not unprecedented. A twelfth-century pseudo-hermetic text, popular with mediaeval and Renaissance Platonists, identifies God as simultaneously the centre and circumference of the world: 'God is an intelligible sphere whose centre is everywhere and circumference nowhere.'[176] It was the imaginative Nicholas of Cusa, positing the equivalence of all divine attributes, who adopted this model as a metaphor of theology itself: 'And so all theology,' he concluded, 'is said to be arranged in a circle.'[177] It is not fortuitous that in the *Ratio* Erasmus terms Scripture, that textual presence of Christ, an orb and its doctrine a circle. He instructs the exegete, diligently opening both testaments, to consider 'that wondrous orb and consensus of the entire fable of Christ.'[178] Not only do old and new covenants harmonize in him, but also the probity of his life agrees with that 'whole circle of doctrine which is his.'[179] The scholar may claim a consensus with Christian teaching in the writings of Plato or Seneca or Socrates, Erasmus notes in obvious allusion to his Italian contemporaries. 'But this circle,' he claims, 'and the congruent harmony of all things among themselves you will find in Christ alone.'[180] Erasmus especially remarks the 'rotating circle' in Jn 12 and 13 which commends Christian society as an image of trinitarian communion. The binding force of that divine community, he explains, dictates that the knowledge or rejection of Christ includes the knowledge or rejection of Father and Spirit.[181] To pretend the role of theologian without fixing on Christ, the courier of revelation, is to miss the mark. What is the use of reviving a Platonic theology when there can be no true theology without Christ as its central focus? To exclude Christ from vision's scope is to reject God. 'For thus you read in the epistle,' Erasmus reminds us with that citation which was to stir notorious controversy, ' "Three are they who give testimony in heaven, Father, Speech (sermo), and Holy Spirit, and these three are one." '[182] Christ, who is the incarnate articulation of divine society, draws his disciples, his bodily members, into that same circular consort, conciliating all things.[183]

What is the sacred geometry of the Erasmian circles? The first circle is the harmony of trinitarian communion. This is the emblem of eternal perfection. In the contemporary cosmology the physical order of nature copies this in the concord of the spheres, nested concentrically and orbiting with circular perfection. Microcosmic earth, groaning around on its axis, bears the additional circles of the geographical zones, the locations of the three estates. Into the circular consort of the Trinity Christ draws the social orders which reflect both divine and natural perfection by a sphere of human concord. *Circulus* was a common classical synonym for a social company as well as for the celestial circuits. In its circularity the Christian commonwealth imitates divine perfection, rotating on the axial Christ. And binding all things together at the axis of intelligibility is Christ's 'orb of doctrine.'

Those readers who had studied Quintilian, as Erasmus advised, would have recognized in the term *orbis doctrinae* the Greek *egkuklios paideia*, the cycle of cultured learning.[184] Christ is an encyclopaedist who draws his disciples into the true circle of learning, the discursive communion of the Trinity. As revelatory discourse itself, as *sermo*, Christ witnesses to divine harmony and bids men imitate it. By imitating the eloquence of Christ humanly, the theologian may share the intelligible harmony of all things created through that *sermo* and their creative source. If speech mirrors human spirit just as Christ reflects imaginatively the author of all life, then speech explicitly about Christ draws the analogy of divine and human societies most sharply. A faithful imitation of Christ in theological discourse cannot but restore humanity to itself in a great renaissance, for it returns humanity to its divine origin. It cannot but promote that cultured community of men building cities and inventing arts: civilization.

In this divine eloquence who is Christ the axial road through, *methodus*, and the circumferal road around, *periodus*, converge. For Erasmus Christ is a circuit, a fully rounded style of discourse, complete in itself. 'For this reason Christ is called *sermo*,' he apologizes, 'because whatsoever the Father speaks, he speaks through the Son.'[185] He is the plenitude of language, the copious discourse of God to men. In the classical theory of oratorical rhythm a *periodus* or *circuitus* was most simply a 'thought expressed in a number of words, duly rounded to a close.'[186] Quintilian instructed that it must complete the thought which it expresses with clarity and intelligibility. Its length should encompass a single breath and not be too unrestrained to retain in memory.[187] As *sermo* Christ fulfils the definition: the complete, clear, memorable discourse of the Father. Like the construction of a periodic style in which the 'whole passage is made to converge at the end,'[188] theology ought to refer everything to its end, Christ, with regular cadence. When the exegete reads Scripture, whether old or new covenant, he must sight Christ alone, considering 'that wondrous orb and consensus of the entire fable of Christ'[189] which defines the Bible. The oratorical circuity which suggests the definition of *sermo* ought to be the exemplar of theological style also: complete, clear, memorable discourse, converging at its end. If for platonizing Cusa theology is round because the divine attributes are circular, for rhetorizing Erasmus theology is circular because the whole world turns on a period.

Like the navigator sighting the pole star through the pin holes of his cross-staff, the theologian sights a single point (*scopus*). This periodic Christ is the point of reference. Erasmus has explained in the *Ratio* that each discipline claims a unique point of reference, and theology has Christ.[190] 'Refer everything to Christ,'[191] he admonishes again and again. Such is not vague pious counsel, but rather, methodological advice that the theologian adopt the rhetorical art of invention. Invention was the primary classical procedure by which the orator found through searching (*invenire*) examples or precepts which might motivate his audience. Invention resorted to 'places' (*loci*) or 'topics' (*topoi*) which were seats of argumentation. From these places the speaker derived devices and maxims to amplify his oration.[192] In the *De copia* Erasmus had ennumerated varieties of commonplaces which the student would find useful, mentioning that the theologian ought to extract his from Scripture.[193] The pastiche of biblical texts which comprises the volume of the *Ratio* is partly an exercise in commonplaces. These places offer the candidate a model for his own first foray into Scripture. They exhibit Erasmus' hermeneutical rules by a pedagogy which is not merely normative but also exemplary.

An examination of this prolix addition to the leaner *Methodus* discloses an order of commonplaces directing the collation of illustrative texts. Because the discourse of Christ is so often 'obscure' Erasmus advises the student to collate texts. 'Repeatedly a collation of passages explains the knot of the difficulty, for what here is said more covertly, there is referred to more lucidly. And whereas almost all discourse (*sermo*) of Christ is hidden in figures and tropes, the candidate of theology will by diligence get an inkling of what the speaker intends.'[194] Erasmus' first exemplary collation centres, as the reader might expect, on Christ: what Christ forbids, what Christ instructs, what Christ solicits but does not exact, what Christ contemns, and what Christ is indifferent to.[195] This gathering of texts for clarity of understanding is not unlike the theologian's personal virtue of collection (*collatio*) in the midst of disputation,[196] an alignment of method and virtue.

The rule of biblical hermeneutics, an appropriation of classical commonplaces, follows. Erasmus advises, 'Tend not only to what is said, but also by whom it is said, to whom it is said, with what words it is said, in which time, on what occasion, what precedes and what follows.' The language of John the Baptist, for example, is not that of Christ. Nor does Christ address the rude populace in the same manner as he does his own disciples. He responds differently to men questioning him insidiously from men inquiring of him in simple spirit.[197] The theologian, Erasmus teaches, must discern these variations of speech with the rule of commonplaces.

Erasmus illustrates the commonplace of persons with the New Testament tropes of the head and members, the shepherd and the flock.[198] No perfunctory catalogue of texts, this section of the *Ratio* discourses rhetorically on the office of the Christian pastor. While this might have seemed digressive to scholastic readers, for Erasmus the people of God who surround theology's *scopus* are integral to the definition and purpose of the discipline. Theological questions and issues are not to be discussed abstractly, but oriented towards the practical and common life of the Christian republic. One sights Christ in order to transform men. The second commonplace, time, parallels this. In sectioning history into five eras, each illustrated with appropriate biblical texts, Erasmus comments on the contemporary state of the Church. Texts exemplary of the Pentecostal age, for example, provide him an excuse for criticizing ecclesiastical law and ritual.[199] The era of Church empire is a springboard to a discourse on peace.[200] And so forth. The extensive use of commonplaces in the *Ratio* not only offers a model for collating biblical pericopes in order to clarify the meaning of the text, it also commends the theologian to render his exegesis of service to the people. The technique must foster the theological goal of expounding Scripture wisely, so that the crowd will depart the learned assembly, better men.

The method of commonplaces which Erasmus advocates in the *Ratio* affords another opportunity for discerning the grammar of his method. For these places are so many headings by which the theologian may refer everything to the one head, the singular commonplace, Christ. When Erasmus admonishes the theologian to 'refer everything to Christ,' he alludes to the method of rhetorical invention, considering Christ as a 'place.' Furthermore, Christ is the central place: 'Do not move Christ from his own central position,'[201] he warns. Cicero had advised his son that 'when the line of discussion is decided upon, the speaker must have before him a point of reference to which to refer all the lines of argumentation obtained from the topics of invention.' Such a point of reference, to which the diverse arguments derived from the topics might be referred comprehensively, was called a 'commonplace.'[202] In this collective sense of 'commonplace,'[203] Christ is the commonplace of theology. He is that single 'topic,' that point of reference to which all scriptural passages and the commentary upon them which comprises theology must be referred for verification and understanding. He is the fountain, storehouse, or head from which the theologian derives the rhetorical argument for amplifying his speech. This is, in my reading, the foundation of Erasmus' term *ratio verae theologiae*: Christ himself as *ratio*, the head or principle of theology. Such is Christ as the paradigm of Erasmus' methodology: that plenitudinous and summary principle from which the theologian may invent the art of human eloquence.

Erasmus here seems inspired by the Pauline doctrine of recapitulation. In his annotation of Eph 1:10 Erasmus displays his semantic knowledge of *anakephalaiōsasthai* as *recapitulari*, 'to gather up to the highest points.' He mentions the use of the term by orators to designate the summary repetition for judgement of matters which have been stated diffusely. He remarks on the theological interpretation of the word in Greek patristic literature; namely, 'that Christ has become the head (*caput*) of angels and men, Jews and Gentiles.' Erasmus suggests that this interpretation is supported by verse 22, '[God] has made him the head over all things for the church,' and that the Greek word has the sense of referring to the head (*revocare ad caput*).[204] But it is in his paraphrase of the epistle that Erasmus evidences his own appreciation for the doctrine of recapitulation, a doctrine which he has emphasized variously in earlier works by insisting on the primacy of Christ as the single head, sighting, source, and Lord of truth and life. His famous dictum, 'Consider, moreover, that any truth you come upon is Christ's,'[205] is recapitulated itself in the paraphrase when he claims that the highest things which pertain to true innocence and beatitude, which some men sought through the observance of the Mosaic law, others through the study of philosophy, still others through superstitious religion and the daemonic cult, are now 'gathered upwards into the one Christ.' He is the 'single fount' from which whatever good there may be in heaven or on earth must be sought. 'For God the Father willed him to be the head of all and willed every man to depend upon this one man.'[206] This economic function of Christ as Lord of the universe and head of the Church, the divine summation of reality, seems to me to secure its methodological counterpart in Christ as *ratio verae theologiae*. And as often as the theologian applies the method of invention, referring texts to Christ, he imitates that saving recapitulation of things in the divine economy, God's plan in Christ. He fulfils Erasmus' ideal of the Christian orator, saviour of the commonwealth.

Erasmus' singular vision of the harmony of the Christian body in its head and the organization of theology under that same head demands the slaying of the many-headed monster, the Hydra scholasticism. As quickly as one might lop off a single premise, six hundred new syllogisms would sprout.[207] Erasmus was convinced that theology ought to be referred to one single head, Christ. By stylistic play the *Paraclesis* had already asserted the tension of the one and the many which was to characterize his methodology. The rhetorical shift is between the concord of Christ and the divisions of the schoolmen, the loquacity of the theologians and the *Logos*. In the business of Christ 'what we desire is that nothing may stand forth with greater certainty than the truth itself, whose expression is the more powerful, the simpler it is.'[208] Erasmus complains that while human industry is applied ardently to all other branches of learning, the singular philosophy of Christ is derided, neglected, or coldly discussed. While sects of Platonists, Pythagoreans, Academics, Stoics, Cynics, Peripatetics, and Epicureans multiply, who embraces Christ's philosophy alone? he asks. 'Let them magnify the leaders of their sect as much as they can or wish. Certainly he alone was a teacher who came forth from heaven; he alone could teach certain doctrine, since it is eternal wisdom; he alone, the sole author of human salvation, taught what pertains to salvation, he alone vouches for whatsoever he taught, he alone is able to grant whatsoever he has promised.'[209]

The motif of the sufficiency of Christ continues compellingly. That wondrous author descended to teach after so *many* families of distinguished philosophers, after so *many* remarkable prophets. His wisdom, 'so extraordinary that once for all it renders foolish the entire wisdom of this world, may be drawn from its *few* books as from the most limpid springs with far *less* labour than Aristotle's doctrine is extracted from so *many* obscure volumes, from those *huge* commentaries of interpreters at odds with one another – and I shall not add with how much *greater* reward. Indeed, here there is no requirement that you approach with so *many* troublesome sciences. The journey is *simple* and it is ready for anyone.' The doctrine of Christ is more common and accessible than the sun.[210]

What men jealously restrict, Christ wishes to be public. The noisy disputations, everywhere in contradiction, must be replaced by co-operation in Christ. Theological quarrels about instances, relations, quiddities, and formalities, so obscure and irksome, should be abandoned for what Christ taught simply. By devoutly philosophizing at the single source of Scripture, the theologian will discover in compendium the entire wisdom of men. 'Although you may cite a thousand rules, can anything be holier than this?' It surpasses the combined learning of the scholastics. The authority of the author needs no endorsement from the schools, for his testimony is from the Father. 'Certainly he is the one and only teacher, let us be disciples of him alone. Let each one extol in his own studies his own author as much as he wishes, this utterance ["This is my beloved Son in whom I am well pleased; hear him"] has been said without exception of Christ alone.'[211]

This tension of unity and multiplicity is reinforced in Erasmus' theological tracts and correspondence. The proportion is inverse: the more symbols, the less faith; the more articles, the less sincerity.[212] In one balance are the multiplied disputes of the schoolmen, in the other the exclusive teaching of Christ. The 'swarms of schoolmen,' their ears attuned to 'propositions, conclusions, and corollaries,' indulge in 'absurdities, quarrelsome and insipid questions,' 'frivolous quibblings,' 'petty fallacies of logic,' 'thorny and intricate arguments,' a 'maze of disputations.'[213] Erasmus complains that 'there are almost as many commentaries on the *Sententiae* [of Peter Lombard] as there are theologians. What other kind or category of manual writer is there except those who blend over and over again one manual with another and, in the fashion of the pharmacist, repeatedly concoct the old out of the new, the new out of the old, one out of many, and many out of one?' In many volumes about 'innumerable' matters, they 'examine minutely each single topic ... yet they fail to agree among themselves.'[214] 'There are many problems which it would be better to pass over than to examine,' but alas, Erasmus sighs, there is 'no end of these little questions.'[215] The scholastic method of ennumerating doctrines and of dissecting them into *quaestio, utrum, videtur quod, sed contra est, responsio* sends Christians 'scurrying in all directions' instead of striving 'in *this* direction,'[216] i.e., Christ as the central sighting. In Erasmus' judgement the scholastic balance, though weighted with verbiage, is featherweight. 'They are more stupid than any pig and lack common sense, they think they themselves occupy the whole citadel of learning. They bring everyone to task; they condemn; they pontificate; they are never in doubt; they have no hesitations; they know everything. And yet few in number as they are, these people are causing tremendous commotion.'[217] An alternative is pressing. Amid 'so great variety of human opinions,' the sure recourse must be the 'reliable sheet-anchor of the gospel teaching.'[218] And that is the anchor emblematic of the *Ratio*.

If divisive quantification is the mark of scholastic method, concord is the unmistakable sign of true theology. The parallel between the critique of scholastic method and the critique of writing with which he opens the *De copia* is striking. Counselling condensation as the mark of an admirable style, Erasmus deplores those who practice 'futile and amorphous loquacity, as with a multitude of inane thoughts and words thrown together without discrimination, they alike obscure the subject and burden the ears of their wretched hearers.' While speech with a rich *copia* is splendid, it must be disciplined by principles, examples, and rules.[219] He who desires to be divinely eloquent must first travel by compendium to the fount, the head, the *ratio* of true theology: *Logos* itself, Christ.

In distinction to the oral bombast of the Scotists, the philosophy of Christ is simple eloquence. Theology ought not to foster division, but to reflect methodologically, as well as doctrinally, the singular Christ and the concord of all men in his body. Instead of complicating the discipline, Erasmus advised, 'rather we must strive to render this art as simple as possible and accessible to all.'[220] Christ is sufficient. He is the 'one head,' the 'captain,' the 'only light,' the 'one and only good,' the 'one Lord of all,' 'sole master and sole Lord,' the 'only source both of true understanding and a happy life,' the 'one ... mightier than all the rest,' and the 'sole archetype.'[221] All must unite under this one head and everything must be referred to him.[222] The rule of the Christian is 'that you set Christ before you as the only goal of your whole life and direct all your efforts, all your activities, all your leisure, all your business in his direction ... Look at Christ alone as the absolute good, so that you may love nothing, marvel at nothing, want nothing but Christ or because of Christ.'[223]

Christ is the centre of theological attention. From his central position at the axis of reality, he will teach the theologian how to read the Father's discourse engraved both in the biblical text and in the human spirit, those mirrors of Christ's own colloquial self. The 'simple and clear eye of the gospel'[224] becomes one's visionary organ for discerning this *sermo*, interior to interior. To the man who watches Christ steadily the 'within' of Scripture discloses its secret alphabet, lending intelligibility to the cosmos.

Christ is the 'sole archetype,'[225] *archē*: beginning and foundation principle. 'In the beginning was the speech and the speech was with God and the speech was God. He was in the beginning with God; all things were made through him, and without him was not anything made that was made.'[226] Erasmus' diagrammatic allegory concentrates the intelligibility of existence as he perceives it. Christ is the archetype from whom all laws flow.[227] And who else is this Christ but *sermo*, the Father's copious oration to men. Whoever departs from this sole archetype, Erasmus warns, 'even by a finger's breadth, wanders from correctness and misses the path.'[228] Such is the path of true theology, the *methodus* (*meta-hodos*) which requires the journeyman to fix his eye on the archetypal Christ. In Erasmus' grammar Christ is the head, the commonplace, the *ratio verae theologiae*. This function complements his identity as divine rhetoric, *sermo, oratio*, in a suggestive parallel to the Stoic doctrine of the *logos endiathetos* or *ratio* and the *logos prophorikos* or *oratio* which some Church Fathers appropriated.[229] From classical oratory through the Renaissance, the commonplace was considered not only the source of amplification, but also itself an *oratio*,[230] a crystallized speech which might be set like a polished ornament into the larger oration. To seek Christ then is to find by invention that most eloquent *oratio*, that divine amplification of the Father which contains all possibilities for human discourse.

SYMBOLIC MATRICES

Erasmus' diagrammatic allegory has two symbolic matrices in an ingenious fusion of macrocosm and microcosm: astronomic models and urban plans. Let these matrices represent the allegorical setting, the scenic backdrop for the staged characters of the Christian commonwealth. Let the metamorphosis of these symbols be the plot of his renaissance.

Anaximander's cosmology is the matrix of a symbolic order which Erasmus' diagram mirrors in reverse. For the first cartographer of Western civilization the universe copied strict mathematical ratios as the visible symbol of the idea of proportion. The universe was not a Homeric disk but a complete sphere hanging in free space with earth at its centre. The courses of all heavenly bodies were circular, with each celestial orbit at a distance three times the diameter of earth. Credited with the 'spiritual discovery of the cosmos,' Anaximander recognized a systematic justice ruling natural phenomena in a continuous process of coming-to-be and passing-away.

The nest of concentric circles which portrays Anaximander's natural universe was modelled on the proportioned life of the Greek city state.[231] Erasmus restores this cosmological projection, which by the sixteenth century was a common model for the political order, to its anthropological origin. He adopts the astronomical model to allegorize Christendom, as Anaximander had borrowed the city state to explain the natural universe. Corresponding to Anaximander's vision is Dante's allegorical pilgrimage from the dense centre of earthly hell to the outermost circle of the sun, his prominent metaphor for God.[232] But Erasmus' allegory proclaims a renaissance of the cosmos, with Christ at the centre and the pilgrims on the perimeters. The exteriorizing drive towards ever-widening horizons which characterizes Dante's plot is replaced in Erasmus by an interiorizing movement. Concentration on Christ, not the eccentricity of scholasticism, becomes the rule of the republic and of the theology which serves it. Law, justice, and transformation – the foundations of Anaximander's cosmopolis – are baptized by Erasmus. The law of Christ, the archetype of law, is poetic justice. This establishes and sustains a transforming Christian society.

Plato's more developed cosmology and the later Ptolemaic system[233] also assist in interpreting Erasmus' concentric spheres. In the TIMAIOS, which Erasmus quotes knowledgeably,[234] Plato describes how the Demiurge fashioned the world's body in perfect spherical shape, with an axial rotation symbolizing the superior movement of reason: 'He turned its shape round and spherical, equidistant every way from centre to extremity – a figure the most perfect and uniform of all.' This uniform body then received in its centre a soul; the soul extended also throughout the whole and enveloped the body. Body and soul of the world were thus fitted into the same frame, centre to centre. The Demiurge fashioned circles within the world-soul. He cut a band of pliable matter into two lengthwise strips, and bent them to touch at the middle, forming two rings. One of these rings he cut into seven smaller rings of unequal size which he fit around a common centre. This armillary sphere represented the motions of the outermost sphere of the fixed stars and planets. The planets therefore do not stray, Plato concluded, but rather circle on a track; they behave with the regularity of intelligence.[235]

Cicero's anagoge on the labours of a statesman, 'Somnium Scipionis,' from *De re publica* mirrors this cosmology. The outermost concentric circle of the statesman's dream 'contains all the rest, and is itself the supreme God, holding and embracing within itself all the other spheres.'[236] The earlier Greek notion that the gods occupied certain heavenly regions has been superseded in Cicero's identification of the empyrean *as* God. In the Stoic tradition this deity is imagined as an all-encircling sea of fire, formless yet capable of assuming all forms and in its association with the universe spherical in shape.[237] The manifestation of deity is *logos*, a rational and intelligent substance which pervades the entire world and which pressures the outermost particles towards the centre with centripetal force.[238] This *logos* acts as gravity to bind both the universe and the state,[239] collecting everything at its centre with universal equilibrium.[240] The central sphere of earth is in Cicero's cosmology 'immovable and lowest of all, and toward it all ponderable bodies are drawn by their own natural tendency downward.' In unison the celestial spheres produce a harmony which men on the unharmonious earth must imitate.[241] The proper function of the microcosmopolis, the *civitas Romana*, is the virtuous imitation of heavenly concord in *logos*.

In the *Querela pacis* Erasmus had indicated the harmony of the spheres as a model for human consideration: 'And the confederation of so many celestial circles, albeit their motion and power is not all one, yet they continue and live thus many years. The powers of the elements, striving among themselves, do defend with equal weight eternal peace; and they, in so great a discord, with a mutual consent and exchange do nourish concord.'[242] For Erasmus, committed to classical ideals, it is such concord which theology must promote, that gathering together of men through oratory which distinguishes civilization from brutality. But in his Christian republic concord depends not on the imitation of the divine empyrean as in Cicero's vision, a Stoic *logos*, but on the imitation of Christ who binds reality together at his own intelligibilizing centre. The injunction to imitate Christ is Erasmus' pedagogical instruction that the Christian imitate the divine oration as a schoolboy copies his master's paradigms. God is the supreme author who has engraved his literature both in his Son and in the human spirit. By focusing on Christ the theologian discovers how to read this text. By imitating Christ the theologian acquires godly eloquence and enhances his own humanity, which was created through that divine discourse.

The theological method of imitation which Erasmus advocates is grounded in the pedagogy of classical rhetoric more probably than in the piety of the Modern Devotion as scholars have previously insisted.[243] Critics misinformed about Erasmus' schooling have claimed the influence of Thomas à Kempis' devotional *Imitatio Christi*.[244] The culling of coincidental words like 'piety' and 'interiority' has embellished the theory of dependence, without sensitivity to the very distinct theological tonalities which common vocabulary may and does here assume in the writings of Erasmus and à Kempis. One scholar states gratuitously that Erasmus 'surely at Steyn read and re-read the *Imitation of Jesus Christ*.'[245] Erasmus, however, never acknowledges à Kempis' method of imitation; he does acknowledge Cicero's. Imitation: 'the best teacher of eloquence.'[246] The Erasmian pursuit of eloquence decisively counters à Kempis' counsel that the imitation of Christ requires a preference for silence rather than for speech.[247] Erasmus' humanist theology is the very imitation of Speech. The cultivation of interior disposition is in his advice is not self-contained asceticism; it flowers in good conversation, the spirit's perfect mirror which mediates man to man in social concord and reflects the divine colloquy.

Because of Erasmus' concern for the practice of speech in the commonwealth, the grammar of theological method merges so intimately with its rhetorical expression that it becomes difficult and even undesirable to distinguish them.[248] Grammatically the word *logos* denotes rhetoric: *oratio*. The meaning of Christ as *logos* is not the word in isolation but a revealing discourse or conversation, an eloquent persuasion to an audience which comes into its humanity in the imitation of the holy colloquy. Erasmus' social theory, his ideas on the education of the Christian prince and the government of the Church are not subsidiary applications of an a priori christological principle. They mark the translation of grammar to rhetoric, for the archetypal discourse is already engaged in the affairs of men, abidingly present in the biblical text, ready for conversation with any reader. To concentrate on Christ is to sight the *ratio* of everything and to understand that the meaning (grammar) of reality cannot be divorced from human persuasion (rhetoric). To take one's fix on Christ at the axis of the commonwealth is thus to ensure the concord of the human circles.

The astrotheology of the Renaissance Platonists is a foil to this christocentrism. According to astrotheological doctrine, the human spirit originated in the stars and acquired the 'aetheric vehicle' as it passed through various astral bodies during its descent into the body of man. The human spirit had particular likeness to the harmony of the spheres since its proper shape before inhabiting the body was spherical and its proper motion was circular. The human spirit was unusually sensitive to the movement of the heavens, and the astral bodies in turn were thought to be subject to the physical effects of vapours, scents, and sounds. The Italian Platonists indulged in theurgic practices such as fasting, lustrations, incensing, and incantations as theological methods. They appealed to the intercession of magicians. And guiding the course of city and Church was not Christ, but the astrologers who served the princes of Europe as counsellors.[249]

The belief of classical mythology that the gods might be identified with planets and stars flourished in the Renaissance. The iconography of the age includes circular diagrams to which Erasmus' allegory is a suggestive counterpart. Particularly fascinating is the conjunction of the circular motif and the human figure in the same diagram, just as in Erasmus' letter to Volz. The dissemination of astrological doctrines in the late Middle Ages inspired drawings which coalesced macrocosm and microcosm by distributing the zodiacal symbols over areas of the human body. Prayer books contemporary with Erasmus often bore these as frontispieces. But even more illuminating is the appearance of the human figure circumscribed, not by a single circle but by concentric circles. The parts of the anatomy are attached by rays to these circles. As one critic describes it, man appears 'as a victim or martyr, fettered, helpless, pierced as if with arrows by the rays of the twelve constellations, his body divided into segments each of which belongs to a given planet or star.[250] Those readers familiar with alchemical diagrams will recall the prominence of the same motifs in them.

Erasmus' diagram is an instructive counterpart to such popular illustrations. It resembles the figure of a man, the body of Christendom, enclosed in a series of concentric circles. In the allegory each band in the nest of circles also represents a part of the human anatomy. The outermost ring is the legs and loins (common man), the next inner ring is the arms (princes), the inner ring is the eyes (prelates), and the centre is the head (Christ). But unlike the iconographic man who is prisoner to the tyranny of the stars, the body of Christendom is subject to the liberating rule of its Lord. Knowledge of true astrotheology, 'the heavenly philosophy of Christ,'[251] will divulge the cure for the ills of society. Erasmus' contemporaries would not have needed to research his meaning, as the modern scholar does: Forsake your court astrologers and common magicians. What need have you for multiplied devotions to the external spheres of heaven? The philosophy of Christ alone is celestial. Take Christ for your intimate counsellor.

Erasmus' allegory challenges also the popular Renaissance illustrations of the planets with their 'children.'[252] Unlike Mercury, for example, who may only preside over those classes of artisans alloted him by Fate, Christ rules over all the earth's children. As *scopus*, he is not only the sighting upon which the theologian must fix his eye. He is also the overseer, the lookout-man. He is the true cosmocrat who oversees all vocations of the world estates, Church, government, and common life. Erasmus deplored as inanities the cabbalistic texts which captured in his estimation, the attention of too many intellectuals.[253] 'I would rather see Christ infected by Scotus, than by that rubbish,' he asserted.[254] For Erasmus such philosophy could only voice empty sounds because it gawked about the universe, instead of steadily focusing on the *Logos* at the centre. Only by sighting Christ could man speak a language full of divine, true meaning and full of persuasion for the good of society.

The microcosmic city of the Renaissance reflected this spherical perfection of the macrocosm. Its architectonic design provides the second matrix for Erasmus' concentric diagram. The history of urban development reveals that the strategy of cities reflects the religious or cosmological faith of a culture. The oldest cities of which there are reliable records, the Sumerian city states of the fourth millennium, were 'concentric, single-focused and centrifugal,' spreading outward from the sacred precinct. This temple was a ziggurat or world-mountain from where the gods, through the priests, 'arbitrated the disputes of a democratic society.' Urban piety claimed to have created a microcosm equal to the galaxies. 'The construction of a ziggurat, despite excruciatingly difficult handicaps of materials and skills, established a city-state in the dead centre of earth and sky ... Man at the centre of the universe was not a geographical fact but a truth.'[255]

The concentric planning concept became more practical than cosmological with the erection of the fortified citadel. Herodotus, travelling in the fifth century BC, described the capital of the Iranian Medes as a perfectly circular city. The concentric walls divided the population into seven castes (like an armillary sphere), each occupying one ring. The kings and nobles inhabited the innermost circle. The island community of Atlantis in Plato's TIMAIOS similarly had seven innerwalled circles whose height rose towards the centre. There each ring-wall was coloured for a planet, with the innermost painted gold for the sun and for the location of the city treasury. Later the Arabs founded Baghdad as a zodiac, oriented within an astrolabic circle, to reflect the impartial order of celestial law.[256]

Christian artists who had never seen Jerusalem portrayed this prototypical capital of the spirit as also concentric in design, with Solomon's temple at the centre.[257] Augustine's foundation of a City of God[258] and the practical necessity of defence dictated concentric city plans for Western Europe following the nomadic invasions. As an urban historian comments, 'Like their far-distant ancestors at the dawn of the Bronze Age, each town became again its own state with the cathedral as *axis mundi*, reaching from the dead centre of the community toward salvation in the sky.' Many concentric towns still thriving in Erasmus' day 'put a magic "blue stone" in the centre of the market place to claim their very own world navel, or erected a seven- or nine-stepped miniature "world mountain" with a

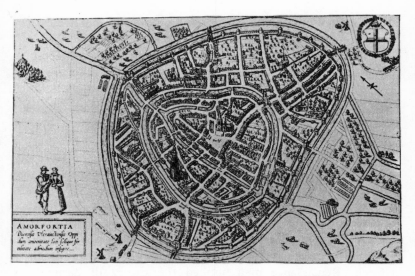

Fig. 3 The Concentric Dutch Town of Amersfoort
Civitas orbis terrarum, edited by G. Braun with engravings
by F. Hogenberg, 1572–1618

"column of justice" – a dim memory of a ziggurat as centre of the world.'[259]

The innermost ring of the typical concentric town in Europe was the original stronghold; the outermost ring, the defensive walls. In the town centre was located the market place with the church, the town hall, the clock, and the market cross.[260] Emphasis was on this city core. As Pierre Lavedan defines it, 'The essential fact of medieval urbanism is the constitution of the city in such a fashion that all lines converge toward a centre, and that the contour is usually circular. Contemporary theorists of urban development term this the radio-concentric system.'[261] The town is characterized as 'a central quarter or core, surrounded by a series of irregular rings, which have the effect of enclosing or protecting the core, while by devious passages, approaching more closely to it.'[262] So writes Lewis Mumford. The key structure of this town plan was the cathedral. Even though the church and the market occupied the same geographical centre, the church was venerated as the true centre. Its services were regular, while those of the market were occasional. The market settled around the church where the populace gathered most frequently and most solemnly.[263]

This telescoped history suggests that Erasmus' concentric model of the commonwealth is profoundly religious, even in its urbanity. If one reads it as a city map, mirroring the cosmos, it discloses his perception of divine method again. Just inside the city walls of the Christian republic are the commoners, with the princes in the next inner section, and the prelates in the church. But Christ stands at the centre of the city. The city of God on earth, the Christian commonwealth, ideally reflects the *logos* of an ordered, centred universe in which everything collects about Christ.

Inspired by the revival of Neo-platonic philosophy, Renaissance architects imagined that a church ought to serve as a microcosmic vehicle for divine revelation by imitating cosmic perfection. Whereas mediaeval man had designed in his city centre a cruciform church, Renaissance man applied the theory of harmonious proportion whereby all radii converged in the ideal centre of an ideal circle. Some architects even argued that the Mass ought to be celebrated dead in the centre of a centrally planned church, and not in the chancel. This was to make the analogy of God as the ubiquitous central point in whom realities meet. From Alberti's eulogy of the circle in *De re aedificatoria*, the first Renaissance architectural tract, the intellectual craze for circular temples flourished, until sainted Carlo Borromeo demanded in Tridentine spirit that the Latin cruciform be reinstated. Could not one see that circular forms were pagan? he asked.[264]

In Erasmus' *Ratio* true theology is portrayed by the architectural metaphor of a building.[265] The candidate lingers on the threshold, preparing himself by piety and learning languages to enter the inner chambers. Once within the sacred precinct he will venerate the altar[266] at the cosmic axis. This sacred place stands at the centre of Christendom's city; it coincides with the place of Christ. Erasmus describes Christ as building material: the solid pillar and safe foundation upon which the good theological architect constructs.[267] Scholasticism, too, is a building, but one that is constructed with the 'stubbles and hay of human commentaries.' It is a pagan ziggurat: the 'tower of Babel' he calls it.[268] This ziggurat, the symbol of the ancient city's relationship to divine realities, is a sign of confusion, a false cosmic centre which disperses the human community into factions. For as in the Genesis legend, the scholastics have the people babbling again, unintelligible to one another.

The ancient theologians who fathered the Church 'raised to heaven an edifice supported on the solid foundation of Scripture.' The moderns are raising a 'superconstructed machine, not less inane than monstrous, upon the futile arguments and adulations of men.'[269] Erasmus bids his candidate enter the true temple of God's earthly city. He is not, however, inviting him to enter a church. This is not the building consecrated with episcopal words and unction, but the temple within: a man's spirit in the image of God, without any idols. This temple is a classroom (*schola*). This temple is Christ himself.[270] The theologian is to matriculate in the school of Christ, joining in spirit that circle of learning which promotes and sustains civilization. He is not to fancy himself a pillar of Christianity, as the scholastics do,[271] but to establish everything on the solid foundation of Christ's oration. As early as his own student days at Paris, Erasmus sensed that he himself would 'overthrow the foundations' of scholasticism. This caused him such anxiety that he withdrew from his studies.[272] But he constructed anew, as the architect of the Renaissance city of God, a temple of learning on the firm foundation of Scripture and invited men to enter and so be taught of God.

The concentration of the universe on the earth and of the city on the temple focuses the symbolism of the centre in Erasmus' allegory. It shifts the cosmological order of Anaximander and the allegorical order of Dante, both of whom located God at the perimeter of empyrean light. Erasmus fixes Christ at the axis of the cosmopolis, the centre of the earthly city. The modern judgement that the Renaissance marks the 'revolution from a theocentric to an anthropocentric view of life'[273] imposes a modern equivalence of 'centre' and 'importance' upon a mediaeval culture which equated 'periphery' with 'importance.' For it was from that empyrean perimeter of the cosmos, where *Logos* dwelled, that meaning was strictly passed down the ladder of descent to man in his earthly centre. What Erasmus allegorizes then is not a shift from a God-centred universe to a man-centred one, but a focus on the cosmic *centre*, what historians have discerned as secularization. Distinguishing Erasmus' Renaissance from what will emerge as modern secularism is a convergence of orders, the sacralization of the secular through the presence of the incarnate *Logos*. At reality's centre is God-man, Christ, a divine presence in the affairs of men. This is a holy city. From his new conceptual location at the city core, Christ persuades men. Zeus *Agoraios* has yielded his place, at least for a Renaissance, to true eloquence. Erasmus' renewal of theology promotes the translation, spatial and linguistic, of Christ to the centre of social attention: the forum, the market place, and the church. To grasp the impact of his diagrammatic allegory, one need only compare his vision with the mediaeval icons of men ascending concentric ranks towards their peripheral Lord. Now Christ emerges in the forum of the Christian commonwealth, in the theological market place, as he once preached effectively in his own public life. With centrifugal force he binds reality to its axis. It is the eloquent imitation of this incarnate *Logos* which translates Christ from the eccentricity of scholastic disputation to his true central place. This is the grammar of method phrased in diagrammatic allegory.

Modern critics repeat conventionally that Erasmus was not a speculative thinker; any apparent originality is subjected to suspicion. Yet this diagrammatic allegory, which Erasmus enjoins the theologian to remember as a model for his discipline, appears to be original. Captivated by the 'geometric mysticism' of the ancients, Renaissance Platonists echoed the hermetic doctrine of God as the intelligible sphere whose centre was everywhere and circumference nowhere.[274] But in every exegesis of this text the symbol is posited of God, not of Christ, in his relation to the microcosmic world-soul. Additionally the centre or mid-point is always conceptualized in tandem with the circumference, so that the orbicular model, rather than the focal centre, is the theological symbol. As promising an alliance as the Neo-platonic mystique appears superficially, Erasmus' model is distinct in conception. It is thoroughly Christian. It is centripetal.

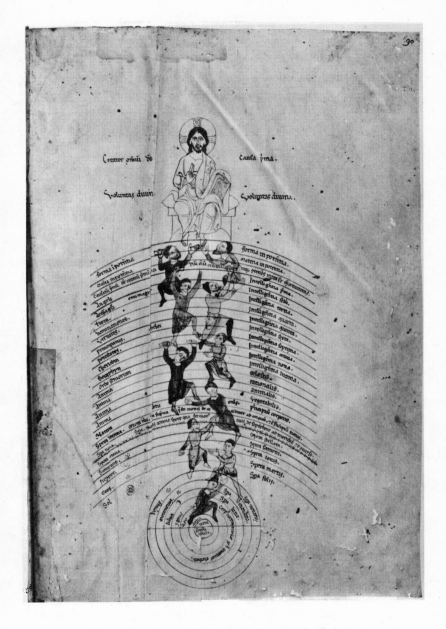

Fig. 4 The Ascent of the Soul through the Spheres
Anonymous Hermetic Ms. of the late 12th century
Photo. Bibl. nat. Paris.

There is of course Bonaventure's independent designation of Christ as a circle or as a centre;[275] there is Nicholas of Cusa's location of Christ as a centre.[276] But I know of only one text before Erasmus' writings which explicitly centres Christ in a circle. That is the round dance with his apostles from the apocryphal Acts of John:

> So he told us to form a circle, holding one another's hands, and he himself stood in the middle. And he said, 'Answer Amen to me.' So he began to sing the hymn: 'Glory be to thee, Father!' And we circled round him and answered him 'Amen.'
>
> > 'Glory be to the, Logos:
> > 'Glory be to thee, Grace. – Amen.'[277]

This glimpse of Christ at the centre of society's circle becomes in Erasmus a focal vision. The rhythm of the dance and the song complements that oratorical rhythm of circuity which secures perfect harmony in Christ. One recalls the imaginative text of the cosmic dance in Plotinus' ENNEAS where man forms a company of singing dancers who centre harmoniously around the supreme choirmaster.[278] Erasmus, who was little given to the Neo-platonic sentiments of his contemporaries, could have subscribed to that metaphor, nevertheless. Perhaps he even borrowed inspiration from John Colet who finally published at Erasmus' own insistence those lectures on the Pauline epistles which had strengthened his resolution for the renewal of Scripture. In his commentary on 1 Cor 7 Colet writes of the imitation of Christ: 'Toward it [Christ's life], as towards a common mark, set up for all, they must direct their lives; that, almost as if shooting at life, if I may so speak, they may gain the life they aim at, which will be the measure of all. Moreover, just as each one here upon earth is nearer that mark or farther off, in just such a degree will he undoubtedly be reckoned, for condemnation or for life.'[279] In the margin of the original manuscript, opposite these words, is a faint sketch of a target with several arrows approaching it.[280] Although Colet's model is an archery target, more obviously Pauline in its athletic imagery than Erasmus' diagram,[281] it does offer another humanist's correlative paradigm of Christian life. By some scholarly symbiosis, whether Erasmus borrowed from Colet or Colet from Erasmus, there also occurs in

Colet's unpublished commentary on Romans a comparison of Christ in the centre of a circle. The line of extreme tolerance, which must not be stretched or broken, forms the circumference of a circle. Christ stands at the centre. The space between the circumference and the centre affords room for counsel.[282] Such are the vague approximations to Erasmus' forthright vision of Christ at the centre of the universe and the city, binding reality together.

There are many ancient implications of the centricity of Christ in New Testament and patristic symbols: the cross as the cosmic tree; the cornerstone of the temple, its inner sanctuary; paradise and Golgotha as world centres; the door and the gate, especially the gaping gate of hell. Modern phenomenology of religion, with its analysis of the centre as the pre-eminent zone of the sacred, may be misleading however. Does this theory apply well to Western religious forms? Mircea Eliade proposes that 'every microcosm, every inhabited region, has what may be called a "Centre"; that is to say, a place that is sacred above all. It is there, in that Centre, that the sacred manifests itself in its totality ...' Even with the understanding that the centre is not to be equated with profane, homogenous, geometrical space, but is rather the spiritual intersection of the cosmic regions,[283] an objection remains.

Before the Renaissance, Latin Christianity did not extend the veneration of the sacred to include the planet earth as the sacred centre of the cosmos. For Western man earth may have claimed its sacred zones, especially the temple erected on the site of hierophany, but planet earth was not the sacred region of the cosmos. Rather it was the least spiritual place in the universe, at whose own densest centre ruled the demonic kingdom. Like Lortz's judgement about the shift from theo- to anthropocentrism, Eliade's theory presupposes the adoption of the Erasmian universe in which meaning finds its place at the centre. The pre-Renaissance grammar of religion derived from a hierarchical or multistrata cosmos, not a centred one. A popular conceptual model was the ladder of ascent, ascent to the seat of meaning, above and beyond.[284] Unlike its Eastern counterpart, Latin theology did not promote a very sturdy belief in the intimacy of earth with Christ, in whose image it was both created and recreated. But Erasmus newly secures Christ at the centre of things.

His diagrammatic allegory of concentric circles imitates both cosmological and urban realities. The more familiar model of the organic body superimposed upon the geometry deserves only summary notice here. The body is a prolific image of allegorical literature. The obvious theological exemplar for Erasmus is the Pauline description of the harmony of organs constituting the body of the Church, and the Church as the body of its ruling head Christ.[285] By transference the sacred body became the standard metaphor towards the end of the Middle Ages for the organizational constitution of the state.[286] But such metaphors of the mystical body of Christ and the mystical body-politic are too well explored by theologians and scholars of the Renaissance both to merit chronicling here. A less obvious reference may be operative, however; namely, the image of the body of discourse. In the PHAIDROS, Plato's dialogue on rhetoric which has already proved so instructive, Socrates proposes that 'every discourse (*logos*) ought to be a living creature, having a body of its own and a head and feet; there should be a middle, beginning, and end, adapted to one another and to the whole.'[287] Suppose one imagines Erasmus' digrammatic allegory as a paradigm, not only of Christendom, but of theology. Its discourse then must be living and integrated, reflecting the harmony of the body of Christ which it serves. The head or *ratio* of theology must always be Christ, and its body of discourse, well-chosen words to accommodate the varying needs and functions of its members, promoting their transformation. Whatever symbolic matrices are examined, whether by scholarly or imaginative mind, the constant grammar of method is disclosed: Christ, the Father's eloquent persuasion, binding together reality.

THE PLOT OF RENAISSANCE

The allegorical action of Erasmus' diagram is a double plot of translocation and transformation, mirroring the transition which marked the Renaissance as an age. The aim of theology, he writes in the *Ratio*, is to speak metamorphically.[288] Translocation, the directive movement of Christendom's characters from lower to higher places within a zone, or from zone to zone, is the geometric or spatial plot. Erasmus appeals to the law of nature to sanction this translocation in which men approach the central Christ. He likens this mobility to the mutations of the four elements which contemporary physics, in the Greek tradition, designated as the primary constituents of matter. Each element has its place, Erasmus instructs the candidate, whether earth, air, fire, or water. But fire, located nearest to the moon, most resembles heavenly nature. In its highest part it is very pure and liquid; in its lowest region it resembles the density of air. Air, on the upper margin of its circle, is very like fire; in its lower part, which borders on water, it is more dense. The same rule applies to the last element, earth. The four constituents of matter transform nature by mutual interaction. Fire consumes the earth, earth refines into water, water evaporates into air. By a kind of natural pedagogy the elements accommodate one another, allowing a transformation from denser into purer matter.[289] This is like, Erasmus observes, Christ's accommodation towards his weaker disciples, or Paul's indulgence of the Corinthians.[290] Christ is at the centre of the cosmos like a purifying fire which melts ice[291] and transforms every element which touches him. It was the Stoics who imagined the *logos* as elemental fire, although the encircling rim of the universe;[292] here Erasmus' imagination is closer to Pythagoras' doctrine of the central hearth which transmutes everything from within.[293] The lesson of the allegory is that the theologian needs a fiery tongue[294] which will accommodate men so as to promote the same transforming movement of human elements from a lower to a higher, purer region of the estate.[295] The mnemonic device of republican men moving closer to the transfiguring Christ reminds the theologian, too, that his discipline is meant to promote such mobility from lower to higher states. The theologian should learn from the law of elemental transformation that his own pedagogy must duplicate the activity of nature: to seize, to transform, to convert. The same verbs with which Erasmus describes the force of nature he applies to the goal of theology.[296] Finally, the theologian should learn that his pedagogy

E

will only succeed, as does nature's, by promoting the accommodation of one element to another.

Unlike mediaeval versions of estates-literature, which proscribed any change of one's lot,[297] Erasmus' allegory reflects new social mobility. Whether Erasmus took to heart Paul's preaching that in Christ there is neither Jew nor Greek, slave nor free, male nor female[298], or whether he simply perceived the burgeoning society in which a butcher's son might become cardinal-statesman, he omits the warning about transgressing one's station. After all, was not he, the cynosure of Europe, only recently a poor bastard? The prescription for the ills of Christendom is not categorically to accept the lot of one's birthright and to adhere to its duties. One may elect to alter one's estate for the progress of the republic. Erasmus himself did this in procuring dispensation from his monastic vows so that he might devote himself wholly to the renaissance of theological letters. The three companies of men circling around the central Christ are not stationary members of a hierarchy. The diagram admits mobility as individual Christians pass the boundaries. This new social mobility between estates is a Christian rite / right of passage, conferred by the common citizenship of baptism.

The second plot, transformation, in which the members of the body are metamorphosed, is organic. Its theological paradigm is the transfiguration of the body in the heavenly city. Accepting the biblical preaching of the redemption of the whole man, Erasmus believed that resurrection would restore the body and effect a perfect correspondence of the whole body of man to its head, Christ.[299] The process of transformation begins in this life by the governance of animality and by the maturation of spiritual man. Erasmus' allegorical plot of the foot (commoner) becoming the eye (prelate) reflects a Christian social order. Erasmus' world is one in which the foot may want to be an eye, and in which the ability to so transform oneself is regarded as a virtue. The mutability of man was a prime conviction of Renaissance humanists, expressed most familiarly in Pico deila Mirandola's *De hominis dignitate*. What distinguishes man from angel or brute, Pico explains, is his mutability, his unique power to mirror all orbits of the macrocosm and to simulate them by will. Pico advises chameleon man, a veritable Proteus, to decide the shape of his own being, whether to degenerate in bestiality or rule with divinity.[300] It is the prelates of the Church whom Erasmus designates the 'eyes' of Christendom.[301] They are the watchmen.[302] The pastoral model is the bishop,[303] the man who is located nearest the focal point, *epi-scopus*. Gazing nowhere except at the glory of Christ,[304] he receives this vision (cf. *phantasiai*) into his heart and so speaks eloquently to his people. But in the Christian republic Erasmus invites the common layman to keep watch also. In Christ there is a mobility which dissolves more primitive rites of passage. In the republic of Christ indeed 'the foot may become an eye,'[305] and it is such conversion that theology must promote.

The rhetoric which Erasmus adapted to serve belief is a persuasion of the will which presupposes just such mutability. Transformation, Erasmus stated, is the goal of theological discourse.[306] Classical metamorphosis expresses a power of transference which is essentially a metaphorical act. Like Circe turning men into swine, or Lucius transformed into an ass, such acts are subject to capricious fortune, but not to providence. There is no suggestion that the transformation fits into an order or plan; the magical act remains discrete, isolated, localized, like a single metaphor. Metamorphosis is a pagan plot. But there is also transfiguration which is Christian mystery. It is this allegorical order which Erasmus' methodology reflects. There is intelligibility and providence in Christ.

The Roman goddess Fortuna had multivalent status. Originally a spherical goddess of sun and moon, she absorbed all other deities in Roman culture. 'She was goddess of the state as well as of the individual; the goddess of the lower classes as well as of the higher; the goddess of women, and of young men too.' She was 'practically a goddess of the city.' Fortuna is, of course, the goddess of chance. Whereas Fate expresses a hidden law, Fortuna is anomic. Without logic or morality she bestows success or inflicts tragedy. Indiscriminately she gives to the poor, and dashes the exalted. She governs the distribution of material goods; as an overseer of worldly interests, she is blind to spiritual advancement. Divination and augury accompany her cult. Her common attribute in Roman art was the ball or wheel, symbolizing the transitoriness of life. She is blind and a harlot. She stands unsteadily on earth's globe, remaining in no place for long.[307]

In the Erasmian scheme, Christ replaces Fortuna's ever-turning wheel of caprice. His head which rotates the spinning bands of priesthood, government, and common life has also the power to liberate and to transform. Like Fortuna, the Erasmian Christ rules from the central sphere of the cosmos, but unlike her his stance is steady. Like Fortuna he is the God of the Renaissance city and all its stratified inhabitants. Like Fortuna he humbles the exalted and raises up the lowly, but his transformations conform to the law of his wisdom, which is poetic justice. Whoever would know this hidden law of Christ must imitate his wisdom with interior purity. Divination and augury are useless, for they are external influences. Christ does not assail men from above like the gods of antiquity, but works through the interiority of speech in civilization. While Fortuna is a blind harlot, Christ is the faithful bridegroom of the Church. He has eyes to see, the prelates of the allegory. Christians should look with faith's eye to perceive the abiding truth beneath the shifting surface of Fortuna.

Erasmus' plot provides an alternative not only to the metamorphoses of antique religion, but also to the transmutations of occult science practised by his contemporaries. This Christian gnosis, alchemy, with its metallurgical procedures as operational symbols for spiritual metamorphosis, shares some motifs with Erasmus' theology. There is the same insistence on interior disposition and transformation. The symbolism of the centre is again salient, as is the intelligible axis. The interior of the earth coincides with the interior of the human body, at whose depths rests the round philosopher's stone. But for Erasmus there is no need for the occult mediation of the symbolic Christ (the stone) when the real Christ is already so accessible in the text of Scripture. Unlike alchemic doctrine, sequestered in riddles, the philosophy of Christ, while mysterious, is accessible to Everyman. Both alchemist and humanist allegorize. But Erasmus claims to know the grammar.

The drive towards interiority is a theological motif well

recognized as characteristically Erasmian. This reductive rhythm is a passage from the without to the within of things, from the surface to the depth of the text, from the visible to the hidden reality, from external devotions to interior piety.[308] He often invokes the Sileni Alcibiadis as models of this mysterious interiority. In his *Adagia* Erasmus identifies the classical figure of Silenus as 'a thing which in appearance (at first blush, as they say) seems ridiculous and contemptible, but on closer and deeper examination proves to be admirable, or else with reference to a person whose looks and dress do not correspond at all to what he conceals in his soul. For it seems that the Sileni were small images divided in half, and so constructed that they could be opened out and displayed; when closed they represented some ridiculous, ugly flute-player, but when opened they suddenly revealed the figure of a god, so that the amusing deception would show off the art of the carver.'[309]

Classical examples of the Sileni were Socrates, Antisthenes, Diogenes, Epictetus. 'But is not Christ,' Erasmus asks, 'the most extraordinary Silenus of all?' His prototypes were the prophets, especially John the Baptist, and his own apostles imitated his apparent ridiculousness. The sacraments of the Church are Sileni too, as is Scripture. The Christian should not adopt what is superficially striking, but strive 'only for the things which are least obvious at a glance ... judging everything by its inner value.'[310] Like the alchemist he should 'visit the interior of the earth,'[311] but there he ought to encounter Christ, who alone transforms. The scholastics were pharmacists too, but in Erasmus' estimation, 'quacks.' 'In the manner of a pharmacist, [they] repeatedly concoct the old out of the new, the new out of the old, one out of many, and many out of one.[312] Such science has no ability to transform the republic. It is futile loquacity, superficial, and not grounded in interior *ratio*. The method of true theology which fully reflects interiority and which does have the power to transform is the veiled and mutable language of allegory.

ALLEGORY UNVEILED

The only book on the hermeneutics of Erasmus never mentions the word allegory[313] and a major biographer has decided that 'all symbolism and allegory were fundamentally alien to him and indifferent, though he occasionally tried his hand at an allegory.'[314] But other scholars have observed Erasmus' emphasis on allegory as a theological method, at least in his pre-Reformation writings. Significant passages have been compiled, locating the function of allegory within the fourfold hermeneutic and within Erasmus' theology.[315] What is the rationale of allegory? Why does Erasmus elect this technique from the galaxy of available methods, and impress his candidate in the *Ratio* with the importance of allegorical method? How does allegory reflect and foster his conviction that theological discourse ought to imitate that divine paradigm, Christ the copious conversation of the Father?

An immediate answer is its divine sanction: allegory is Christ's own pedagogical technique, as recorded in Scripture. This was adopted by the apostles, especially Paul, and by the wise ancients, especially Origen.[316] Should not the theologian imitate the best masters? To do theology is to emulate those ancient men who most closely imitated the gospel, which most perfectly reproduces Christ, who is the reflexive speech of the Father. In a letter to Colet Erasmus characterized theology as the 'principal part of all literature.'[317] In the *De copia* he exposed the human art of imitation, advising that the faculty of elegant writing is trained by committing precepts to memory and by making as many variations on them as possible. The creative method is the emulation of good authors, and excellence consists in improving on *their* unusually rich passages. Erasmus instructs, 'Note all the figures in them, store up in our memory what we have noted, imitate what we have stored up, and by frequent use make it a habit to have them ready at hand.'[318] Note, memorize, imitate – so as to acquire the habit of theology too. Erasmus considered the Fathers the prime practitioners of this technique in their cultivation of that perfect reflection of the mind of Christ traced in Scripture. Rather than expend energy in rational inquiry, one ought to study their allegorical commentaries.[319]

Theology is not a discipline of rigorous exploration into God, as in the scholastic *quaestio*, but a linguistic appropriation of the archetypal text: Christ, *oratio*. As Erasmus asserted in his paraphrase of Jn 1:1, to question mysteries was temerarious; rather one was to hold them fast. Not to scrutinize the mysteries by logical inquiry but to scrutinize the text by grammar and its ally rhetoric was the theologian's business. 'The theologian derives his name from divine oracles, not from human opinions,' he teaches his tyro in the *Ratio*.[320] Classical scholasticism, which defined theology as *sacra pagina* also, used the text as a springboard to reflection, transcending the limitations of its words in an enlargement of faith through reason. In Erasmus' evangelical humanism, the text is instead an exemplar to be clarified linguistically at the threshold of mystery, but above all to be imitated in man's intellectual and affective paraphrase of divine speech. Erasmus proclaims Christ as speech distilled from the Father's inmost heart, and Scripture as speech distilled from the most secret recesses of Christ's heart.[321] Upon this divine process of generation, by which God authors and publishes his text, Erasmus supports his notion of theology as human participation through speech in the living colloquy which is Christ. Christ as the conversation of the Father's heart → gospel as the conversation of Christ's heart → theology as the conversation of the gospel's heart. Theology artfully discloses the hidden meaning of the gospel, the heart which beats beneath the skin of the letters. A prominent technique by which it may accomplish this purpose is allegory.

'In unveiling the hidden sense,' Erasmus had cautioned, 'one ought not to follow conjectures of his own mind but acquire a method and, so to speak, a kind of technique.'[322] His reference is to allegory. In Erasmus' vocabulary the word *allegoria* fluidly ranges from the single act of transference which is metaphor to a sustained figurative interpretation, such as Origen's allegory on Abraham's sacrifice which is introduced early in the *Ratio*.[323] Erasmus succinctly defines it as a theological technique in his ennumeration of the four senses of Scripture: 'It treats the sacred mysteries of the head and whole mystical body.'[324] Thus the mnemonic sphere of Christendom, forming Christ's body around his central head, may be interpreted imaginatively as an allegory of allegory itself. There is perfect coincidence in the theologian's appropriation of that model as an exemplar for directing his discipline, and the aim of allegory. Both are constituted by the same elements, Christ and his people. Both claim the same plot, transformation.

As a technique allegory promotes that transformation which is the general aim of theological discourse through the linguistic act of transferring meaning. The transfer of meaning stirs man to a new comprehension of things, which may eventually flower in the transformation of life. According to Aristotle's theory of poetics man learns his earliest lessons through linguistic mimesis. Metaphor is an inductive device. 'The reason of the delight in seeing the picture is that one is at the same time learning – gathering the meaning of things, e.g. that the man there is so-and-so.'[325] Figurative language exercises the human spirit in the act of straining to discern meaning. The delight of discovery is true learning. Christ's discourse, as Erasmus understands it in the *Ratio*, suggests conformity to these classical principles of pedagogy. Christ conceals his meanings with tropes and allegories, with similes and parables, Erasmus explains, so that he might 'exercise our sluggishness.' The student's difficulty in perceiving the meaning of the scriptural text yields afterwards a 'pleasanter fruit.' Christ's parabolic method is an efficacious device for teaching and persuading,[326] a conviction about figures shared by classical rhetors too.

Allegory not only stirs the mind, it also delights.[327] Delight was for Erasmus the hallmark of humanity (*humanitas*), the certain promise of excellence in learning. Commenting favourably on the pedagogical theory of the ancients, he says, 'It was their doctrine also that excellence in true learning was only to be obtained by those who find pleasure in its pursuit; for this cause the liberal arts were called by them "Humanitas." '[328] Erasmus applauded the canon *dulce et utile*, and advised masters to 'choose such subjects as are pleasant and attractive, in which the young mind will fill recreation rather than toil.'[329] The parable of the prodigal son, Erasmus explains to his theological candidate, strikes the human spirit more sharply than the nude declaration that God freely receives the sinner. With more delight does the listener receive the parable of Abraham excavating wells than the bare command to draw the precepts of right living from Scripture.[330] If the theologian would not lull a yawning audience to sleep, he must 'add the wrap of allegory'[331] to his exhortations. Allegory provokes a recognition which is pleasurable; this is true learning. 'Thus more enjoyably is truth seized upon which first tested us under the wrap of enigma.'[332] With its play in the discrepancy of signifier and signified, allegory is a pleasant way to do theology. Sighting Christ, the theologian invents a poetic interpretation which will leave the reader to exclaim, 'Ah, that is He.' The pleasure of allegorical literature thus anticipates the beatitude of final recognition (heavenly *anagnōrisis*) and confirms the Christian in wisdom.

For adolescent Erasmus, first discovering manuscripts in the library at Steyn, scholarship was pleasure. This was not the gentle felicity (*felicitas*) of mediaeval monks at their *lectio divina*,[333] but a sensuously spiritual enjoyment (*voluptas*).[334] Erasmus' humanist conviction that literature imitated the divine act of creation through speech allowed him the indulgence of allegory, despite his practical urgency about being useful. Pleasure was in fact useful. His scenario of a relevant Church was to be set, improbably for modern man, in an ideal garden.[335] Those were the years before religious practicality demanded austere economy of image, both in language and art. What Wisdom did first, Erasmus agreed, was to play. Some reformers thought that sixteenth-century man needed the plain word of the gospel and blunt advice from the pulpit. But Erasmus thought figurative language the better method, for it secured its lesson by pleasure. He expected allegory to be tempered, however, by the good sense which grammar demands. If the literal sense of the text was instructive, then that sufficed. But if the text was ambiguous or even scandalous, if the audience required an interpretation which could accommodate itself to different spirits, then an allegory was to be devised.[336] In any event, the theologian was not to bore God's people with spiritless language which failed to stir humanity.

The scholastics might have imagined Erasmus a spiritual sybarite for his advocacy in the *Ratio* of ornamental language. For him in turn the language of the schoolmen was naked. Schoolish method was 'frigid' and 'sterile.' If the academic theologians played with the words of Scripture, it was only to rape their sense. Their play was a brutal violation, a distortion of language. 'Desiring eagerly to seem festive,' Erasmus protested, 'they deprave mystical words to scurrilous jokes.' Could anything be further from the style of Christ and his disciples than the disputes of the followers of Thomas and Scotus? Erasmus asks.[337] The language of the ancient and true theologians was, in contrast, sensuously clothed. By a kind of holy seduction it prompted the pleasure of understanding and the transformation of life. A theologian ought to be well schooled in rhetorical figures, both for the discernment of Scripture and for the ornamentation of his own discourse. Erasmus provides his tyro with examples in the *Ratio* of tropes and figures which he might study with profit.[338]

If scholastic words were 'frigid,' the discourse of true theologians 'burned' with charity, the interior life which prompted good language. As the fire of Christ melted ice,[339] so this fiery language of charity accommodated itself to the varying needs of men. The pedagogical efficacy of patristic allegory lay in such mutability: its accommodation to the protean interpretation of many readers.

Accommodation was the classical pedagogue's hallmark.[340] Christ was protean in the variety of his doctrine and life, testifying with mutability now to divine nature, now to human; calling some men while rejecting others; granting or refusing miracles; exacting silence, demanding witness; fleeing from the crowd, embracing it. Erasmus collates in his *Ratio* many New Testament texts which disclose this variety of Christ. And he does not hesitate to call Christ, Proteus.[341] The text of Scripture he thought the perfect reflection of Christ's protean method: 'In an equal degree [it] accommodates itself to all,' lowering, adjusting, nourishing, bearing, fostering, sustaining, serving, doing everything until we grow in Christ.[342] If Christ was Proteus, his disciples did not fail to imitate the method of their master. The apostle Paul especially was a chameleon and a polypus, the ingenious sea-creature which could mutate his colouring at will to deceive fishermen.[343] Erasmus called his own theological labour a Proteus.[344] The theologian could accommodate both protean text and his varied readers simultaneously with the response of allegory. The polysemous language of allegory better imitates variety than does the restrictive uniformity of a logical proposition. It metamorphoses meaning linguistically in anticipation of the transformation of the listener's understanding, then life.

This polysemy, which imitates both the accommodating meaning and method of Christ, is complemented by allegorical plenitude. Allegory is a synechdoche suggesting a larger organization of symbols to which it relates integrally.[345] Just as within Erasmus' diagrammatic allegory of theology there are ranked estates, all tending towards the central Christ, so allegory can be a small and partial cosmos participating in the larger and whole ornament (*kosmos*)[346] of divine eloquence: Christ, *oratio*. This microcosmic speech roundly imitates the periodic discourse which is Christ and relates imaginatively the visible and invisible orders.

The relationship of part to whole in true allegory is never a progressive mathematics of meaning, as in dialectic. Allegory transcends the summation of its elements by an organic configuration, a Gestalt. Allegory is not only quantified symbolism, although extension is necessary in its true form. Quantification accounts for the consecutive succesion of words, but not for the association in that succession, or what Maurice Merleau-Ponty terms the 'intersection' of words.[347] However many metaphors are arranged in ornamentation, like brightly coloured beads on a string, they do not compose allegory. Allegory is rather a plenitude which is an ornamental cosmos of ordered meanings. The 'levels of meaning,' in a modern term, are teleologically controlled.

Polysemy requires some literal bedrock, and true theological allegory never deserts its foundation. It is defined by a tension of meanings in which the historical sense always remains, like Christ, the centre of gravity. In Erasmian hermeneutics the control centre is Christ, the measure who computes multivalent meanings in their properly ordered values. The variety of Christ's life and speech, Erasmus reminds the student in the *Ratio*, composes a whole. By imitating this whole, the exegete can harmonize textual contra- dictions, referring them all to the summary Christ.[348] Christ is the grammatical axis at which all language intersects. As a new Hermes he directs the interpretation of the text's symbolic organization, in a folding-back of meaning upon meaning. The boundaries of sense are established by divine utterance, and this *Logos* alone beckons exegetes across the limits of meaning to himself. 'In these matters,' Erasmus advised, 'this rule ought to be observed, that the sense, which we elicit from obscure words, correspond to that orb of Christian doctrine, correspond to his life, and then correspond to the natural symmetry.'[349] The grammatical circuit is full, round, complete, because 'whatsoever the Father speaks, he speaks through the Son.'[350]

A grammatical Christ confers meaning on man, rounding out a world by his creative speech. The theological relation of word to meaning is not one:one, but one:the whole because Christ is the plenitude of speech and the grammar of all meaning. In Plato's dialogue on language, CRATULOS, the dialectician Socrates argued that the meaning of discourse (*logos*) equals the sum of its parts. Letter + letter = syllable. Syllable + syllable = word. Word + word = sentence. Sentence + sentence = discourse.[351] The meaning of language inheres atomistically in the verbal chain. It is susceptible therefore of discrete analysis by logical definition. In Plato's grammar the original signification of a word, rather than its usage, is normative. The double consequence is that in his philosophical republic speech becomes the charge, not of the orators, but of the lawmakers who are guided by dialecticians. Lawyers form rules for proper usage. Second, hermeneutics is mostly etymology; etymology comprises more than half of the dialogue.[352] Allegory is not judged the proper theological method, even if Plato does resort to such invention. Socrates complains that 'this sort of crude philosophy will take up a great deal of time ... Now I quite acknowledge that these allegories [about the gods] are very nice, but he is not to be envied who has to invent them.' As for himself, he has not the leisure to indulge in allegory. 'I must first know myself, as the Delphian inscription says; to be curious about that which is not my concern, while I am still in ignorance of my own self, would be ridiculous.'[353] The straightforward method to knowledge is dialectic.

It was this confidence in reason's ability to discern truth directly, without the mediation of the linguistic arts, which informed scholastic method. Unlike this procedure from the basic unit of language as the letter of the alphabet, Erasmus' humanist methodology originates in the whole oration: the *Logos*. Abstract word (dialectic) vs speech act (rhetoric). This is the irreconcilable conflict between scholasticism and Erasmian humanism: for dialectic the primary unit of expressed meaning is the word (*verbum*); for rhetoric, the discourse (*oratio*). And it is *oratio* for Erasmus which reflects the universal *ratio* which is Christ. His insistent programme for the restoration of rhetorical theology, established on grammar, proceeding by the methods of common-place and allegory, derives from this conviction: it is Christ who is the focal text of true theology and the name of Christ is *oratio*, the eloquent persuasion of God.

Christ has the wisdom to discern the true significances of things and their true relations because he is their grammarian. With the share in this divine wisdom which allegorical method promises, the theologian may also penetrate through the superficiality of words and things to their *logos*. The interiorizing movement of allegory, from the surface to the secret of the text, aligns the human spirit with its own invisible law. The theologian anticipates the knowledge of Christ by his transformation from external, corporeal man to inner, spiritual man. That is the grammar of piety as the disposition of the learner. Like Christ, like the Scripture, the theologian too becomes an imitative Silenus, apparently foolish in his humanity, but secreting divine life within. Allegory is the perfect alignment of language and spirit. It is the method of humanity (*humanitas*) because it is the method of Christ through whom humanity was created and recreated.

The link between Erasmus' rhetorical understanding of grammar and his theological methodology is the *Logos*. In his translation of the Johannine prologue he boldly announces, 'In the beginning was the speech,' correcting Jerome's 'word.' Pointing apologetically to patristic predecessors and to the daily practice of the Church, he argues that Christ is not the single isolated word (*verbum*) but speech (*sermo*). And if 'whatsoever the Father speaks, he speaks through the Son,' then this archetypal discourse is divine plenitude. As human discourse, centring its sight on Christ, theology ought to imitate the Father's oration with a literary plenitude that indicates the divine grammatical order. Allegory is such a little world of language which infers the plenitude of *logos* itself. It capsulizes a hierarchy of orders, just as the *Logos* sums up all reasons in his own method. The verbosity of the scholastics in imitation of Greek philosophy is not the oratorical copy of this fullness of Christ, as one may infer from Erasmus' repudiation of it. It is a mathematical multiplication and division of discrete elements. Scholasticism relies on the geometrical method of syllogism; it subjects divine reality to atomistic analysis by conforming Scripture to logic. In Erasmus' grammar the paradigmatic text is not reducible to a discrete, atomistic word. It remains forever the full revelation of God. Erasmus insists upon a methodical, organized theology, but one ordered by the discipline which bears the same name as Christ himself: *oratio*.

The theologian's task is the faithful transmission of creative Speech for the rebirth of civilization. Even unlettered men may aspire to this profession because its method begins simply enough in the cultivation of one's own humanity, in the maturation through learning of that inner spirit which is a true imitation of Christ. Anyone can learn to imitate, especially with Erasmus for tutor. The ultimate goal of the candidate, however, is to graduate. 'We pass our entire lives under tutors,' Erasmus regrets, 'always subject to supervision and without ever aspiring to liberty of spirit or to growing up in the fullness of charity.'[354] The theologian must mature to be 'taught of God,' *Theodidaktos*. He must matriculate in the school of Christ, learning the methods which imitate the Father's Method. The genius of the *Ratio* is not its catalogue of hermeneutical techniques, but Erasmus' well-spoken vision that the method of true theology is Christ. To Christ by Christ: that is the Father's circular strategem of grace which Erasmus' methodology imitates. 'He accommodated himself to those whom he wished to draw to himself.'[355]

At once arresting and prolix, this treatise eludes kinds of analysis which are theologically conventional. It cannot be systematized, for example, without violating the text. It can only be seized and bound like Proteus by the recognition of its own organizing principle. Other scholars have argued that this principle is the search for mystery as the source of beauty,[356] or the dialectic of theory and practice;[357] one finds the wellspring of Erasmus' theology in the Neo-platonic doctrine of flesh and spirit,[358] another in the experiences of people.[359] Erasmus' rhetorical theology is both rich and diffuse enough to accommodate generously many perceptions of its designing genius, even conflicting ones. His contemporaries too thought him parataxic and protean.[360] But if one apprentices himself to that master theologian, and takes up the angle of vision which Erasmus advises, then he cannot avoid sighting that grammar which measures and sums all interpretations at the intelligibilizing axis. The grammar of method secures itself in Christ, and the name of that Christ who promises the comprehension of Erasmian realities is the *Logos*.

While Erasmus' christocentrism has been forwarded with some scholarly conviction,[361] the word *logos* has surfaced rarely and in eccentric contexts.[362] In my reading it is his archetypal word, the paradigm for his renaissance of true theology in imitation of God's own eloquent oration. This grammar of theological method is not to be found in any appendix to the *Ratio*. It must be inferred from the text by discerning that universe of discourse which his methodology implies. It forces an interpretative engagement in which the reader only comprehends Erasmus' plot by playing from the grammatical axis to the allegorical circumference in an imitative universe of discourse. The compression of his grammar to a single word, *logos* as *sermo*, is not the diminishment of his art, as in a scholastic reduction of many meanings to one logic. For this is the word in which every word is spoken and it is prior to every logic. It is Speech itself. It is the copious Christ: the grammar of many meanings, engaged in the ever-shifting interpretation of God to man and man to God.

FOUR

❧ Confabulatio ❧

WITH ITS BEARINGS ON CHRIST, Erasmus' humanist method
serves in the forum of the republic, educating the intelligence and
will of eloquent men. As orator the theologian is a responsible
citizen of the commonwealth. The discriminating scholarship
which altered *verbum* to *sermo* was not a dry grammatical exercise
but an incentive to conversation, and so, to renaissance. Erasmus
plotted a conversational network which extended from the Father's
utterance of his speech into creation; through the patrimonial words
of men of classical and Christian antiquity, foreshadowing or
witnessing the *Logos* in the world; to himself conversing with them,
the reader joining in, and reader speaking with reader in a ring
around the continent. If Erasmus' fellow humanist Budé scored
him for loitering in grammatical subtleties,[1] he at last
comprehended the reality to which that grammar tended. 'For
Proteus,' he wrote, 'is properly God's *sermo*, transforming himself
into every miraculous thing. Which *sermo*, if we learn to hold in
faith, to cultivate with zeal, to embrace with love, will teach us all
things which are, which were, and which will soon be brought
about.'[2] And so God's conversation was passed on, making
theology through a human colloquy of spirit with spirit.

A more lucid Scripture, reflecting divine eloquence, would
engage human spirit in its proper activity: good speech. 'Let all the
conversations of every Christian be drawn from this one source,'
Erasmus had urged in his *Paraclesis*. 'For in general our daily
conversations reveal what we are. Let each one comprehend what
he can, let him express what he can.'[3] Erasmus penned a world

reborn where even schoolboys could instruct one another in pious conversation (*confabulatio*).[4] He imagined the farmer singing at the plow, the weaver humming to the movement of his shuttle, the traveller lightening a weary journey, all with the text of Scripture.[5] 'Do you think,' he asked archly, 'that the Scriptures are fit only for those with anointed hands?'[6] Against the obscure cant of the scholastics, jealously couching Christ in esoteric erudition, Erasmus flung these words: 'Only a very few can be learned,' he conceded, 'but all can be Christian, all can be devout, and – I shall boldly add – all can be theologians.'[7]

The theologian is colloquial man. He converses with the Text and with its best commentaries. In imitation of Christ, God's own eloquent oration, he shares discourse with others in a renaissance of life and letters. The scholarship of Erasmus, standing bent over his manuscripts alone, is not solitary, but an imitative *sermo*, a textual conversation with ancient and contemporary men. It flowers into a 'godly feast,' a colloquy of devout men wisely explaining Scripture to one another.

Underscoring his bold enterprise, Erasmus wrote, 'Socrates brought philosophy down from heaven to earth; I have brought it even into games, informal conversations, and drinking parties.'[8] If Christ conversed in public, why should the theologian confine his words to a select audience?[9] Can he not philosophize as well in the market as in the monastery?[10] Erasmus circumscribes his theological renaissance in 'Conuiuium religiosum,'[11] a colloquy of new men. The host Eusebius announces his circle of guests to be 'philosophers.'[12] These are philosophers of Christ, not Socrates, however, and they dare to renew the earth with a conversation so piously learned that man rivals nature as an index of God.

The conversation unfolds in the smallest circle: a garden.[13] This is like the garden of the authors into which Erasmus released the schoolboys of Europe, like a swarm of bees: 'And so the student, like the industrious bee, will fly about through all the authors' gardens and light on every small flower of rhetoric, everywhere collecting some honey that he may carry off to his own hive.'[14] But this is the garden of the singular Author who wrote his likeness both in the discourse of his Son and in the human spirit. In this garden every other author's book is subordinate to God's text. Exegeted by a convention of literary gardens, Eusebius' emblematic villa disguises paradise: the garden where man first strolled in intimate conversation with God and mate, and the garden where man recreated in Christ at last will dine in divine fellowship. Erasmus instructed his candidate in the *Ratio* that true theology was a 'most fertile garden' where one might both amuse and complete himself. Scholasticism was underbrush, yielding only sterile thorns of argumentation on which a Christian would lacerate and torture himself. Schoolish method was a pestilence to rot the spirit. The method of true theology was elegant, a 'garden ever-greening with every genus of tree and flower' in allegory of the 'innocent spirit abounding in every kind of virtue.'[15] Into such a garden Erasmus ushers his readers, inviting them to his godly feast.

This colloquy, published just four years after the *Ratio*, famously illustrates Erasmus' vision of an ideal Christian society informed by theological eloquence. The entrance to Eusebius' villa, which opens onto a welcoming garden, is guarded by a gate. Who is its porter but St Peter himself? 'I prefer him as porter to the Mercuries, Centaurs, and other monsters some people paint on their doors,' explains Eusebius with vigorously Christian taste. The doorkeeper is not silent, he continues, but greets callers trilingually. A Latin motto reads, 'If thou wilt enter into life, keep the Commandments.' The Greek inscription says, 'Repent ye, therefore, and be converted.' And the Hebrew, 'The just shall live by his faith.' These biblical sayings are indices of the way to the pursuit of godliness, true Christian life, and life eternal.[16] Once before in an Erasmian colloquy Peter had met a caller at the gate, only to bar entry for that nominal Christian who produced, not the key of evangelical knowledge, but the key of power.[17] Eusebius' villa is only an earthly fiction of paradise and Peter only a painted icon. The callers, however, demonstrate evangelical learning by reading the sacred inscriptions trilingually. Unlike Julius II, who is restricted from heaven by a righteous Peter, the host and his elderly guest Timothy gain easy access through the gate.

Here the garden path forks, with one walk leading to a chapel. Timothy observes, 'On the altar Jesus Christ gazes heavenward, whence his Father and the Holy Spirit look out, and he points to heaven with his right hand while with his left he seems to beckon and invite the passerby.' Not the beatific vision, to be sure, but at least a worldly glimpse at divine society. Eusebius mentions again that the image does not receive them in silence, but with trilingual mottos: 'I am the way, and the truth, and the life,' 'I am the Alpha and the Omega,' and 'Come, ye children, hearken unto me; I will teach you the fear of the Lord.' Whereas the mottos on the gate were preparatory injunctions to observe the law, repent, and live by faith, these mottos are the very testimonials of Christ to himself and his mission. The host invites his guests to return this greeting with a prayer, begging that Christ 'draw us to himself by himself,'[18] in a circular strategem of grace.

Once Timothy has been introduced to this attraction of the estate, the biblical texts which witness to Christ, the pair continue to stroll and to marvel at the grounds. Eusebius has plotted his estate to solicit astonishment and inquiry from his guests, two dispositions which permit him to play pedagogue. Timothy is a willing pupil and prods him on, questioning the emblematic character of every object. There is a merry fountain which bubbles excellent water. This symbolizes, as Eusebius interprets it, 'that unique fountain which refreshes with its heavenly stream all those who labour and are heavily laden, and for which the soul, wearied by the evils of this world, pants.'[19] In the renewal of theology *ad fontes* which popularly characterizes Erasmus' hermeneutics, he often describes Scripture as a fountain and the ancient theologians as golden streams of eloquence. The scholastics drink from muddied rivulets;[20] Scotus' fountain is a frog pond.[21] Timothy is invited, as Erasmus invites all theologians, to tap the pure, clear fountain of Christ. Host and guest proceed to the more cultivated garden enclosed by the walls of the house. Timothy exclaims in delight that these gardens are truly Epicurean. 'This entire place is intended for pleasure,' Eusebius replies, 'honest pleasure, that is; to feast the eyes, refresh the nostrils, restore the soul.'[22] A well-rounded culture does not starve the senses for the intellect, and, as Erasmus knew, such pleasure promotes excellence in true learning.[23] A hallmark of humanity, pleasure is a perfect tutor to theological excellence, imitating in corporeal man the spiritual beatification of divine communion.

Expressing humanist indulgence, Eusebius continues, 'Other men have luxurious homes; I have one where there's plenty of talk.'[24] Could any place have pleased Erasmus more? Lest appearances deceive, Eusebius the true humanist has graced dumb nature and art with 'sayings.' By his human invention, for example, the garden associates in the universe of discourse. It is planted with 'talking' herbs, each species boasting an inscribed banner and a label announcing its special virtue. The botanical frescos in the gallery which skirts the garden also speak by human design. In this loquacious zoo the painted owl advises in Greek, 'Be prudent: I don't fly for everyone.' While the exterior of the house is lavishly illustrated with a panorama of natural history, the interior is graced with scenes more immediately evocative of classical and Christian texts. In Eusebius' study are murals of the global regions and murals of famous teachers, with Christ on the Mount, accompanied by Father and Spirit, occupying the chief place. On the walls of the left upper gallery are gospel scenes with place names and summary captions as mnemonic devices. On the walls of the opposite gallery are painted the complementary Old Testament figures and prophecies, completing the circle of Scripture. It is here, Eusebius discloses, that he retires alone to converse with himself or in a circle of friends, meditating on the divine economy. Timothy is certain that in this pedagogical house no student could be bored. The plan merits his admiration: 'A wonderful variety, and nothing inactive, nothing that's not doing or saying something.' This is emblematic earth where the student's mind can be teased and trained, an Erasmian school. There is a fluid movement from things to words and words to things which encompasses the kitchen garden, the walls of the house, the dinner service, the party favours, and even the names of the characters. Eusebius the evangelical humanist can elicit a conversation from nature of art so well that in his theological inventiveness he even turns a question about his estate's sewer system into a pious moral.[25]

In such a Christian civilization where the visual image was properly subordinated to its linguistic interpretation, Erasmus could afford to modify his earlier depreciation of art as a Christian symbol.[26] In this colloquy Eusebius capsizes Plato's theory of imitation, teaching: 'We are twice pleased when we see a painted flower competing with a real one. In one we admire the cleverness of Nature, in the other the inventiveness of the painter; in each the goodness of God, who gives all these things for our use and is equally wonderful and kind in everything.'[27] This is the new cosmos in which human artistry is not a dim remembrance of nature's original design, but an invention which may even rival nature in pleasure and practicality both. Nature may suggest the Creator with reflexive immediacy, but art may entice man to meditate on the marvel of God who invents a creature capable of imitating his creation in an active prolongation of divine energy. If human language participates in the act of the Father disclosing his mind in speech, then human art might be an analogue of the divine phantasm, Christ the icon of the Father, tending towards that completion in speech. Whatever epistemology might be inferred from the exchange of aesthetic theories which Erasmus inserts in this colloquy, it is plain enough that his Renaissance man, Eusebius, thinks it expedient to confer the gift of language on dumb nature and art. He distills the moral of the image into an articulate maxim. The visitor to the estate is not permitted to infer his own associations when he views the painted owl. He is told its meaning in the picture alphabetized, the inscribed Greek caption, 'Be prudent: I don't fly for everyone.'

A man needs the eye to discern God's trace in the world, and Timothy, being initiated to this emblematic cosmos in old age, is not always perceptive. Eusebius' repeated question, 'But don't you recognize?'[28] chides him. The theologian who had studied Theophrastos' *De plantis, ventis, ac gemmis*, Nicander's *De noxiis bestiis*, Oppianus' *De piscium ac ferarum naturis*, as well as the natural histories of Pliny, Macrobius, Athanaeus, Dioscorides and Seneca – precisely as Erasmus had advised in the *Ratio* –[29] would have recognized the species painted on the gallery walls. As Erasmus had said, 'Not rarely from the very peculiar nature of the thing depends the comprehension of the mystery.'[30] The exercise in reading trilingual mottos at the garden gate and the instruction in animal lore dramatize the grammatical knowledge which the tyro must acquire before he is admitted to the sacred banquet of theology. He must learn to read scriptural verses in the original Hebrew, Greek, and Latin. He must know the vocabulary of the text and not be like the scholastics, confusing fish for tree.

An uneducated eye is not the worst sin, however, and Timothy still has opportunity to prove himself a lay theologian at the text. 'These sights feast the eyes but don't fill the belly,'[31] Eusebius concludes the preliminaries, hurrying his guest forward to the luncheon. Such emblems are like the mnemonic devices which capture memory's vision but are never digested viscerally. In the *Ratio* Erasmus had urged a single vow: that the theologian transform himself into what he learns. 'It is food for the spirit, thus at length useful, not if it remains in the memory as in a stomach, but if it is passed into the very feelings and the very viscera of the mind.'[32] A meal to satisfy a Christian's hunger would be, not such pictorial appetizers, but the full banquet of Scripture itself.

'The most sumptuous feasts are the study of the Holy Scriptures,' Erasmus had taught. He perpetuated in his lessons the biblical metaphor of the word of the Lord as nourishment. 'As bread is food for the body,' he wrote, 'God's Word is food for the soul.' The manna which God rained on the Israelites adumbrated the exegete's knowledge of the Bible. The text should be retained and its nourishing kernel digested like manna. Whoever vomits the words distastefully suffers from an ailing spiritual palate.[33] In this colloquy the 'godly feast' is not the table of victuals which Eusebius supplies from the resources of his estate, but the nourishment of Scripture and its exegesis in which the company engages. The guests circling Eusebius relish the textual meal more than the menu served at table, in a proper Christian ordering of body to spirit. Their task of interpretation is co-operative. They acknowledge the banquet as an imitation of the Eucharistic meal which Christ ate with his disciples,[34] a meal which for Erasmus symbolized the concord which theology must promote. In the *Querela pacis* he had styled the sacred liturgy as a banquet of peace where the Eucharistic bread and wine are signs of love and amity.[35] In his paraphrase on Matthew's gospel he explains the Eucharistic symbols as that conciliation in friendship by which Christ both devotes himself to us and binds us together.[36] Those who sit to feast on the text in Eusebius' garden will not bicker about the just interpretation, but will assist one another towards common appreciation. Thus scholarship recapitulates humanly the economy of Christ, drawing men together in a bond of charity.

This colloquial meal implements in many details the Erasmian renaissance of theological method, dramatizing the *Ratio*'s principles in a more obvious and entertaining way than that sober treatise afforded. The host instructs the guests to wash 'that we may approach the table with hands and hearts both clean.'[37] In the *Ratio* too Erasmus had invited the candidate to spiritual lustration before exegesis. As in the *Ratio*, here also the example of the holy pagans stirs these Christians to an even more exact observance of the ablution.[38] Erasmus thought it almost sacrilegious to approach Scripture unwashed,[39] and precisely what he meant by his recurring admonition is stated in the adage *illotis manibus*. 'Unwashed hands' is the symbol for the impiety of undertaking the exegesis of Scripture without preparatory knowledge of the biblical languages.[40] In the *Ratio* the adage is broadened to include the unclean spirit,[41] so that the rite of washing may be understood here as a spiritual cleansing also, aligning outer and inner man in this emblematic villa where human actions suggest divine realities. The washing may also recall baptism, which initiates in Erasmus' thought the profession of theology.[42]

After this preparation the plot turns on the imitation of Christ and concentration on his presence. Eusebius blesses the food with a hymn, in explicit imitation of Christ at the Last Supper. He recites, with the consent of the guests, not a ditty of popular piety but an eloquent prayer which the ancient father John Chrysostom had both recommended and interpreted.[43] Prayer, Erasmus had advised in the *Ratio*, was always to accompany the exegesis of Scripture.[44] Prayers said, the nine muses sit to lunch, not without (like Christ's own disciples) a squabble about the seating arrangement. Eusebius invites Christ 'to attend our feast and rejoice our hearts by his presence.' When Timothy indicates that all the chairs are occupied, Eusebius prays, 'May he mingle with all our food and drink, so that

everything taste of him, but most of all may he penetrate our hearts!'
To attract Christ's presence and to ready the guests for it, the host
proposes a reading from Scripture.[45] Had not Erasmus once
assured his readers that the text would 'render him so fully present
that you would see less if you gazed upon him with your very
eyes?'[46]

Commentary on Scripture seems to this enlightened host more
profitable table conversation than the foolish yarns and bawdy
stories which customarily accompanied the meals of decadent
Christendom. 'True gaity,' he teaches, 'comes from a clean, sincere
conscience. And truly enjoyable conversations are those which are
always pleasant to have held or heard and always delightful to recall,
not those which soon cause one to be ashamed and conscience-
stricken.' To season the meal with Christ's own savour then, the
servant boy reads Prov 21: 1–3 in a clear and distinct voice.
Eusebius reiterates the compendious method of the *Ratio*. Brevity
is enjoined. 'That will do,' he dismisses the boy, 'for it is more
beneficial to learn a few things eagerly than to swallow many in
boredom.' The perfect pedagogue! Timothy remarks that Proverbs
is a little book which may be carried profitably at all times.[47]
Erasmus, of course, thought that wisdom ought to be portable:
ready at hand for society's newly mobile man. Was not his
acclaimed *Enchiridion* compact?[48] He despised the unwieldy, ever
multiplying, scholastic volumes which no student could secrete in
his pocket, or in his heart. 'Who can carry around with him
Aquinas' *Secunda secundae*?'[49] he cried in exasperation. Scripture
was a totable compendium of wisdom to lighten the traveller's
load.[50]

Eusebius hesitates to comment on the passage. 'I wish we had
here a good theologian who not only understood these matters but
had taste as well. I don't know whether it's permissible for us
laymen to discuss these topics.' Timothy alleviates Eusebius'
scruple by voicing Erasmus' proclamation that 'all can be
theologians.' 'Permissible even for sailors, in my opinion,' he
replies, 'provided they're cautious about passing judgement. And
perhaps Christ,' he reassures Eusebius, 'who promised to be
present wherever two men are gathered together in his name, will

help us, since we are so many.'[51] To be gathered concordantly in Christ's name is to invite the disclosure of that eloquent reality which his name promises: *oratio*, the revelation of God. These Christians, gathered together to collect their readings of the text into understanding, imitate Christ as *ratio* also as he gathers up the meanings of things into his own grammar. And so Christ is fulfilled by charity and learning in this third circle of his body.

The Christian muses agree to divide the verses among themselves for a co-operative reading of the text.[52] The reader who anticipates that Eusebius has convened a compact lay synod, about to arrive at a consensus on the pericope, will be frustrated in the desire for easy intellectual agreement. The interpretations by the members exemplify various techniques which Erasmus had advocated in the *Ratio*: collation of texts, grammatical analysis, allegorical reference to Christ, and others. Although all are approved methods of scriptural exegesis, they do not yield in conjunction an unequivocal interpretation. Rather they indicate various senses of the text, approached from this road or that, suggesting that even Erasmian shortcuts to the theological knowledge can leave the journeyman irresolute. Although divine grammar assimilates these protean truths in the mind of God, they remain refracted in the human mind. And man is left to puzzle and seek, and puzzle again.

Eusebius examines the moral sense of the verse, collating other Old Testament texts by resorting to the topic of kings and also contributing an allegory of his own invention. Timothy undertakes to accommodate the verse to a deeper meaning. He allegorizes the king to be the perfect man and assists his exegesis with carefully chosen Pauline texts. Sophronius suggests that the verse corresponds to the Pauline doctrine that piety accommodates various modes of life, and he illustrates this with equally various examples from the apostle's letters. Theophilus comments on the third verse, referring everything to Christ, explaining how the prophetic revelation is effectively interpreted by and in the Lord Jesus. Pressed by his host to explain two particular words in the verse, he complies competently by referring to other illuminating texts, to the Hebrew idiom, and to etymology. In a later query about the sense of 1 Cor 6:12, another guest, Eulalius, tries to align that verse with Stoic teaching, attend to the context of the discourse (as Erasmus had taught in the *Ratio*), and appeal to the exegesis of an ancient theologian, Ambrose. The extemporaneous exegesis of this company implies a Christian society so well-versed in Scripture that common men may discourse convincingly, without excusing themselves from table to consult lexicons, commentaries, or divines from the university. Timothy exclaims to Eusebius, 'What do you mean, "layman?" Were I a Bachelor of Divinity I'd be very little ashamed of this interpretation.' When an embarrassed guest likens himself as an exegete to a shadow who sheds light on textual darkness, the host reassures him that such shadows are suitable for human eyes, which only see 'through a glass darkly.'[53]

The exegesis of Prov 21:1–3 does not concentrate the attention of the party exclusively on Scripture, but prompts the circle to receive all good literature as suffused with Christ's own spirit. The purity of expression in classical letters contributes to good morals, disclosing humanity, they decide. Such literature even hints of divine inspiration. The writings of the Scotists are by comparison 'dull' and 'lacking in feeling'; they leave the reader less enthusiastic for virtue. The conversation of Christian monks, the company thinks, could learn much from that of the old pagans which is touched with the spirit of immortality. The guests discuss how Ciceronian sentiments may be harmonized with Pauline and Petrine teaching,[54] an exercise which for many modern scholars constitutes the definition of Erasmus' 'Christian humanism,' a baptism of pagan letters.

Meditation on the text also promotes lively reflection on the contemporary life of the Church. Ceremony and charity are earnestly discussed in counterpoint. The feast is crowned with a reading from a treasured gospel codex (Matt 6:24–25), and it concludes circularly as it began with a ritual ablution and the earlier hymn. While Eusebius welcomes the guests to linger and explore other features of his estate, he excuses himself to visit the sick and conciliate a quarrel.[55] Thus the godly feast, a conversation of Christian life and letters, terminates where scholastic disputation seldom does: in a charity which goes forth amiably into other villages. It imitates perfectly the apostolic activity recorded in the

New Testament where the *agapē* was an incitement to such evangelization. Timothy blesses that departure with a circular prayer which ends the colloquy, 'May the Lord Jesus prosper your going and coming!'[56] And so the colloquy copies that movement from text to life which Erasmus thought the dynamic of true theology. From philology to praxis, from the study to the village, is the plot of renaissance for that humanist theologian who affirmed language as the stuff of life.

In this emblematic villa, a microcosm of the Christian commonwealth, every image is a pedagogue and every thing is wisely ordered within God's gracious plan. Appearances may deceive, as the Greeks warned, but appearances may also teach if only human inventiveness orders them towards good. This estate, established on the foundations of *humanitas*, boasts a marvelous variety of busy and useful things in which nature and art compete for the attention of men. The devices which stir memory and delight the senses prompt the maturation of human spirit. And this spirit expresses itself most naturally and most divinely in good discourse. Here is a circle of Renaissance men for whom *bene dicendi* means not rhetorical artifice but that true eloquence which springs from spirit and promotes community. The host Eusebius is 'orthodoxy,' that patristic complement of pious living and right thinking couched in the word *eusebeia* before the more restrictive *orthodoxia* became fashionable.[57] His guests bear emblematic names, and their conversation coincides with the reputation which the names confer in a sympathy of spirit and speech. Timothy is 'honouring God,' Theophilus, 'lover of God,' Chrysoglottus, 'golden-tongued,' Eulalius, 'sweetly speaking,' Theodidactus, 'taught of God.' The biblical text is the meal which feeds and revives them. It tutors them in that mutual eloquence and piety which distinguishes Erasmus' school from the faculty of divinity at Paris. He thought the disputations of scholastic theologians more childish and fierce than the inimical carousing of philosophers in Lucian's SUMPOSION H LAPITHAI.[58] If young Erasmus had declined to return to the monastery at Steyn because of the 'conversations so cold and inept, with no savour of Christ,'[59] he had at last forged an alternative.

With their remarkable perception of the harmony of human

colloquy with divine oratory, the circle of host and guests is never unaware that it feasts in imitation of Christ with his twelve.[60] They are but nine like the Muses;[61] as laymen they cannot succeed, as do bishops, in the place of the apostles.[62] Rather they dedicate themselves to the vocation of common man; in this third circle of his body are lay and married men.[63] In this new school of Christ they need not abandon the Muses, like Erasmus wailing his fate at Paris,[64] but can delight in good letters. This republican circle of theologians, which imitates Master and disciples, finally reflects the trinitarian circles painted in the villa's chapel and library. Whether a man goes to pray or to study, his colloquy imitates the society in which the Father confers, the Son discourses, and the Spirit overshadows.[65] Binding celestial and terrestrial globes at his intelligibilizing axis, Christ points to heaven with one hand and with the other beckons men to join the conversation,[66] becoming as every true theologian should be, *Theodidaktos*. And how to become 'taught of God?' One might begin by enlisting Erasmus for tutor.

In this literary fiction the implementation of the method of true theology, witnessed in the knowledge of grammar and so in the wisely learned exegesis of Scripture, above all in concentration on the textual presence of Christ, ensures the concordant discourse which defines society reborn. This colloquy is a cameo of the human imitation of Christ, the archetypal conversation, civilizing the commonwealth through language. The circle closes: divine and human orders in alignment, fulfilling the economy of creation.

In a translation from text to life, this book has progressed from a scholar's concern with the translation of one biblical word to the ideal fulfilment of his paradigm in a theological republic. If modern scholars of Erasmus cannot congregate in his study to discuss with piety and learning the grammar of theological method, we can at least all meet where that grammar becomes syntax, in Eusebius' garden where *logos* is truly flesh in Everyman. The more who journey the method, the merrier the round of tales. As in the beginning there was speech, so let there be in the end.

⚜ Abbreviations ⚜

AB	The Anchor Bible
AS	Approaches to Semiotics
ASD	*Opera omnia.* Amsterdam: North Holland, 1971 –
BHR	*Bibliothèque d'Humanisme et Renaissance*
BN	Bibliothèque de la Faculté de Philosophie et Lettres de Namur
BST	Basel Studies of Theology
Byz	*Byzantion*
CCSL	Corpus Christianorum series latina
CGMA	Corpus grammaticorum medii aevi
CSEL	Corpus scriptorum ecclesiasticorum latinorum
CSEP	Collectio selecta SS Ecclesiae Patrum
CSLP	Corpus scriptorum latinorum Paravianum
EE	*Erasmi Epistolae,* ed. P.S. Allen et al. 12 vols. Oxford: Clarendon, 1906–58
GRB	*Greek, Roman and Byzantine Studies*
H	*Ausgewählte Werke,* ed. Hajo Holborn and Annemarie Holborn. Munich: C.H. Beck, 1964
HB	Humanistische Bibliothek: Abhandlungen und Texte
HR	*History of Religion*
JBL	*Journal of Biblical Literature*
JHI	*Journal of the History of Ideas*
JL	Janua linguarum
JThS	*Journal of Theological Studies*
LB	*Opera omnia,* ed. J. Clericus, 11 vols. Leiden, 1703–6

LThK	*Lexicon für Theologie und Kirche*, ed. Jösef Höfer and Karl Rahner. 10 vols. Freiberg: Herder, 1957–65
MGP	Monumenta Germaniae Pedagogica
MPPR	Monumenta politica et philosophica rariora
N et E	Notices et extraits des manuscrits de la Bibliothèque Impériale et autres Bibliothèques
PB	Les philosophes belges
PG	*Patrologia graeca*, ed. J.-P. Migne
PL	*Patrologia latina*, ed. J.-P. Migne
PLS	*Patrologia latina: supplementum*, ed. Adalbert Hamman
PRG	Realencyclopädie für protestantische Theologie und Kirche, ed. J.J. Herzog. 22 vols. Leipzig: J.C. Heinrich, 1896
RBMAS	Rerum Britannicarum Medii Aevi Scriptores
RLV	*Revue des langues vivantes*
RQ	*Renaissance Quarterly*
RR	*Romanic Review*
SC	Source chrétiennes
SCBO	Scriptorum classicorum bibliotheca Oxoniensis
SMRT	Studies in Medieval and Reformation Thought
SP	*Studies in Philology*
SR	*Studies in the Renaissance*
ST	Thomas Aquinas, *Summa Theologiae* in *Opera omnia*. 16 vols. Rome: Polyglota S.C. De Propaganda Fide, 1882–1948
THR	Travaux d'Humanisme et Renaissance
ThT	*Theology Today*
ThZ	*Theologische Zeitschrift*
Tr	*Traditio*
VAAS	Vorträge der Aeneas-Silvius-Siftung an der Universität Basel
ZNTW	*Zeitschrift für die neuentestamentliche Wissenschaft*

❧ Notes ❧

THE EPIGRAPHS ARE FROM PLATO, CRATULOS, 391e, trans.
Benjamin Jowett, *The Dialogues of Plato* (New York: Random House, 1937),
I, 181; and from Erasmus, *Enchiridion militis Christiani, H,* p. 96, 4–5; *LB,* V,
43A. Transliteration of Greek texts throughout this book follows the style of *A
Manual of Style* (12th ed. rev.; Chicago: University of Chicago Press, 1969),
with the exception of *chi* which is transliterated *ch* rather than *kh*.

ONE: SERMO

1 This first Greek and Latin edition of the New Testament was
   printed in Basel by Johann Froben. Both Nikolaus Gerbel and
   Joannes Oecolampadius assisted with the scholarship, although
   Erasmus is credited as editor. The New Testament of the
   Complutensian Polyglot Bible was already prepared for press in
   1514, but was not published until 1520, pending papal approval.
      Since this chapter concerns the translation of the Johannine
   prologue, it should be indicated that Erasmus' edition of that Greek
   text was twice preceded. In 1504 the first six chapters of John were
   printed at Venice in a book containing a Latin translation of the
   poems of Gregory Nazianzen. Erasmus refers in correspondence to
   having seen the Aldine (?) edition of Gregory's prose compositions,
   but not the poems, and requests a copy. To Wolfgang Lachner, *EE,*
   III, 53 (no. 629, 12–14). In 1514 the prologue was reprinted in
   Greek at Tubingen. Bruce Metzger, *The Text of the New
   Testament: Its Transmission, Corruption, and Restoration* (2d ed.
   rev.; Oxford: Clarendon Press, 1968), p. 96, n. 1.

F

Reference to the *Erasmi Epistolae*, ed. P.S. Allen et al. (Oxford: Clarendon Press, 1906–47), will be given in both styles to which Erasmus scholars are accustomed: first the volume and page number, and then in parenthesis the letter number and line of citation where appropriate.

2 Erasmus confesses 'ego laboribus enecor' in a letter to Gianpietro Carafa, *EE*, II, 176 (no. 377, 6). To Urbanus Regius he writes that 'multorum etiam mensium perpetuis laboribus enecto verius quam fatigato,' *EE*, II, 204 (no. 392, 4–5).

3 From Leo x, *EE*, II, 114–115 (no. 338)

4 '... sic itur ad astra.' From Andrea Ammonio, *EE*, II, 200 (no. 389, 52)

5 'Nouum Testamentum plurimos amicos mihi conciliauit vbique.' To Johann Reuchlin, *EE*, II, 331 (no. 457, 48–49). Trans., Francis M. Nichols, *The Epistles of Erasmus* (New York: Longmans, Green, 1901–18), II, 374. Cf. To Sir Thomas More, *EE*, II, 242–243 (no. 412); To Thomas Linacre, *EE*, II, 247 (no. 415); To John Fisher, *EE*, II, 244–246 (no. 413)

6 Erasmus resided at the Collège de Montaigu, Paris, but withdrew after several fitful attempts at study interrupted by illness. *EE*, I, 146ff. He did accept a doctorate in theology in 1506, but only at the urging of friends. To Servatius Rogerus, *EE*, I, 431–432 (no. 200); To Jan Obrecht, *EE*, I, 432 (no. 201). P.S. Allen states that the doctorate was from Turin, *EE*, I, 426, in the note to no. 194. Also, Léon-E. Halkin, 'Erasme docteur' in *Religion et Politique: Mélanges offerts à M. le Doyen André Latreille*, Collection du Centre d'Histoire du Catholicisime, II (Lyon: Université de Lyon, 1972), pp. 39–47.

The degree represented an honour different from the achievement of passing the theological examinations at Paris. Cf. 'After the middle of the fourteenth century there were chairs of theology in the arts faculties and the *collegia doctorum* authorised to confer degrees in theology, but no separate faculties of theology organised for the training of theologians after the manner of Paris, Oxford or other Northern universities.' Paul O. Kristeller, commenting on the Italian universities, in 'Renaissance Aristotelianism,' *GRB*, VI (1965), 162, n. 13

7 To Publio Fausto Andrelini, *EE*, I, 235–236 (no. 96–100)

8 To Maarten Bartholomeuszoon van Dorp, *EE*, II, 90–114 (no. 337); To Johann Maier von Eck, *EE*, III, 330–338 (no. 844); *Apologia ad ex. virum Iacobum Fabrum Stapulensem, LB*, IX, 17A–50E; *Apologia duae contra Latomum, LB*, IX, 79B–106E

9 'Nouum Testamentum quod pridem Basileae praecipitatum fuit verius quam editum.' To Willibald Pirckheimer, *EE*, III, 117 (no. 694, 17–18)

10 Erasmus stresses the importance of Leo x's prospective approval in letters To Silvestro Gigli, *EE*, III, 72 (no. 649, 12); To Thomas Wolsey, *EE*, III, 81 (no.658, 39); To Erard de la Marck, *EE*, III, 194 (no. 757, 25); To Antoon van Bergen, *EE*, III, 198 (no. 761, 11); To Cuthbert Tunstall, *EE*, 111, 302 (no. 832, 3); To Antonio Pucci, *EE*, III, 380 (no. 860, 13)

11 '... rumpantur vt ilia Codris.' To Cuthbert Tunstall, *EE*, III, 302 (no. 832, 3)

12 'Iam quod cauillantur, ob id me parare nouam editionem quod prior mihi non satisfaciat, fingamus ita esse; quid est quod reprehendat? si studeam meipso melior esse, et id facere quod ab Origene, quod ab Hieronymo factum est et ab Augustino?' To Mark Lauwerijns, *EE*, III, 265 (no. 809, 56–59)

'... praesertim cum id ingenue testatus sim in prima editione me facturum si foret vsus.' Ibid., ll. 59–61. Cf. '... paratissimus ad palinodiam, sicubi more hominum lapsus sim,' in the *Apologia* prefaced to the 1516 edition, *H*, 165, 21–22; *LB*, VI, **2

'Contemnant hanc primam editionem, nisi multos in ea locos explicui in quibus Thomas Aquinas hallucinatus est, ne quid dicam de caeteris. Aut negent hoc, aut refellant si queant.' To Mark Lauwerijns, *EE*, III, 265 (no. 809, 70–72). Trans., Nichols, III, 325

13 'Si optandum est vt diuinos libros habeamus quam emendatissimos, hic meus labor non solum amolitur mendas sacrorum voluminum, verùmetiam obstat ne posthac queant deprauari.' To Antonio Pucci, *EE*, III, 381 (no. 860, 50–52). 'Si optando vt huic disputatrici theologiae, quae pene plus satis pollet in scholis, accedat fontium cognitio, huc peculiariter hoc opus conducit.' Ibid., ll. 55–57. Trans., Nichols, II, 431. 'Nullum igitur studii genus laeditur hoc meo labore, sed adiuuantur omnia.' Ibid., ll. 57–58

14 To Hermann von Neuenar, *EE*, III, 151 (no. 722). To Sir Thomas
    More, *EE*, III, 153 (no. 726); To Wolfgang, Faber Capito, *EE*, III,
    163–164 (no. 734); To William, 4th Lord Mountjoy, Blount, *EE*,
    III, 235–236 (no. 783); To John Fisher, *EE*, III, 236–238 (no. 784);
    To More, *EE*, III, 238–240 (no. 785); To Henry Bullock, *EE*, III,
    292–293 (no. 826); To Henry VIII, *EE*, III, 304–305 (no. 834)

15 'Odi hunc meum laborem, quoties quorundam ingratitudo venit in
    mentem.' To Pierre Barbier, *EE*, III, 189 (no. 752, 7–8). 'Sic
    quorundam spectatorum peruersissima malignitas facit vt me tam
    immensi laboris nonnunquam capiat tedium.' To Philip of
    Burgundy, *EE*, III, 195 (no. 758, 10–12)

16 To Anton van Bergen, *EE*, III, 198 (no. 761, 9–10); To Paschasius
    Berselius, *EE*, III, 192 (no. 756, 15); To Philip of Burgundy, *EE*,
    III, 195 (no. 758, 7). To Paschasius Berselius, *EE*, III, 192 (no. 756,
    21)

17 'Sum totus nunc in Nouo Testamento, quod me propemodum non
    solum exo[s]culauit sed exanimauit.' To Gerard Geldenhouwer, *EE*,
    III, 103 (no. 682, 3–5). Cf. To Willibald Pirckheimer, *EE*, III, 360
    (no. 856).

18 '... Tamen hec peragenda est fabula.' To Hermann Neuenar, *EE*,
    III, 151 (no. 722, 16). Trans., Nichols, III, 165. Cf. 'Siue huc natus
    sum, non oportet *theomachein* gigantum exemplo; siue ipse hoc mihi
    intriui mortarium, par est vt idem exedam.' To Philip of Burgundy,
    EE, III, 195 (no. 758, 14–15). 'His fatis natus sum, mi Bouille; sed
    non oportet *theomachein*.' To Henry Bullock, *EE*, III, 220 (no. 777,
    22–23). 'His fatis sum natus.' To John Colet, *EE*, III, 240 (no. 786,
    19)

19 To Gerard Geldenhouwer, *EE*, III, 103, 144–145 (no. 682, no. 714).
    To Willibald Pirckheimer, *EE*, III, 117 (no. 694, 17–20); To Pierre
    Barbier, *EE*, III, 120 (no. 695, 19–21); To Erard de la Marck, *EE*,
    III, 194 (no. 757, 21–24); To Gerard Geldenhouwer, *EE*, III, 196
    (no. 759, 16–18)

20 'Sed ex aduerso consolatur me bonorum profectus.' To Pierre
    Barbier, *EE*, III, 189 (no. 752, 8–9). 'Rursum me consolatur recti
    conscientia et, ni fallor, non mediocris hinc ad bonos reditura
    vtilitatis.' To Philip of Burgundy, *EE*, III, 195 (no. 758, 12–13)

21 'Certum est enim aut immori negocio semel suscepto, aut tale

reddere vt et Leone decimo dignum videtur et posteritate.' To
Erard de la Marck, *EE*, III, 194 (no. 757, 24–26)

22 'Nouum Testamentum ... retexo ac recudo, et ita recudo vt aliud
opus sit futurum.' To Willibald Pirckheimer, *EE*, III, 117 (no. 694,
17–19). 'Noui Testamenti bonam partem recognouimus, et ita
recognouimus vt aliud sit opus futurum.' To Henricus Glareanus
(Heinrich Loriti), *EE*, III, 134 (no. 707, 16–17)

23 'Nunc non hoc ago, verum idem molior quod iam tercio factum est
in edendis Prouerbiis.' To Mark Lauwerijns, *EE*, III, 265 (no. 809,
61–62)

The third major edition of adages, the *Adagiorum Chiliades*, was
published by Froben in 1515. Margaret Mann Phillips describes it:
'The whole book has undergone revision and expansion. Comments
on proverbs, which previously called for erudition only, now have
sentences or whole paragraphs neatly inserted in the original text,
turning them into sharp criticisms of contemporary society. Among
these extensions which alter the atmosphere and intention of the
book, there are a number of long essays which are brand new in
1515, some of them among the most important writings of
Erasmus.' *The 'Adages' of Erasmus: A Study with Translations*
(Cambridge: University Press, 1964), p. 96

24 'Ad haec, in translatione priore parcius mutaui, ne nimis
offenderem istorum animos nimium morosos: nunc adhortantibus
eruditis viris plusculum hac in parte sum ausus. Deinde locos
immutatos crebriore autorum nomenclatura communio, ne quid
habeant quo tergiuersentur *hoi duspeitheis*. Postremo loca tum
festinanti praeterita adiicio.' To Mark Lauwerijns, *EE*, III, 265 (no.
809, 62–67)

25 Concerning the MSS which Erasmus used for his NT editions, see
C.C. Tarelli, 'Erasmus' Manuscripts of the Gospels,' *JThS*, XLIV
(1943), 155–162; Bo Reicke, 'Erasmus und die neutestamentliche
Textgeschichte,' *ThZ*, XXII (1966), 254–265

26 '... et ita vertimus vt primum studuerimus, quoad licuit, integritati
sermonis Romani, sed incolumi tamen Apostolici sermonis
simplicitate. Deinde dedimus operam vt quae prius lectorem
torquebant vel amphibologia vel obscuritate sermonis vel orationis
vitiis aut incommodis, iam explanata sint ac dilucida; parcissime

interim recedentes a verbis, a sensu nusquam.' To Antonio Pucci, *EE*, III, 381 (no. 860, 34–40). Trans., Nichols, III, 430. '... tamen non ex nobisipsis somniamus, sed ex Origine, Basilio, Chrysostomo, Cyrillo, Hieronymo, Cypriano, Ambrosio, Augustino, petimus.' Ibid., ll. 40–42

'... plusquam sexcentos locos aperuimus.' Ibid., l. 53. Cf. '... et supra mille loca annotaui.' To Servatius Rogerus, *EE*, I, 570 (no. 296, 156)

'Vulgatam hanc aeditionem non conuellimus ... sed indicamus vbi sit deprauata; submonentes sicubi insigniter dormitauit interpres, explicantes si quid inuolutum ac spinosum.' To Antonio Pucci, *EE*, III, 380 (no. 860, 44–49). Trans., Nichols III, 431. 'Porro lectionis varietas non solum non officit studio sacrarum Scripturarum verumetiam conducit, autore diuo Augustino. Neque tamen vsquam tanta est varietas vt ad orthodoxae fidei periculum pertineat.' Ibid., 381–382, ll. 61–64

27 To Pierre Barbier, *EE*, III, 188 (no. 752, 5); To Jan of Friesland, *EE*, III, 217 (no. 775, 3); To Henry Bullock, *EE*, III, 220 (no. 777, 22); To William Warham, *EE*, III, 233 (no. 781, 5); To Pierre Barbier, *EE*, III, 248 (no. 794, 61–62). To John Fisher, *EE*, III, 236 (no. 784, 3–4); cf. To Josse Bade, *EE*, III, 286 (no. 815, 2–3); To Pierre Vitré, *EE*, III, 287 (no. 817, 2–3); To Richard Pace, *EE*, III, 290 (no. 821, 13–14). To Pierre Barbier, *EE*, III, 248–249 (no. 794, 62–65); cf. To Beatus Rhenanus (Beat Bild), *EE*, III, 251 (no. 796, 14–17); To Joannes Oecolampadius, *EE*, III, 252 (no. 797, 5–7). To Pierre Barbier, *EE*, III, 340 (no. 847); To Sir Thomas More, *EE*, III, 340–341 (no. 848). '... ipse mihi geminum senium.' To Erard de la Marck, *EE*, III, 194 (no. 757, 23–24)

28 To Jan Šlechta, *EE*, III, 552 (no. 950, 38–41); To Maarten Lips, *EE*, IV, 559 (no. 955)

29 'Ob hanc vnam omnia: in hac profecto me iudice nostra dependet victoria, praemium tot disceptationum, tanti laboris ouatio atque triumphus.' From Maarten Lips, *EE*, III, 499 (no. 922, 46–48)

30 Modern scholarship does not attribute the authorship of this prologue to the evangelist John, but supposes it to be an early Christian hymn. See, e.g., Raymond E. Brown in his notes to *The*

Gospel According to John (i–xii) (Garden City, N.Y.: Doubleday, 1966), pp. 18–23.

31 *Annotationum in Evangelium Joannis*, 1:2, *LB*, VI, 336A

32 'Nos tametsi videbamus *sermonis* vocabulo rectius exprimi Graecam vocem, qua usus est Evangelista, *logon*, tamen in Editione prima superstitioso quodam metu non mutaueramus *verbum*, quod posuerat Interpres: ne quam ansam daremus iis, qui quidvis ad quamvis occasionem calumniantur.' *Annotationum in Evangelium Joannis*, 1:2, *LB*, VI, 335A–B

33 'Ad haec, in translatione priore parcius mutaui, ne nimis offenderem istorum animos nimium morosos: nunc adhortantibus eruditis viris plusculum hac in parte sum ausus.' To Mark Lauwerijns, *EE*, III, 265 (no. 809, 62–65). As an example of friendly persuasion, see From Sir Thomas More, *EE*, II, 370–372 (no. 481).

34 The unnamed preacher who is described as a theologian, a professed religious, and a bishop in *Apologia de 'In principio erat sermo,' LB*, IX, 111F, is Henry Standish. Although Erasmus spares naming him there, he does identify him in a letter reporting the incident To Hermann von dem Busche, *EE*, IV, 311 (no. 1126, 53, 70, 78, 86). Erasmus' intelligence of the sermon was probably through his friend Sir Thomas More, who must be the married courtier who refuted Standish at a court dinner that evening. See also, *The Correspondence of Sir Thomas More*, ed. Elizabeth F. Rogers (Princeton: University Press, 1947), To a Monk, pp. 179–184 (no. 83, 526–691). Cf. To Martin Luther, *EE*, VIII, xlv–xlvii (no. 1127a) in which Erasmus explicitly names More as his protector. The letter to von dem Busche mentioned above reports the sermon in substance, the banquet scene, and a third incident when Standish denounces Erasmus before the king and queen of England for doctrinal heresies. Standish was a lackey of Edward Lee, Erasmus' chief English opponent.

35 'Nam hactenus annis plus mille tota Ecclesia legerit, "In principio erat verbum," nunc tandem, si superis placet, Graeculus quispiam docebit nos, legendum esse, "In principio erat sermo." ' *Apologia de 'In principio erat sermo,' LB*, IX, 111F; cf. 111D

36 The Carmelite, dubbed 'Camelita' for his dull spirit, is only described as titled with a baccalaureate in theology. Ibid., 113A.

P.S. Allen (*EE*, IV, 194 in the introductory note to no. 1072) and Augustin Renaudet (*Érasme: sa pensée religieuse et son action d'après sa correspondence (1518–1521)* [Paris: Felix Alcan, 1926], pp. 67, 78, 96–99) both identify him as the friar Nicolaas Baechem. Known as Egmondanus or Edmondanus, Baechem was a member of the theological faculty of Louvain and a professed enemy of Erasmus.

This assignation seems dubious to me, however, on three counts: first, Baechem received a Doctor of Divinity degree from Louvain in 1505; second, at the time when this second edition was published, and in the following years, Baechem was prior of the Carmelites at Louvain, having already completed his pastoral service in Brussels. These facts are noted by Allen but not reconciled with his assignation, *EE*, III, 416–417, n. 13. Third, Erasmus labels the preacher a 'sychophant' who is enacting the 'initiation rite' into the theological sodality of Louvain. While it may be possible that the preacher was acting at Baechem's instigation, the characterization of him does not fit Baechem. The preacher whom Erasmus mentions is a young man, of junior status academically; he has only a bachelor's degree. Erasmus mentions his 'obtuse youthful audacity.' *LB*, IX, 112D. Baechem, on the contrary, was a man of stature, both academically because of his doctor's degree and faculty position and ecclesiastically because of his appointment as prior of the Carmelite community. There is no record either of Baechem's involvement with the *sermo* controversy, although it is recorded that he attacked another translation in the same edition. Erasmus replied to that in his *Apologia de loco*, '*Omnes quidem resurgemus*,' *LB*, IX, 433. Records also survive that Baechem preached in the same year against the foundation of the Collegium Trilinguum and publicly denounced Erasmus' love of Greek as a sign of heresy. See, Renaudet, ibid. But *sermo* is not mentioned.

37 '... quendam Erasmum qui non vereretur corrigere Euangelium sancti Joannis.' *Apologia de 'In principio erat sermo*,' *LB*, IX, 112D. The verdict was, 'sed arbitratur me damnare quod ipse scripsit Euangelista.' Ibid., 113A

38 'Lutetiae non dissimilem huic fuisse tumultum, ex amicorum litteris cognovi.' Ibid., 112D

39 Impudence and sedition are paired, ibid., 112B, 113B, 114B. The
charge of sedition refers to the attempt to win the political support
of the Mayor of London, ibid., 112B–C; and to incite the populace,
ibid., 112F–113A, 114A–B, 120E, 121A, 121E–122A, 122C–D, 122E, and
cf. *Annotationum in Evangelium Joannis*, 1:2, *LB*, VI, 336B. Erasmus
may have also had in mind the scholastic performance at the court
banquet before the king and queen of England. See this chapter, n. 34.

40 The *Bibliotheca Erasmiana: Répertoire des oeuvres d'Erasme*, ed. F.
Vander Haeghen (Nieuwkoop: B. De Graaf, 1961) lists six editions
published in 1520 at Basel, Cologne, and Louvain. The edition
dated the month of February at Dirk Martens' press was the first
printing of the early version. Another early version not listed by
Vander Haeghen is: *Apologia Erasmi Roterodami palam refellens
quorundam seditiosos clamores apud Populum ac Magnates, quibus ut
impie factum iactitant, quod in evangelio Ioannis verterit, in principio
erat sermo*. Without printer or date, the edition is identified in a
letter from Sir Roger Mynors as, Nürnberg: Friedrich Peypus, ca.
1520. The copy is in the Erasmus collection at the Centre for
Reformation and Renaissance Studies, Victoria University in the
University of Toronto. Willem de Vreese, *Bibliotheca Erasmiana
Rotterdamensis* (Rotterdam: Bibliothek des Gemeente, 1936), I, 61,
lists another copy of this same edition in the collection of the
Rotterdam Public Library. The augmented version of the *Apologia*
appeared first from Froben's press, bound with the *Epistolae aliquot
eruditorum virorum*. For complete listings, see *Bibliotheca
Erasmiana*, ed. Vander Haeghen, 1st series, p. 12.

While the *sermo* translation and its ensuing controversy is noted
briefly in a number of Erasmus studies, there is but a single,
sketchy article devoted to it: C.A.L. Jarrott, 'Erasmus' *In principio
erat sermo*: A Controversial Translation,' *SP*, LXI (1964), 35–40. I
agree with the author's thesis that the use of *sermo* (conversation)
suggests the intellectual commitment of the humanists to dialogue
and reflects also the 'idea of dialogue which is essential to the Logos
as the Second Person of the Trinity,' pp. 35, 37. I should like to
note here, however, Jarrott's theological misunderstanding of this
function of the *Logos*, which is a conversation *ad extra*, i.e. to
creatures, and not *in se*, i.e., to the other persons of the Trinity. See

this chapter, n. 152. Jarrott fails, therefore, to consider the economic role of Christ as *sermo* in the forum of the Christian republic which is thematic of this book. Her translation and interpretation of the text on other crucial issues are also disputable. See this chapter, nn. 144, 152, and Chapter 2, n. 2.

The comments of Jean-Claude Margolin and James D. Tracy provide conjecture rather than sound theological scholarship. Margolin, who mentions the translation as an example of Erasmus' interpretation of the dogma of the Incarnation, suggests that: '*Verbum* risque d'être pris pour une Parole transcendante, tombant verticalement sur les humains, dont l'intellect se contenterait d'accueillir passivement la lumière; au contraire, *sermo* est la parole dialoguée, celle qui instruit familièrement, qui tisse entre les consciences des liens horizontaux, disons une parole humaine, quoique d'essence divine: triomphe de l'immanence sur la transcendance, humanisation de Dieu dans la personne du Christ.' *L'Idée de nature dans la pensée d'Erasme*, VAAS, VII (Basel and Stuttgart: Helbing and Lichtenhahn, 1967), p. 35. There is neither semantic nor theological evidence to support Margolin's notion that *verbum* designates a transcendent word and *sermo* an immanent one. In theological fact, the *sermo* which is Christ is first the transcendent utterance of the Father. While Margolin admits that 'cette dernière interprétation n'est pas explicitée par Érasme,' he nevertheless imagines 'je ne pense pas néanmoins forcer sa pensée,' and refers the reader to Jarrott's article. Ibid., 61, n. 152.

Tracy's distinction has no semantic or theological basis either: 'Others before Erasmus had used *sermo* to translate *logos* (114B, 119A) but the choice seems also to be significant in terms of his characteristic effort to substitute a more general, spiritual meaning (sermo = speech) for the particular with overtones of sacredness (verbum = word).' *Erasmus: The Growth of a Mind* (Geneva: Droz, 1972), p. 77, n. 52.

Near the conclusion of his book on Erasmus' hermeneutic, which is not favourably reviewed, John W. Aldridge, *The Hermeneutic of Erasmus*, BST, II (Zürich: EVZ, 1966), p. 144, comments that 'Had Erasmus known Koine Greek he would no doubt have rendered *logos* differently.' Without guessing what the innuendo means, one

may ask what evidence there is that Erasmus, who translated the
Greek NT several times, did not know koine Greek. It ought to be
noted that Erasmus recognized that NT Greek was colloquial rather
than classical. See, e.g., From Johann Maier of Eck, citing Erasmus,
EE, III, 210 (no. 769, 60–62); To Johann von Botzheim, *EE*, VIII,
259 (no. 2206, 36–37).

Dietrich Harth devotes a few pages to the *sermo* translation in
Philologie und Praktische Philosophie (Munich: Wilhelm Fink, 1970).
He interprets Erasmus' motive in translating *logos* as an attempt to
overcome the breach between thought and speech which characterized mediaeval logic. He points to Erasmus' analogy of the speech
of the tacit concept and the reason of God as an illustration of this
identity, pp. 42–43. Without discounting Harth's interpretation as a
possible philosophical reading, I should indicate that it would be
difficult to support this from the texts. Although Erasmus lists *ratio*
as a Latin cognate for *logos*, he does not state that *logos* means the
unity of thought and speech, or that he intends to ensure that
meaning by his translation. Moreover, what philosophical advantage
would *sermo* gain over *verbum* since both can indicate the unity of
thought with its oral expression? Rather, Erasmus takes the *Logos* of
the Johannine prologue to be 'speech' and indicates that it means
God's full oration. While it is true that in rhetorical theory *sermo*
implies an expression of human rationality (as Harth discusses in
his introduction and I in Chapter 2), his reading of Erasmus'
intention seems to me strained. I also think his reading of the
analogy between the speech of the tacit concept and God's reason is
another misunderstanding of the text. Erasmus states that the *Logos*
is neither a tacit concept nor sounded speech, but rather that
analogously what in man is the tacit concept in God is the Son
eternally one with the Father, what in man is speech in God is the
Son eternally generated. See this chapter, n. 143. One may extra-
polate from this philosophically that there is unity of thought and
speech in God, but that is not what Erasmus is establishing in his
argument. He is presenting an analogy of God and man in language.

41 'Et tamen qui molestissime vociferantur haec apud populum non
legerunt annotationem nostram in eum locum.' *Apologia de 'In
principio erat sermo,'* *LB*, IX, 120F. Erasmus knew from the

demonstration of Sir Thomas More that Standish had not read this annotation. To Hermann von dem Busche, *EE*, IV, 311 (no. 1126, 51–53). Erasmus often complains that his detractors never read his works. See, e.g., To Mark Lauwerijns, *EE*, III, 263–264 (no. 809, 12–17).

42 *Apologia de 'In principio erat sermo,' LB*, IX, 111A–113B; 120E–122F. This dissemblance before the people was not a fresh problem for Erasmus. He complains of such chicanery over the first edition. To Henry Bullock, *EE*, III, 293 (no. 826, 5–8)

43 Nunc evulgant, quod erat inter eruditos disputandum, et evulgant apud coriarios ...' *Apologia de 'In principio erat sermo,' LB*, IX, 112F. 'Nos illa doctis scripsimus, non populo.' Ibid., 112E. For documentation and interpretation of his doctrine of lay theology see my article, 'Weavers, farmers, tailors, travellers, masons, prostitutes, pimps, Turks, little women, and Other Theologians,' *Erasmus in English*, 3 (1971), 1–7. Jarrott also notes the discrepancy and concludes, 'Of course there is no real contradiction here; obviously the important thing for the weaver singing Scripture at his loom is that he sings of the Son of God, not whether he thinks of Him as "sermo" or "verbum." ' 'Erasmus' *In principio erat sermo*: A Controversial Translation,' 39. It is also possible that Erasmus wished the NT to be available to all, but the debate about certain issues confined to scholars.

44 'Ista nihil apud populum, in Scholis suum habitura locum.' *Apologia de 'In principio erat sermo,' LB*, IX, 121B–C. Ibid., 112D–E, 112F

45 Ibid., 112F–113A, 114A–B, 120E, 121A, 121E–122A, 122C–D, 122E. *Annotationum in Evangelium Joannis*, 1:2, *LB*, VI, 336B–C. Cf. Acts 7:55–61. If Erasmus criticized his opponents for rousing the mob to a stoning mood, he was not above advocating that fate for his enemies. '... oportebat non solum esse ludibrio pueris verumetiam foras lapidari publicitus.' To Gerardus Listrius, *EE*, III, 83 (no. 660, 21–22)

46 *Apologia de 'In principio erat sermo,' LB*, IX, 122A–B

47 To Thomas Wolsey, *EE*, IV, 157–158 (no. 1060)

48 '... quanto justius nos imploraverimus eorundem opem adversus malitiosam stolidorum rabularum conspirationem, adversus

hujusmodi seditiosam petulantiam.' *Apologia de 'In principio erat sermo,' LB*, IX, 122A

49 I.e., the mendicant friars. Standish was a Franciscan.

50 See n. 47.

51 The many instances of the words 'scholastic' and 'schoolmen' in this book are meant to be understood within the context of humanist argument, even propaganda, in particular, Erasmus' criticisms. This book does not evaluate the justice of Erasmus' condemnation of scholasticism.

52 'Sunt enim qui cum sibi pulchre docti videantur, vix norint Joannem aliter scripsisse quam Latine.' *Apologia de 'In principio erat sermo,' LB*, IX, 113B. 'Ac principio quidem negari non potest, ab ipso Euangelista, qui haud dubie Graece scripsit, *Christum* dici *logon*, Ibid., 113D–E. 'Certe negari non potest, Graecam dictionem *logon*, qua sine controversia usus est Euangelista.' Ibid., 114A

53 '... *logon*, quae vox cum sit polysemos, nunc *sermonem* aut *verbum*, nunc *orationem*, nunc *rationem*, nunc *sapientiam*, nunc *computum* significans.' Ibid., 113E. '*Logos* Graecis varia significat, *verbum*, *orationem*, *sermonem*, *rationem*, *modum*, *supputationem*, nonunquam et pro *libro* usurpatur, a verbo *legō*, quod est *dico*, sive *colligo*.' *Annotationum in Evangelium Joannis*, 1:2, *LB*, VI, 335A

54 'Horum pleraque divus Hieronymus aliqua ratione putat competere in Filium Dei. Miror autem cur *verbum* Latinis placuerit magis quam *sermo*.' Ibid. *Apologia de 'In principio erat sermo,' LB*, IX, 113E

55 Note the repeated phrase 'apud Latinos auctores,' 'apud Latine loquentes' in the following note.

56 '... apud Latinos auctores aliquoties *verbum* usurpari pro dicto quopiam brevi, veluti proverbio, aut sententia.' Ibid., 113F. '... apud Latine loquentes *verbum* non sonet totam orationem, sed unam aliquam dictionem; raro tamen dictum aliquod breve, veluti sententia aut proverbium vetus, *verbum* est.' *Annotationum in Evangelium Joannis*, 1:2, *LB*, VI, 335C

57 '... *verbum* frequentur usurpatur pro certa parte orationis, non pro quavis dictione, quam, ut dixi, Graeci *rhēma* vocant.' *Apologia de 'In principio erat sermo,' LB*, IX, 113F

58 'Caeterum quoties significamus orationem, *verba* potius dicimus multitudinis numero, quam *verbum*, ut *verba facere*, pro loqui: et,

multis verbis mecum egit, pro eo quod erat, egit mecum prolixa oratione.' Ibid.

59 'Certe negari non potest, Graecam dictionem *logon*, qua sine controversia usus est Euangelista, verius et usitatius exprimi Latinis per *sermonis*, quam per *verbi* vocabulum.' Ibid., 114A. In addition to the six citations ennumerated here from the formal apologies, cf. '... aut quasi *sermo* non melius exprimat Graecam vocem *logos* quam *verbum*.' To Thomas Wolsey, *EE*, IV, 158 (no. 1060, 26–27)

60 'Nos tametsi videbamus *sermonis* vocabulo rectius exprimi Graecam vocem, qua usus est Evangelista, *logon*.' *Annotationum in Evangelium Joannis*, 1:2, *LB*, VI, 335A

61 '... quum *sermo* multis nominibus rectius et aptius exprimat Graecam vocem quam *verbum*.' Ibid., 335B

62 '... imo cum *sermonis* vocabulum non uno nomine commodius sit, atque etiam molius, cum vocem Graecam *logon* rectius exprimat.' *Apologia de 'In principio erat sermo,'* *LB*, IX, 121D

63 '... imo *sermonis* vocabulum aptius exprimere Graecam vocem *logos*, qua usus est Euangelista.' Ibid., 122D

64 'Primum, *sermo* commodius explicat quod Evangelista posuit *logon*. *Annotationum in Evangelium Joannis*, 1:2, *LB*, VI, 335C

65 'Primum, sermo commodius explicat quod Evangelista posuit *logon*, quod apud Latine loquentes *verbum* non sonet totam orationem, sed unam aliquam dictionem.' Ibid.

66 'At Christus ideo dicitur *logos*, quod quicquid loquitur Pater, per Filium loquatur.' Ibid.

67 'Levia sunt haec, fateor, sed tamen quamlibet levis accessio huc aut illuc impellit, cum alioqui res est in aequilibrio.' *Apologia de 'In principio erat sermo,'* *LB*, IX, 114A

68 'Denique nescio quo modo magis arridet animo meo in nugis admiscere seria quam in magnis rebus nugari.' To Guillaume Budé, *EE*, II, 255 (no. 421, 105–106). Trans., R.A.B. Mynors and D.F.S. Thomson, *The Correspondence of Erasmus* (Toronto: University of Toronto Press, 1976), III, 307

69 'Sed indignum se iudicant ad istas grammaticorum minutias descendere; sic enim vocare solent eos qui bonas didicere literas, atrox esse conuicium existimantes grammatici cognomen; quasi vero laudi vertendum sit theologo si grammaticen nesciat. Non facit

theologum sola grammaticae cognitio. At multo minus theologum facit ignorata grammatica.' To Henry Bullock, *EE*, II, 325 (no. 456, 130–136). Trans., Nichols, II, 328

70 The entire *Apologia de 'In principio erat sermo'* is a refutation of this charge, but see especially, *LB*, IX, 122C, and the *Annotationum in Evangelium Joannis*, 1:2, *LB*, VI, 336A

71 *Apologia de 'In principio erat sermo,'* *LB*, IX, 114A, 115A, 115C, 121D

72 'At in hoc meo proposito, quo major est varietas, hoc plus est fructus.' *Annotationum in Evangelium Joannis*, 1:2, *LB*, VI, 336D

73 '... divinam hanc virtutem.' *De copia*, *LB*, I, 3B. Trans., Donald B. King and H. David Rix (Milwaukee: Marquette University, 1963), p. 11. 'Vt non est aliud vel admirabilis, vel magnificentius quam oratio, divite quadam sententiarum verborumque copia, aurei flumenis instar, exuberans.' Ibid., 3A. Trans., ibid. Ibid., 6C–D. Trans., ibid., 16

74 Ibid., 8D–9C

75 *Apologia de 'In principio erat sermo,'* *LB*, IX, 113C. *Annotationum in Evangelium Joannis*, 1:2, *LB*, VI, 335B

76 'Proinde dicturo delectus adhibendus, ut ex omnibus optima sumat. In promendo judicum requiritur, in condendo sedulitas.' *De copia*, *LB*, I, 9A. Trans., King and Rix, p. 20

Margaret Mann Phillips notes that 'words for Erasmus have a certain uniqueness. There are hardly any real synonyms, though some may be more suited to the poet or the orator and certain centuries have their own words (the historical approach is very clear),' in 'Erasmus and the Art of Writing,' in *Scrinium Erasmianum*, ed. J. Coppens (Leiden: E.J. Brill, 1969), I, 343.

77 Erasmus considered such books a stupid source for learning Latin and often commented unfavourably on the scholastic resort to them. See, e.g., *Ratio seu methodus compendio perveniendi ad veram theologiam*, *H*, p. 186, 30–34; *LB*, V, 80D.

78 'Postremo, ut demus nihil interesse inter *sermonem* et *verbum*, certe generis congruentia magis commendat *sermonis* vocabulum.' *Apologia de 'In principio erat sermo,'* *LB*, IX, 114A. 'Deinde generis congruentia facit.' *Annotationum in Evangelium Joannis*, 1:2, *LB*, VI, 335C. For amplification of this argument, see Chapter 2, pp. 33–35.

79 'Nam ut mollius est, *sermo factus est homo*: ita durius est, *verbum*

caro factum est, nisi molliret consuetudo, quae nihil non mollit.'
Apologia de 'In principio erat sermo,' LB, IX, 114A. '... ut mollior sit
oratio, quoties dicimus, *Sermo Dei factus est caro,* quam *Verbum Dei
factum est caro.' Annotationum in Evangelium Joannis,* 1:2, *LB,* VI,
335C. For amplification, see Chapter 2, p. 35.

80 '... etiamsi nusquam hactenus Dei Filius dictus esset *sermo.'
Apologia de 'In principio erat sermo,' LB,* IX, 114B

81 '... quod sane mihi liberum opinor fuisset.' Ibid., 113D

82 See this chapter, p. 28, n. 205, for an example. Erasmus'
correspondence and religious writing in the years enveloping the
first and second editions of his NT reveal that he had to contend
seriously with the misattribution of authority to Jerome's translation
by influential theologians.

83 '... privatim legi cupimus, non publice.' *Apologia de 'In principio
erat sermo.' LB,* IX, 112E; '... in opere, duntaxat in hoc parato ut
privatim legatur.' Ibid., 113D; '... in libro qui privatim legitur.'
Ibid., 114B; '... quod in opere, quod nec in Templis, nec in Scholis
legitur, sed in cubiculis duntaxat, ubi quid tandem non est fas legere?'
Ibid., 121D; '... sed privatim domi legatur.' Ibid., 122E; '... qui privatim
legitur.' *Annotationum in Evangelium Joannis,* 1:2, *LB,* VI, 335B

84 '... neque mutat Ecclesiasticam publicamque lectionem.' *Apologia de
'In principio erat sermo,' LB,* IX, 114B. 'Nolim, ut nunc res
habent, in templis recitare, *In principio erat sermo.' Annotationum in
Evangelium Joannis,* 1:2, *LB,* VI, 336B; 'Non in Templis, sed in
Musaeis legenda.' Ibid., 335B

85 '... et hunc hominis laborem comprobari summo Pontifici.' *Apologia
de 'In principio erat sermo,' LB,* IX, 122D

86 On consensus see James K. McConica, 'Erasmus and the Grammar
of Consent,' *Scrinium Erasmianum,* ed. Coppens, II, 76–99.

87 'Non est meum aut mei similium convellere, quod usu publico
receptum est.' *Ratio, H,* p. 208, 29–30; *LB,* V, 91B

88 '... claris ac probatis scriptoribus est habenda, qui multis ante nos
saeculis in terram uersi, diuinis ingeñs institutisque sanctisimis,
nobiscum uiuunt, cohabitant, colloquuntur.' Petrarch, *De remediis
utriusque fortunae* in *Operum* (Basel: Henrichus Petri, n.d.), I, Bk. I,
praef., p. 2

89 'Nam vera emendate loquendi facultas optime paratur, cum ex

castigate loquentium colloquio conuictuque, tum ex eloquentium
auctorum assidua lectione, e quibus ii primum sunt imbibendi,
quorum oratio, praeterquam quod est castigatissima, argumenti
quoque illecebra aliqua discentibus blandiatur.' *De ratione studii*, ed.
Margolin, *ASD*, 1–2, p. 115, 5–8; *LB*, I, 521C–D

90 '... aut imperitos sacrarum Litterarum, qui hoc nescierint: aut
stupidos, qui non animadverterint: aut sychophantas, qui tam
seditiose calumnientur, quod tam multiplici comprobatur
auctoritate.' *Apologia de 'In principio erat sermo,'* *LB*, IX, 114B

91 Ibid., 111F–112B. See this chapter, n. 92. Ibid., 112D

92 ' "At divus," inquit, "Augustinus cum ostendat Graecam dictionem
logos Latine significare et *verbum*, et *rationem*, tamen placet ei magis
verbi, quam *rationis* vocabulum in hoc sane loco. Siquidem *verbum*
magis quadrat ad significandam secundam Personam in divinis (his
enim verbis utebatur) propter rationes quas allegat Augustinus. Sed
eas," inquit, "rationes isti Graeculi non intelligunt, et audent tamen
contaminare Scripturas." ' Ibid., 111F–112A. Cf. the text of this
sermon as reported to Hermann von dem Busche, *EE*, IV, 310 (no.
1126, 17–28). The passage from Augustine to which Standish refers
is *De trinitate* (CCSL, La), ed. W.J. Mountain (Turnholt: Brepols,
1968), Bk. XV, xvi, p. 500. The disputed word, however, is not
ratio, but *cogitatio*. I have verified this also in the second edition of
the work (Venice: Paganinus de Paganinis, 1489), f. 1 1, but
Erasmus' edition of Augustine was not available to me for
consultation.

93 'Nam quod Augustinus docet, *verbi* vocabulum aptius notare Filium
Dei, quam rationis aut caeterorum, nihil ad me pertinet, cum ego
sermonem cum *verbo* conferam, non cum *ratione*, et ita praeferam
sermonem, ut *verbum* non rejiciam.' *Apologia de 'In principio erat
sermo,'* *LB*, IX, 113E

94 ' "Assentior," inquit alter, "de ratione; sed quid istud ad
sermonem? Nec enim Erasmus vertit, "In principio erat ratio," sed
"In principio erat sermo." ' To Hermann von dem Busche, *EE*, IV,
311 (no. 1126, 64–66)

95 By this date Erasmus had edited Athanasius, Basil, Cyprian, and
Jerome. *Bibliotheca Erasmiana*, ed. Vander Haegen, 2d series, pp.
11, 13, 23, 29

96 *Apologia de 'In principio erat sermo,' LB*, IX, 114C. Erasmus had edited the *Opera* of Cyprian, published by Froben's press, in the same month (February) as the appearance of the first version of the apology for *sermo*. Thus his detractors could play the coincidence of publication into a scandal.

97 '... consulant vetustos codices manu descriptos, consulant aliorum Editiones (sunt enim aliquot) et intelligent a me nihil immutatum hoc loco, nec alibi, nisi ex fide vetustorum Exemplarium.' *Apologia de 'In principio erat sermo,' LB*, IX, 114D. There were seven earlier editions of Cyprian; the *editio princeps* was from the Roman press of Conrad Sweinheim and Arnold Pannartz in 1471. Cyprian, *Opera omnia*, ed. Guilelmus Hartel (Vienna: C. Geroldi, 1871), III, lxx–lxxvii

98 '... Cyprianus aut legerit, "In Principio erat sermo," aut putarit nihil prorsus interesse inter *verbum* et *sermonem*.' *Apologia de 'In principio erat sermo,' LB*, IX, 115A

99 Ibid., 113D, 114B, 121D, 121E. *Annotationum in Evangelium secundum Joannis*, 1:2, *LB*, VI, 335B

100 *Apologia de 'In principio erat sermo,' LB*, IX, 114C. Cf. *Annotationum in Evangelium Joannis*, 1:2, *LB*, VI, 335C. The reference is to Cyprian, *Adversus Iudeos ad Quirinum* (CCSL, III), ed. R. Weber (Turnholt: Brepols, 1972), Bk. II, vi, p. 37. The citation is from Chapter 6, and not Chapter 5 as Erasmus states.

101 'En habent ipsum locum, de quo movent hanc tragoediam: habent auctorem tam antiquum, tam modis omnibus probatum a probantissimis, ut nemo possit contemnere.' *Apologia de 'In principio erat sermo,' LB*, IX, 114C

102 Ibid., 114D. The reference is to Cyprian, *Adversus Iudeos ad Quirinum*, ed. Weber, Bk. II, iii, pp. 31–32. The first citation which Erasmus offers is Ps 44:2. The next reference is telescoped from two. It should read Ps 32:6, not Ps 22: 'Sermone Dei coeli firmati sunt, et spiritu oris ejus omnis virtus eorum'; next, the verse attributed to Isaiah is Rom 9:28: 'Verbum consummans, et brevians in justitia, quoniam sermonem breviatum faciet Deus in toto orbe terrae.' The third reference is Ps 106:20. Finally, Erasmus, probably confused by the second verse, incorrectly identifies the last reference as Rev 6. It is Rev 9:11–13.

103 *LThK*, II, 381

104 *Apologia de 'In principio erat sermo,'* *LB*, IX, 115A. The reference
is: 'Hanc Graeci *logon* dicunt, quo uocabulo etiam sermonem
appellamus ideoque iam in usu est nostrorum per simplicitatem
interpretationis sermonem dicere in primordio apud Deum fuisse,
cum magis rationem competat antiquiorem haberi, quia non
sermonalis a principio sed rationalis Deus etiam ante principium, et
quia ipse quoque sermo ratione consistens priorem eam ut
substantiam suam ostendat.' Tertullian, *Adversus Praxean* (CCSL, II),
ed. Aem. Kroymann and Ernest Evans (Turnholt: Brepols, 1954),
Bk. V, iii, pp. 1163–1164

105 Ibid. Erasmus gives *De resurrectione carnis* as the locus of the
quotation; it does not occur, however, in the modern critical edition
of that work. Erasmus may have had in mind '... quia ex dei
uoluntate uerbum caro factum est,' from *De carne Christi*, XIX, 2,
p. 907. He overlooks the opening passage of *De oratione* (CCSL, I) in
which Tertullian writes of Christ as 'Dei spiritus et Dei sermo et
Dei ratio,' Bk. I, i, p. 257.

106 Ibid., 115B–C. *Annotationum in Evangelium Joannis*, 1:2, *LB*, VI,
335D. The citation is from Augustine, *In Ioannis Evangelium
Tractatus* (CCSL, XXXVI), ed. Radbodus Willems (Turnholt: Brepols,
1954), CVIII, p. 617.

107 Ibid., 115C

108 Ibid., 115D–F. The references are to Augustine, *In Ioannis
Evangelium Tractatus*, ed. Willems, LIV, p. 461; *De trinitate* (CCSL,
L), ed. Mountain, Bk. I, xii, p. 65; *Ennarationes in Psalmos* (CCSL,
XL), ed. Eligius Dekkers and Iohannes Fraipont (Turnholt: Brepols,
1956), cxlvii, 22, p. 2157; ibid., 2158.

109 Ibid., 116E–117C. The references are to Hilary, *De trinitate* in
Lucubrationes quotquot extant, ed. Desiderius Erasmus (Basel:
Eusebium Episcopium and Nicolai Fratris, 1570), Bk. II, pp. 17, 18,
19. There are numerous errors in the citations of the *Apologia* as
compared with the incunabulum (Venice: Paganinus de Paganinis,
1489); with Erasmus' own edition; and with the most modern
edition, which is of the Codex Archivi S. Petri Vaticano D. 182, ed.
Joseph L. Perugi (Turin: Marietti, 1930).

110 Ibid., 117C–E. The references are to Ambrose, *Omnia quotquot*

extant ... opera, ed. Erasmus (Basel: Froben, 1538), II in I, *De fide orthodoxa contra Arianos,* Bk. II, p. 209; IV in II, *Hexameron,* Bk. IV, 13A–B; the third citation does not appear (*LB,* IX, 117D) but cf. *Hexameron,* IV, 16C: 'sermo eius ortus naturae sit.' The final citation commenting on Heb 4:12 is difficult to locate because Ambrose wrote no commentary on Hebrews as he did on the other NT epistles. Modern scholarship attributes the authorship of *De fide orthodoxa contra Arianos,* not to Ambrose as Erasmus does, but to Gregory, bishop of Elvira. See Otto Bardenhewer, *Geschichte der altkirchlichen Literatur* (Freiburg: Herder, 1923), III, 398.

111 Ibid., 117E–F. The references are to Jerome, *Commentariorum in epistola ad Ephesios* in *Omnes quae extant stridonensis lucubrationes,* ed. Erasmus (Basel: Froben: 1537), IX, i, 205B, 209B.

112 Ibid., 117F–118A. Cf. *Annotationum in Evangelium Joannis,* 1:2, *LB,* VI, 336A. The references are to Lactantius, *De Christianae religionis institutio* in *PL,* VI, 467, Bk. IV, viii, and *PL,* VI, 469, ix.

113 Ibid., 118A–B. Cf. *Annotationum in Evangelium Joannis,* 1:2, *LB,* VI, 336A. The reference is to Aurelius Prudentius Clemens, *Carmina* (CCSL, CXXVI), ed. Maurice P. Cunningham (Turnholt: Brepols, 1966), 'Hymnus ante Somnium,' p. 29.

114 Ibid., 118C–D. I have been unable to locate these citations in the modern critical edition, Anselm of Canterbury, *Opera omnia,* ed. Franciscus Salesius Schmitt (Segovia: Abbey Press, 1938–1940), I and II; (Edinburgh: T. Nelson, 1946–1961), III–VI.

115 Ibid., 118E–F. The reference is to Remigius of Auxerre, *Expositio in Epistolam ad Hebraeos* in *Commentarius in Epistolas S. Pauli, PL,* CXVII, 849C; ibid., 849D; ibid., 850C, 851B. In this edition the work is wrongly attributed to Haymo of Falversham. See Maximillianus Manitius, *Geschichte der lateinischen Literatur des Mittelalters* (Munich: Beck, 1911), I, 516–517.

116 Ibid., 118B–C

117 ' "Ista," inquit, "littera de se videtur habere difficultatem, tamen considerando aliam translationem planior est. Ubi enim nos habemus *sermo,* in Graeco habetur *logos,* quod est idem quod *verbum*; unde *sermo,* id est *verbum*." ' Ibid., 116A–B. The citation is from Thomas Aquinas, *In Epistolam ad Hebraos* in *Opera omnia* (New York; Musurgia, 1949), XIII, 705.

118 Ibid., 116B

119 Ibid., 116C. The reference is Nicolas of Lyra, *Biblia sacra cum glossa ordinaria*, ed. Strabo Fuldensis (Paris: Franciscus Fervardentium, 1590), VI, 835–836: '... quia sermo acciptur hic pro verbo, unde et Graeco habetur, *logos*, quod signat idem quod verbum.' See also Anselm of Canterbury, 'Sermo Dei, id est, verbum Patris.' Ibid., 835B.

120 Ibid., 116C. The reference is to Hugh of St Cher, *Opera omnia in universum vetus, et novum testamentum* (Venice: Nicolaus Pezzana, 1732), VII, 246a–d: [Vivus est sermo Dei] 'idest filius Dei, qui dicitur verbum Patris, quia immediate exiit ab eo, sicut sermo a mente, et postea induit carnem, quasi vocem ad narrandum nobis Patrum.' He also cites Jn 17:18 and Wis 18:15, the same passages that Erasmus argues. With reference to Erasmus' apology for *sermo*, Hugh of St Cher (Hugo Cardinalis) is identified incorrectly as a Cardinal Hugo in Werner Schwarz, *Principles and Problems of Biblical Translation: Some Reformation Controversies and their Background* (Cambridge: Cambridge University Press, 1955), p. 146, and in McConica, 'Erasmus and the Grammar of Consent,' p. 93, n. 61.

121 Ibid., 116C. The text to which Erasmus refers is in the interlinear gloss, edited by Nicolas of Lyra, *Biblia sacra cum glossa ordinaria*, VI, 835–836.

122 'Neque dissentit Glossa, quam vocant ordinariam, cui communi Theologorum consensu plurimum est ponderis.' Ibid., 116C.

123 Ibid. The reference is *Glossa ordinaria*, *PL*, CXIV, 651A, as Erasmus cites, except for 'compages'; and CXIII, 1180D: 'Sed tuus, Domine, sermo. Id est, Filius.' The authorship of the *Glossa ordinaria* is mistakenly attributed in this edition to Walafrid Strabo. It is the work of Anselm of Laon and others.

124 'Ecce vir tantus non veretur, Filium Dei vocare sermonem, vocare dictionem, hoc est loquutionem Patris.' Ibid., 118C–D. See this chapter, n. 114.

125 'Vides ut Anselmus Augustino succinens, non veretur Dei Filium appellare sermonem.' Ibid., 118D–E. See this chapter, n. 114.

126 See this chapter, n. 115.

127 'Neque dubito quin innumera possint adduci exempla, quibus

doceamus, probatos Ecclesiae doctores nullo scrupulo fuisse deterritos, quo minus *Christum* appellarent *sermonem Patris,* si cui vacet loca disquirere.' *Apologia de 'In principio erat sermo,' LB,* IX 118F. Unfortunately, research discloses that some of his testimonial texts are misattributed. See this chapter, nn. 105, 110, 147, 153.

128 '... Ecclesia quotannis toties recinens facit ut frequentissime dictum videatur. Et quaenam sunt istorum aures tam surdae, ut ad vocem toties repetitam et inculcatum nondum assueverint?' *Apologia de 'In principio erat sermo,' LB,* IX, 116A

129 'Sic olim legit Ecclesia, sic hodie canit,' *Annotationum in Evangelium Joannis,* 1:2, *LB,* VI, 336A

130 See this chapter, n. 128.

131 See this chapter, n. 117.

132 See this chapter, n. 119.

133 See this chapter, n. 120.

134 See this chapter, n. 121.

135 *Apologia de 'In principio erat sermo,' LB,* IX, 116C–D. The reference is to Hugh of St Cher, *Opera omnia,* III, 166u: 'Hoc est contra multos, qui cum infirmantur, prius ad medicum, quam ad Christum currunt, praeponentes consilium medici corporalis verbo Dei, quod est medicina spiritualis.'

136 Ibid., 116C. The reference is to Nicolas of Lyra , *Biblia sacra cum glossa ordinaria,* ed. Strabo Fuldensis, in the interlinear gloss: 'Id est, filius per quem omnia, cuius potestas vbique,' III, 1960.

137 'Si impium, si blasphemum, si capitale est, Christum appellare *sermonem* aut ante me, aut mecum damnent oportet tot egregios Ecclesiae proceres, Cyprianum, Ambrosium, Hieronymum, Augustinum, Hilarium, Prudentium, Lactantium, cumque his Thomam, Lyranum, Hugonem, glossa ordinariam, imo totam Ecclesiam.' Ibid., 121D–E. *Italics mine.* This argument is similar to Augustine, *Contra Iulianum, PL,* XLIV, Bk. II, x, 701–702.

138 'Natura sum extemporalis et ad recognitionem mire piger.' To Damianus a Gois, *EE,* XI, 207 (no. 3043, 36–37). Cf. *EE,* VII, 48 (no. 2095, 1–8). On Erasmus' extemporaneity of composition, see D.F.S. Thomson, 'The Latinity of Erasmus,' in *Erasmus,* ed. T.A. Dorey (Albuquerque: University of New Mexico Press, 1970), pp. 119–121.

139 In the letter To Martin Luther, *EE*, VIII, xlv (no. 1127a, 11), the
Scotist is identified as a Spaniard imported to England for the
purpose of teaching the philosophy of Duns Scotus.

140 ' "Verbum," inquit, "est conceptus tacitus, quod si Christus recte
dicitur sermo, consequetur ut sermo quoque sit conceptus tacitus,"
quod ille videri volebat vehementer absurdum, "cum sermo," ut
ajebat, "sit conceptus expressus voce." ' *Apologia de 'In principio
erat sermo,' LB*, IX, 119A–B

141 'Hic est syllogismus eximii Theologi, cum aliorum aliquot
hominum, tum ipsius in primis judicio, cujus illum non puduit
apud summos et dignitate et eruditione viros.' Ibid., 119B. 'Quod si
qui conentur sophisticis argutiis docere, Christum recte *verbum*
dici, *sermonem* non recte, quid aliud efficient, quam ut tot eximios
Ecclesiae proceres blasphemos faciant et insanos?' Ibid., 119A. Cf.
121D–E.

142 '... an protinus consequitur, ideo Christum non recte dici
sermonem, quia recte dicitur *verbum*? An ideo Christus non
recte dicitur lux aut veritas, quia dicitur verbum?' Ibid.,
119B

143 'Nam res divinas nullae voces hominum proprie exprimunt.' Ibid.,
113C. 'Siquidem haec nomina varia accommodantur personis ex
consuetudine sermonis humani, quo nostra tarditas commodius
adducatur in aliquam Dei cognitionem.' Ibid., 119B. 'Et nonulla
veluti propria tribuuntur singulis, quae tamen re vera propria non
sunt, sed tamen juxta captum humanae mentis aptius alia de aliis
praedicantur. Id quoties facimus, humanis vocibus abutamur
oportet.' Ibid., 119C. '... alioqui Filius Dei neque tacitus est
conceptus, neque voce expressus, sed quod nobis est animi tacitus
conceptus, hoc est ille manens in Patre, qui cum habet eandem
essentiam: quod nobis est animi sensus sermone prolatus, hoc est
ille semper a Patre nascens, a quo personae proprietate
distinguitur.' Ibid.

144 '... alioqui si Christus nihil aliud est quam verbum internum, quo
sensu dixit Joannes, "Et verbum erat apud Deum?" ' Ibid., 119C.
Jarrott states incorrectly that 'For his interpretation of the
Trinitarian implications of "sermo," Erasmus is not original but
relies on St Augustine,' in 'Erasmus' *In principio erat sermo*: A

Controversial Translation,' 37. Erasmus does not rely on Augustine; rather, he corrects Augustine. Jarrott omits this text from her article, not perceiving that Erasmus' exposition of Augustine's texts is a critical response to the Scotist's syllogism. Jarrott appears to have missed the issue of the argument; namely, that for Augustine *verbum* signifies primarily the mental word, whereas for classical grammar and Erasmus *verbum* means the spoken word. See below for amplification.

145 'Non quod alius assumtus homo, et alius sit sermo qui assumsit, sed quod unus atque idem pro varietate causarum nunc sublimis, nunc humilis praedicatur.' *Apologia de 'In principio erat sermo,' LB,* IX, 117F. The citation is Jerome, *Commentariorum in epistola ad Ephesios* in *Omnes quae extant stridonensis lucubrationes,* ed. Erasmus, IX, 205B.

146 'Nihil enim prohibet idem verbum variis modis expromi ex mente Patris: expromitur cum gignitur, verissimum verbum, quia Patri simillimum. Expromtum est, cum per illud Pater conderet universa, et verbo suo firmaret coelos. Sed crassissime, ac nobis maxime familiari modo expromptum est, cum corpus humanum assumens, nobis humano more loqueretur.' *Apologia de 'In principio erat sermo,' LB,* IX, 119D–E.

147 Ibid., 119E–120B. The references are Augustine, *De trinitate,* ed. Mountain, Bk. IV, xx, p. 196; the supposititious *De cognitione verae vitae,* xiv (incorrectly given as iv), *PL,* XL, 1015; and *In Ioannis Evangelium Tractatus,* no citation.

148 'Proinde uerbum quod foris sonat signum est uerbi quod intus lucet cui magis uerbi competit nomen ... Nam illud quod profertur carnis ore uox uerbi est, uerbumque et ipsum dicitur propter illud a quo ut foris appareret assumptum est.' Augustine, *De trinitate,* ed. Mountain, Bk. XV, xi, pp. 486–487. Trans. Stephen McKenna (Washington: Catholic University of America, 1963), p. 477. Cf. *In Ioannis Evangelium Tractatus* I, 8, ed. Willems, p. 5. *De trinitate,* ibid., 487. '... ad illud uerbum hominis, ad uerbum rationalis animantis, ad uerbum non de deo natae, sed a deo factae imaginis dei, quod neque prolatiuum est in sono neque cogitatiuum in similitudine soni quod alicuius linguae esse necesse sit, sed quod omnia quibus significatur signa praecedit et gignitur de scientia

quae manet in animo quando eadem scientia intus dicitur sicuti est.'
Ibid., 488. Trans., ibid., 478

149 '... magis verbum dicitur quod sonat, quam quod animo
concipitur.' *Apologia de 'In principio erat sermo,' LB,* IX, 120B.

150 ' "Notandum," inquit, "verbum mentis non habet rationem verbi,
nisi prout induit rationem manifestati." ' Ibid. The citation is
Durand of Saint Pourçain, *In Petri Lombardi Sententias Theologicas
Commentariorum libri IIII* (reprint of Venice: Guerraea, 1571;
Ridgewood, N.J.: Gregg, 1964), I, Bk. I, dist. xxvii, q. ii, p. 77, col.
I, n. 7. Erasmus' *Apologia* mistakes the number of the distinction.

151 'Sed quoniam ea quae voce proferuntur, notae sunt earum
affectionum, quae prius insunt in animo, et altera res alteri
respondet, utraque verbum dicitur.' Ibid., 120B. '... ut est verbum
mentis, ita est sermo mentis.' Ibid., 120C

152 'Atque apud Graecos magis ad hanc opinionem respondet
etymologia, quod illis *logos* etiam *rationem* sonet, et *logismos cogitatio*
sit, et *logizomai cogito* sive *reputo. Sermo* cum a *serendo* dici
videatur, unde et *dissero*, propius accedit ad rationem Graecae vocis
quam *verbum,* quod ab aeris verberatu dictum putant Grammatici,
quemadmodum vocem a boando.' Ibid., 120C–D. Cf. Quintilian,
Institutio oratoria, ed. M. Winterbottom (Oxford: Clarendon Press,
1970), I, Bk. I, vi, p. 47; and also Varro's etymology, n. 161.

    Jarrott misconstrues this passage which she considers the 'crucial
point' of Erasmus' argument. She incorrectly translates the text:
'Therefore I argue that *sermo* approaches more closely to the
meaning of the Greek word than *verbum,* since *sermo* is spoken by a
begetting, a bringing forth ...' The causal clause should read rather
in English: '*sermo* seems to be derived from *serare* (to sow), whence
also *dissero* (to speak) ...' Jarrott then misinterprets her
mistranslated text: 'It is this generative discourse between the
Father and the Son which, in the mystery of the Trinity, *is* the
Son.' 'Erasmus' *In principio erat sermo*: A Controversial
Translation,' 38. The reader should recall here that Christian
orthodoxy professes that the Son is the generat*ed* discourse *of* the
Father, and not, as Jarrott claims, the generat*ive* discourse *between*
the Father and the Son.

153 *Apologia de 'In principio erat sermo,' LB,* IX, 120D. The reference is

to a spurious work of Augustine, *Principia dialecticae*, *PL*, XXXII, 412.

154 '... igitur nihil hic sit quod non pro me faciat.' Ibid., 120E

155 'Malim equidem omnibus *aproskopos* esse.' *Annotationum in Evangelium Joannis*, 1:2, *LB*, VI, 336B–C

156 Ibid., 336C. Cf. To Guillaume Budé, *EE*, III, 227–228 (no. 778, 238–250); From Budé, *EE*, III, 271–272 (no. 810, 110–118)

157 'Non hercule magis, quam novatus est Nicolaus, qui posita veste candida sumpsit fuscam.' *Annotationum in Evangelium Joannis*, 1:2 *LB*, VI, 336B

158 *'logos'*, *A Greek-English Lexicon*, ed. Henry G. Liddell and Robert Scott, rev. Henry S. Jones and Roderick McKenzie (9th ed.; Oxford: Clarendon Press, 1940), II, 1058–1059. *'logos,'* *The Vocabulary of the Greek Testament*, ed. James H. Moulton and George Milligan (London: Hodder and Stoughton, 1930), p. 379; *'logos,'* *A Greek-English Lexicon of the New Testament and Other Early Christian Literature*, ed. William F. Arndt and F. Wilbur Gingrich (Cambridge: University Press; Chicago: University Press, 1957), pp. 478–480; *'legō, logos, rhēma, laleō, Theological Dictionary of the New Testament*, ed. Gerhard Kittel, trans. and ed., Geoffrey W. Bromiley (Grand Rapids, Mich.: Wm. B. Eerdmans, 1967), IV, 69–143; *'logos,'* *A Patristic Greek Lexicon*, ed. G.W.H. Lampe (Oxford: Clarendon Press, 1961), I, 807–811

159 '... alioqui propemodum malim *orationis* quam *sermonis*, quod *sermonis* frequenter sit confabulatio familiariter colloquentium.' *Apologia de 'In principio erat sermo,' LB*, IX, 114A. 'Alioqui nihil aptius reddebat emphasin Graecae vocis quam *oratio.' Annotationum in Evangelium Joannis*, 1:2, *LB*, VI, 335C

160 See this chapter, n. 78.

161 'Sermo, opinor, est a *serie* ... sermo enim non potest in uno homine esse solo, sed ubi oratio cum altero coniuncta.' Marcus Terentius Varro, *De linqua latina*, trans. Roland G. Kent (London: William Heinemann; Cambridge: Harvard University Press, 1951), I, Bk. VI, lxiv, pp. 230–232

162 'sermo,' *A Latin Dictionary*, ed. Charleton F. Lewis and Charles Short (Oxford: Clarendon Press, 1879), p. 1679; 'sermo,' *Totius Latinitatis Lexicon*, ed. Aegidio Forcellini (Prati: Giachetti, 1845),

IV, 138; 'sermo,' *Dictionnaire étymologique de la langue latine*, ed. A.
Ernout and A. Meillet (4th ed.; Paris: C. Klincksieck, 1959), p. 617;
'sermo,' *The Oxford Classical Dictionary*, ed. N.G.L. Hammond
and H.H. Scullard (2d ed.; Oxford: Clarendon Press, 1970), p. 979
    Cf. the meanings (1) *tuitio, conductus*; (2) *homilia, concio ad
populum in Ecclesia*; (3) *ratio*; (4) *sermo publicus* or *generalis de fide*,
as e.g. the *actio fidei, auto de inquisición* or *auto da fé*; (5) *contentio,
lis, controversia*. Domenico du Cange, *Glossarium mediae et infimae
latinitatis* (Paris: Libraire des sciences et des arts, 1938), VII, 438.
See also J.–P. Migne, *Lexicon manuale ad scriptores mediae et infimae
latinitatis* (Paris: Garnier Fratres, 1890), col. 2046.

163 Christine Mohrmann, 'Praedicare-tractare-sermo,' in *Etudes sur le
    latin des chrétiens* (Rome: Storia e Letteratura, 1958–1965), II,
    71.

164 See this chapter, n. 159.

165 The literature chronicling and interpreting this christology is too
    ponderous to catalogue here. One might consult an introductory
    bibliography such as that provided in Marguerite Harl, *Origène et la
    fonction révelatrice du Verbe incarné* (Paris: Seuil, 1958), pp. 31–68;
    read also pp. 73–97.

166 The paraphrase begins, 'Natura divina quoniam in immensum
    superat imbecillitatem humani ingenii ...' *Paraphrasis in evangelium
    Joannis, LB*, VII, 497A. The citation of Mt 11:27b occurs at 497C.
    'Itaque rationibus humanis scrutari divinae naturae cognitionem,
    temeritas est: loqui de his, quae nullis verbis explicari queunt,
    dementia est: definire, impietas est ... Et satis est interim ad
    consequendam salutem aeternam, ea de Deo credere, quae palam
    ipse de se prodidit in sacris Litteris ... Haec simplici fide tenere,
    Christiana Philosophia est.' Ibid., 497C–D

167 'Itaque quemadmodum arcanae Litterae summam illam mentem,
    qua nihil cogitari potest neque majus, neque melius, Deum vocant.'
    Ibid., 498F–499A. '... ita hujus Filium unicum, sermonem illius
    appellant.' Ibid., 499A. 'Filius enim quum non sit idem qui Pater,
    tamen similitudine Patrem quasi refert, ut utrumque in altero liceat
    intueri, Patrem in Filio, Filium in Patre. Sed gignentis ac geniti
    similitudo, quae in humana generatione multis modis imperfecta est,
    in Deo Patre et hujus Filio perfectissima est.' Ibid. 'Nec est alia res,

quae plenius et evidentius exprimat occultam mentis imaginem, quam oratio non mendax.' Ibid. 'Haec enim vere speculum est animi, qui corporeis oculis cerni non potest.' Ibid., 499A–B. 'Quod si cui volumus animi nostri voluntatem esse cognitam, nulla re certius id fit, aut celerius, quam oratione, quae ex intimis mentis arcanis depromta, per aures audientis, occulta quadam energia, animum loquentis transfert in animum auditoris.' Ibid., 499B. 'Nec est alia res inter mortales efficacior ad omnem animorum motum excitandum, quam oratio.' Ibid.

168 'Filius itaque dicitur, quod caeteris omnibus par ei unde nascitur, sola personae propietate [*sic*] discernitur.' Ibid. Cf. 'Sic erat indivulsae naturae cum Patre, ut juxta personae proprietatem esset apud Patrem.' Ibid., 500A. '... tamen personae proprietate discretus, non naturae dissimilitudine, erat apud Deum Patrem.' Ibid., 500B. 'Sermo dicitur, quod per hunc Deus, qui in suapte natura nulla ratione comprehendi potest, nobis voluit innotescere.' Ibid., 499B. Cf. 'Verbum autem Patris ideo dictum est, quia per ipsum innotescit Pater.' Augustine, *De fide et symbolo*, iii, 3, in *PL*, XL, 183.

Erasmus confesses the eternity of *sermo*: '... aeternae mentis sermo aeternus, quo sibi semper velut arcana cogitatione loquitur Pater, etiam ante conditum hunc mundum.' *Paraphrasis in evangelium Joannis*, *LB*, VII, 499C. And the act of creation: '... condidit universam hanc mundi machinam, et in hac mentes Angelicas, et humanum genus velut ex Angelis ac pecudibus medium.' Ibid., 499D

'Quemadmodum autem si quis esset Rex omnipotens, quicquid is fieri juberet, id protinus factum esset: ita Pater vere omnipotens per Filium ac sermonem suum condidit universa. Atque hac ratione primum depromsit sermonem suum, per quem nobis veluti loquutus innotesceret: seseque per admirationem pulcherrimae machinae cognitum, in affectus nostros insinuaret.' Ibid., 499D–E. '... sed Filius Dei bis natus est, semel a Patre ante tempora, vel potius sine tempore: ex Deo vero, verus Deus: rursus tempore ab aeterno destinato, ex Maria virgine, ex homine, verus homo. Nam hoc modo visum est Deo, nobis rursum depromere sermonem suum, ut crassius ac familiarius nosci posset.' Ibid., 499E–F

169 'Non est haec temporaria nativitas, nec sermo similis humano.
Nihil corporeum est in Deo, nihil tempore fluidum, aut loco
circumscriptum: neque quicquam omnino initio, progressui, senio,
aut ulli mutationi obnoxium,' etc. Ibid., 499C

170 *Apologia de 'In principio erat sermo,' LB*, IX, 116E–118E

171 The errors which Erasmus singles out are these: that God's
Speech is posterior to God who speaks it; that the Speech came into
being when born in the flesh of the Virgin Mary; that Jesus Christ
was nothing other than mere man, or that he was produced among
other creatures. *Paraphrasis in evangelium Joannis, LB*, VII, 499E–F.
He expounds the orthodox doctrine in 499C and in 499F–500C.

172 'Quod igitur Sol est rebus corporeis, hoc sermo divinus, qui est
Christus Jesus, est mentibus mortalium, quibus per peccatum in
altissimas tenebras et mortem collapsis, ineffabili caritate succurrere
studuit.' Ibid., 500D. Beginning with the phrase, 'Prius enim
vivebant homines in ignorantia ...' Erasmus develops the christology
of light. Ibid., 500D ff.

173 'Origenis operum bonam partem euolui; quo praeceptore mihi
videor non nullum fecisse operaeprecium. Aperit enim quasi fontes
quosdam et rationes indicat artis theologicae.' To John Colet, *EE*, I,
405 (no. 181, 38–41)

174 'Origène rejette l'interpretation que le IIᵉ siècle donnait du titre de
logos en l'attribuant au Christ et refuse d'entendre *logos* dans le sens
de langage ou de parole. Il juge excessive l'assimilation du Fils à
une simple émission, *prophora*, du Père ... La première explication
du titre de *logos* que nous allons lire est de beaucoup la plus
fréquente dans l'ensemble de son oeuvre, elle est meme la seule,
pourrait-on dire: le *logos* est 'ce que ote en nous toute part
irrationelle et nous constitue véritablement capables de raison.'
Harl, *Origène et la fonction révélatrice du Verbe Incarné*, p. 124

175 'Il concoit rarement la relation du Père et du Fils sur le modèle de
celle qui existe entre une intelligence et son expression verbale.'
Ibid.

176 E.-W. Kohls, *Die Theologie des Erasmus* (Basel: Friedrich
Reinhardt, 1966), I, 98. André Godin, 'Erasme et le modèle
origénien de la prédication,' *Colloquia Erasmiana Turonensia*, ed.
Margolin (Toronto: University of Toronto Press, 1972), II,

174 Erasmus on Language and Method in Theology

807–820, especially 810. Cf. 'De Vitrier à Origène,' Ibid., 47–57.

177 Dunatai de kai ho logos huios einai para to apaggellein ta kruphia tou patros ekeinou, analogou tō kaloumenō huiō logō nou tugchanontos. Hōs gar ho par' hēmin logos aggelos esti tōn hupo tou nou horōmenōn, houtōs ho tou Theou logos, egnōkōs ton patera, oudenos tōn genētōn prosbalein autō chōris hodēgou dunamenou, apokaluptei hon egnō patera. Origen, TO KATA IŌANNĒN EUAGGELION EXĒGĒTIKŌN, 1, xxxviii, 277. In the first phrase I am following Harl's inversion of *logos* and *huios*. See *Origène et la fonction révelatrice du Verbe Incarné*, p. 125, n. 17.

178 Erasmus edited the *Opera omnia* of Athanasius, published in 1519 (see Chapter 3, n. 119) and was editing Origen at the time of his death.

179 ho phanerōsas eauton dia Iēsou Christou tou huiou autou, hos estin autou logos apo sigēs proelthōn. EPISTOLAI, ed. Th. Camelot (Paris: Cerf, 1951), MAGNĒSIEUSIN, viii, 2, p. 102

180 kai Logon kalousin, epeidē kai tas para tou Patros omilias pharei tois anthrōpois. PROS TPUPHŌNA IOUDAION DIALOGOS, 28. *PG*, vi, 776A. Cf. the same argument applied to the title *aggelos*, ibid., and also lxi, 613C–616A. I find no evidence yet, however, to support Lewis Spitz's judgment that 'Justin Martyr's theory of the spermatic logos inspiring the ancient Greek philosophers was obviously in evidence here,' i.e. in *LB*, vii, 772. *The Religious Renaissance of the German Humanists* (Cambridge: Harvard University Press, 1963), p. 214

181 In the context of the Son as the Father's unique revelation, Irenaeus writes: 'Agnitio enim Patris est Filii manifestatio: omnia enim per Verbum manifestatur.' The Greek reads *panta gar dia tou Logou phaneroutai*. *Contra haereses* (SC, C) ed. Adelin Rousseau (Paris: Cerf, 1965), II, Bk. IV, 6, 3, p. 442

182 'Atque horum trium summus est consensus: Pater est auctor, Filius nuntius, Spiritus suggestor.' *Paraphrasis in epistolam d. Joannis, primam*, 5:7, *LB*, vii, 1158D

183 As an example of this complaint: 'In theological terms he readily accepted Christ as the supreme teacher of wisdom, but had difficulty in believing the world to be so constituted that man could be delivered from his own wickedness only by the death of God's

only Son.' Tracy, *Erasmus: The Growth of a Mind*, p. 236. That the soteriological theme was not absent from Erasmus' theology has been indicated already by other scholars, e.g., John W. Payne, *Erasmus: His Theology of the Sacraments* (Richmond, Va.: John Knox, 1970), 64–66, 71–96.

184 See, e.g., the figure of Christ in fresco from the cemetery of Domitilla, reproduced in Louis Bréhier, *L'art chrétien* (Paris: Renouard, 1928), p. 39, fig. 12; and the figure in bas-relief, p. 51, with commentary on p. 50.

185 'verbum,' *A Latin Dictionary*, ed. Lewis and Short, p. 1972; 'verbum,' *Totius Latinitatis Lexicon*, ed. Forcellini, p. 618.

186 See this chapter, n. 158.

187 Jerome, *Homilia in Ioannem Evangelistam* in *PLS*, II, 183–188

188 Tertullian, *Opera*, I, *Adversus Hermogenem*, ed. Kroymann, Bk. xx, iv, p. 414; *Adversus Praxean*, ed. Kroymann and Evans, Bk. VII, viii, p. 1166; VIII, iv, 1167; XII, vi, 1173; XIII, iii, 1174; XVI, I, 1180; XIX, vi, 1185; XXI, I, 1186
Cyprian, *Adversus Iudaeos ad Quirinum*, ed. Weber and Bénevot, Bk. II, iii, p. 31; II, vi, p. 37

189 Tertullian, *Adversus Praxean*, Bk. v, iii, pp. 1163–1164. See this chapter, n. 104.

190 For a complete listing of Old Latin Bible MSS, see *Vetus Latina*, ed. Bonifatius Fischer, vol. I: *Verzeichnis der Sigel* (Freiburg: Herder, 1949). For a survey of the most important of these, see Metzger, *The Text of the New Testament*, pp. 72–75.

191 Novatian, *De trinitate*, ed. G.F. Diercks (Turnholt: Brepols, 1972), Bk. XIII, i, p. 32; XV, vii, 37; XXI, xvii, 74

192 Hilary, *Opera* (CSEP, XXVI–XXIX), ed. A.B. Caillau and M.N.S. Guillon (Paris: Méquignon–Havard, 1830), I, *De trinitate*, Bk. I, x, p. 37; II, xii, 68; II, xxiii, 73–74; XII, ix, 228; XII, lvi, 503; II, *De synodis, seu de fide orientalium*, XXIV, p. 23; XXIX, 26; LXIX, 52; III, *Tractatus in Psalmum CXXII*, VII, p. 252

193 Eusebius Vercellensis, *De trinitate* (CCSL, IX), ed. Vincent Bulhart (Turnholt: Brepols, 1957), Bk. III, xlvii, p. 42; v, xx, 70; v, xxii, 71

194 Metzger, *The Text of the New Testament*, p. 73

195 Eusebius Vercellensis, *De trinitate*, ed. Bulhart, Bk. v, xxii, p. 71

196 Isaac Judaeus, *Expositio fidei catholica* (CCSL, IX), ed. A. Hoste (Turnholt: Brepols, 1957), p. 347

197 Zeno Veronensis, *Tractatus 11, 8 'De nativitate Domini'* (CCSL, XXII), ed. B. Löfstedt (Turnholt: Brepols, 1971), p. 176

198 Maximus, *Opera* (CCSL, XXIII), ed. Almut Mutzenberger (Turnholt: Brepols, 1962), *Sermo* XXXIXa, extr., p. 157; *Sermo* LI, p. 207; *Sermo* LXIV, p. 270; *Sermo* CX, extr., p. 428

199 Ambrose, *Opera* (CSEL), ed. Carolus Schenkl et al. (Vienna: F. Tempsky, 1879), I, ed. Schenkl, *Hexameron*, Bk. I, v, p. 15; *De paradiso*, v, p. 283; *De Isaac vel anima*, v, p. 666; II, ed. Schenkl, *De interpellatione Iob et David*, I, ix, p. 232; IV, iv, p. 278; V, ed. M. Petschenig, *Expositio psalmi CXVII*, xiv, 23, p. 313; VIII, ed. Otto Faller, *De fide*, I, 8, p. 24; I, 19, p. 52; I, 8, p. 25; II, 2, p. 66; V, I, p. 223; V, 9, p. 260; IX, ed. Faller, *De spiritu sancto*, I, II, pp. 66–67; I, 15, p. 80; XI, ed. Faller, *Epistularum*, XI, p. 86. *Tractatus in evangelio secundum Lucam* (SC, XXI), ed. Gabriel Tissot (Paris: Cerf, 1956), I, Bk. I, xiii, p. 53; Bk. II, xl, p. 90; 11, Bk. X, cxviii, p. 195

200 Lactantius, *De vera sapientia et religio*, PL, VI, Bk. IV, viii and ix, 467–469

201 Arnobius, *Adversus nationes*, ed. C. Marchesi (Turin: I.B. Paravia, 1934)

202 Marius Victorinus, *De trinitate hymni*, PL, VIII, 1141, 1142, 1144

203 See this chapter, n. 106.

204 The Vulgate translation by Jerome was authorized at the session of 8 April 1546, of the Council of Trent. *Concilium Tridentinum*, ed. Societas Goerresiana (2d ed.; Freiburg: Herder, 1961), V, 91–92. For discussion of the issue of revision at the Council see, Hubert Jedin, *A History of the Council of Trent*, trans. Ernest Graf (London, etc.: Thomas Nelson and Sons, 1957), pp. 92–98.

205 'Porro quod scribis ab hac aeditione non esse recedendum tot videlicet consiliis approbata, more vulgarium theologum facis; qui quicquid vllo modo in publicum vsum irrepsit, ecclesiasticae tribuere solent autoritati. At mihi vel vnam profer synodum in qua sit haec aeditio comprobata.' To Dorp, *EE*, II, 110 (no. 337, 768–772). Trans., Mynors and Thomson, *The Correspondence of Erasmus*, III, 135. Cf. the apology in the letter To Henry Bullock, *EE*, II, 321–329 (no. 456)

206 Metzger, *The Text of the New Testament*, p. 102. The posthumous edition of 1555 discarded the Vulgate again.

207 '[Qui] quomodo numerum sine diuisione patiuntur.' Tertullian, *Adversus Praxean*, ed. Kroymann and Evans, Bk. II, p. 1161

208 '... quod sequitur, "Et verbum erat apud deum," uerbum quidem solus filius accipitur non simul pater et filius tamquam ambo unum verbum.' Augustine, *De trinitate*, ed. Mountain, Bk. VI, ii, p. 230

209 Kenneth Burke, *The Rhetoric of Religion: Studies in Logology* (Boston: Beacon, 1961), p. 114

210 'Quod eadem locutio non constet pluribus verbis, sed sit unum verbum.' Anselm of Canterbury, *Monologion* in *Opera omnia*, ed. Schmitt, I, xxx, p. 48. Trans., S.N. Deane, *Saint Anselm: Basic Writings* (La Salle, Ill.: Open Court, 1965), p. 91. 'Nam si sic est summae naturae consubstantialis, ut non sint duo, sed unus spiritus: utique sicut illa summe simplex est, ita est ista. Non igitur constat pluribus verbis, sed est unum verbum per quod facta sunt omnia.' Ibid. Trans., ibid. Cf. *Epistola de incarnatione verbi* in *Opera omnia*, II, x, pp. 25–26

211 The inconsistency applies with respect to classical grammar. Post-Augustan Latin uses *locutio* by transference to mean an utterance or a word.

212 Thomas Aquinas, *ST*, I, q. XXXIV, art. 1, 2 in *Opera omnia* (Rome: Polyglotta, 1888), IV, 365–368. '... unicum Verbum eius est expressivum non solum Patris, sed etiam creaturarum.' Ibid., art. 3, p. 370. Trans., Anton C. Pegis, *Basic Writings of Saint Thomas Aquinas* (New York: Random House, 1944), I, 337

213 Henri de Lubac, *Exégèse médiévale: Les quatre sens de l'Ecriture* (Paris: Aubier, 1959–1964), III, 187–197. He cites the verse without reference, p. 188; it is Rom 9:28.

214 'A divinis oraculis nomen habet theologus, non ab humanis opinionibus.' *Ratio*, H, p. 305, 14–15; *LB*, V, 138B

215 'an haec propositio: deus est scarabaeus aeque possibilis sit atque haec: deus est homo.' Ibid., H, p. 297, 28–29; *LB*, V, 134B. This occurs in a catalogue of scholastic questions 'quae parum pium sit investigare, sunt, quae citra salutis dispendium possint nesciri, sunt, de quibus eruditius sit ambigere et cum Academicis *epechein* quam

pronuntiari.' Ibid., ll. 22–24; *LB*, v, 134A. Cf. ibid., *H*, p. 180, 3–5;
LB, v, 76E–77A.

216 'Nobis satis est credere, tenere et adorare quod scriptum est.'
Ibid., *H*, p. 298, 25–26; *LB*, v, 134E

217 Cf. this chapter, n. 166, with *Ratio*, *H*, p. 300, 32; *LB*, v, 135E
where he cites Chrysostom's rule 'scrutamini scripturas'

TWO: ORATIO

1 'Alioqui nihil aptius reddebat emphasin Graecae vocis logou quam
oratio.' *Annotationum in Evangelium Joannis*, 1:2, *LB*, vi, 335C

2 'Postremo, ut demus nihil interesse inter *sermonem* et *verbum*, certe
generis congruentia magis commendat *sermonis* vocabulum, alioqui
propemodum malim *orationis* quam *sermonis,* quod *sermo* frequenter
sit confabulatio familiariter colloquentium.' *Apologia de 'In principio
erat sermo,' LB*, ix, 114A. 'Deinde generis congruentia facit.'
Annotationum in Evangelium Joannis, 1:2, *LB*, vi, 335C

C.A.L. Jarrott mistranslates the grammatical expression
'congruentia generis' (agreement of gender) as 'suitability of kind.'
'Erasmus' *In principio erat sermo*: A Controversial Translation,' *SP*,
LXI (1964), 37. She fails, therefore, to notice Erasmus' argument
from gender which I expose here. Dietrich Harth claims that
Erasmus does not offer a reason for wanting to translate *logos* by
oratio but speculates: 'Doch liegt die Vermutung nahe, dass er
damit auf die literarische Überlieferungsform der Offenbarung
anspielte, da zu seiner Zeit der Ausdruck "oratio" längst im Sinne
von literarischer Prosa eingebürgert war.' *Philologie und Praktische
Philosophie: Untersuchungen zum Sprache-und Traditionsverständnis
des Erasmus von Rotterdam*, HB, I / II (Munich: Wilhelm Fink,
1970), pp. 43–44

3 'Ego sum via, et veritas, et vita.' *Annotationum in Evangelium
Joannis*, 4:14, *LB*, vi, 396C

4 Niccolò Perotti, *Rudimenta grammatices* (Bologna: Johannes
Schriber, de Annunciata, 1478), f. a 4–6. It is interesting to note
that on f. a 5 Perotti uses *sermo* as an example of masculine
gender.

Erasmus recommends Perotti thus: 'Inter recentiores haud

multum video discriminis, nisi quod Niolaus Perottus videtur
omnium diligentissimus, citra superstitionem tamen.' *De ratione
studii*, *ASD*, 1–2, pp. 114–115, 14–1; *LB*, 1, 521C

5 'Sic dici virum Perpennam ut Alfenam muliebri forma et contra
parietem ut abietem esse forma similem, quo[m] alterum
vocabulum dicatur virile, alterum muliebre et utrumque natura
neutrum sit. Itaque ea virilia dicimus non quae virum significant,
sed quibus proponimus hic et hi, et sic muliebria in quibus dicere
possumus haec aut hae.' Marcus Terentius Varro, *De lingua latina*,
trans. Roland G. Kent (London: William Heinemann; Cambridge:
Harvard University Press, 1951), II, Bk. IX, xli, pp. 468–469

6 Flavius Sosipater Charisius in *Grammatici Latini*, ed. Henric Keil
(Hildesheim: Georg Olms, 1961), I, *Artis grammaticae*, Bk. I, viii, p.
17; Probus, ibid., IV, *Catholica*, pp. 3–33, and *Instituta artium*, pp.
52–53; Donatus, ibid., *De partibus orationis ars minor*, p. 355, and
Ars grammatica, pp. 375–376; Cledonius, ibid., V, *Ars grammatica*,
pp. 10, 39; Iulianus, ibid., *Excerpta ex commentariis in Donatum*, pp.
318–319; Phocas, ibid., *Ars, de nomine et verbo*, pp. 412–430;
Augustine, ibid., *Regulae*, pp. 496–507; Q. Rhemnius Palaemon,
ibid., *Ars*, pp. 533–541; Asper, ibid., *Ars*, pp. 549–550; and ibid.,
De nomine et pronomime and *De dubiis nominibus* (Fragmentum
Bobiense), pp. 555–594. Also, Isidore of Seville, *Etymologiarum sive
originum*, ed. W.M. Lindsay (Oxford: Clarendon Press, 1911),I, Bk.
VII, xxviii, no pagination

7 'Inter latinos vetustiores Diomedes ...' *De ratione studii*, *ASD*, 1–2,
p. 114, 14; *LB*, 1, 521C.

8 'hoc enim animo auribusque audientis adfertur animalium esse
quidem duo tantum genera, sed sine speciali discriminatione.'
Diomedis in *Grammatici Latini*, ed. Keil, I, *Artis grammaticae*, Bk.
I, p. 320

9 'Genera igitur nominum principalia sunt duo, quae sola novit ratio
naturae, masculinum et femininum. genera enim dicuntur a
generando proprie quae generare possunt, quae sunt masculinum et
femininum. nam commune et neutrum vocis magis qualitate quam
natura dinoscuntur, quae sunt sibi contraria.' Priscian in
Grammatici Latini, ed. Martin Hertz (Hildesheim: Georg Olms,
1961), *Institutionum Grammaticarum*, I, Bk. V, p. 141. Cf. 'Varro

dicit "genera dicta a generando. Quicquid enim gignit aut gignitur, hoc potest genus dici et genus facere." ... Varro ait "genera tantum illa esse quae generant: illa proprie dicuntur genera." ' *De lingua latina*, ed. Kent, II, Fr. 7a, p. 602; Fr. 7b, p. 604

10 'Genera dicta sunt ab eo, quod generant, atque ideo duo sunt tantum genera principalia, masculinum et femininum. haec enim sexus tantum generat. genera autem aut naturalia sunt, aut ex auctoritate descendunt ... in his enim naturalem nullum intellegimus sexum, sed eum sequimur, quem firmavit auctoritas.' Marius Servius Honoratus in *Grammatici Latini*, ed. Keil, IV, *Commentarius in artem Donati*, pp. 407–408. Cf. *Explanationum in artem Donati*, Bk. I, pp. 492–494

11 '... non erunt genera nisi duo, masculinum et femininum. nulla enim genera creare possunt nisi haec duo.' Pompeius in *Grammatici Latini*, ed. Keil, V, *Commentum artis Donati*, p. 159

12 'Genera nominium, quae naturalia sunt, duo sunt, ut quidam volunt, masculinum et femininum, quoniam omne scilicet animal natura necesse est esse aut masculinum aut femininum. dicta autem haec sunt ab eo genera quod generare possunt. denique si simplicibus et veris et naturalibus nominibus utamur, naturale primum masculinum genus mares, femininum feminas appellabimus. sed quoniam [cum dicamus "Cato" aut "Marcia" nominum hominum dicimus quae quia] nullum nomen ipsum aut mas est aut femina, generi tamen subiacet, quia corporis nomen est, recte masculinum genus aut femininum, non mas aut femina dicimus. non enim nomina generant, sed corpora, quorum illa sunt nomina. ita non nomen mas aut femina est, sed homo aut animal, cuius illud est nomen. quod cum ita sit, remanet ut in hac tali dictione nominum, quod masculina potius quam mares, feminina quam feminas dicimus, naturale generis nomen videatur omissum. erunt tamen principalia sub huius modi nominibus genera.' Consentius in *Grammatici Latini*, ed. Keil, V, *Ars, de duabus partibus orationis nomine et verbo*, p. 343

13 Tatwin, *Ars* (CCSL, CXXX pt. 1), ed. Maria de Marco (Turnholt: Brepols, 1968), Bk. I, xxxvi, p. 15

14 'angelicum nomen dabit hic; sed dicito neutra plurali numero Cherubin Seraphinque beata.

est Cherub, est Cherubim, Cherubin, Seraphim Seraphinque, atque Seraph.'
Alexander de Villa–Dei, *Doctrinale* (MGP, XII), ed. Dietrich Reichling (Berlin: A. Hofman, 1893), pt. I, iv, p. 36, ll. 514–517. Cf. p. 35, ll. 501–504. Not all mediaeval grammarians of influence speculated on grammatical gender in this way, however. Cf. Eberhard Bethuniensis, *Graecismus* (CGMA, I), ed. Iohannes Wrobel (Bratislava: G. Koebner, 1887), vi, p. 19, 1 to p. 22, 33; ix, p. 54, 1 to xii, p. 128, 462

15 'Genus *masculinum* est modus significandi rem sub proprietate *agentis,* ut *vir, lapus.* Genus *foemininum* est modus significandi rem sub proprietate *patientis,* ut *petra, mulier.*' Thomas of Erfurt in *Lexicon Scholasticum Philosophico-Theologicum,* ed. Mariani Fernandez Garcia (Quaracchi: College of St Bonaventure, 1910), *Tractatus de modis significandi sive grammatica speculativa,* xvi, p. 13. Cf. i, p. 1, concerning the active and passive modes of signifying.

In this edition the text is erroneously attributed to Duns Scotus. M. Grabmann has corrected the attribution of authorship in a series of documentary articles.

For discussion of gender in Thomas of Erfurt and Siger de Courtrai, see G.L. Bursill-Hall, *Speculative Grammars of the Middle Ages: The Doctrine of Partes Orationis of the Modistae* (AS, II), ed. Thomas A. Sebeck (The Hague and Paris: Mouton, 1971), pp. 162–167. Louis Kukenheim also remarks that the gender of nouns occupied an important place in mediaeval grammars. *Contributions à l'histoire de la grammaire grecque, latine, et hébraïque à l'époque de la Renaissance* (Leiden: E.J. Brill, 1951), p. 63

Modist grammar was a speculative restatement of Priscian's grammar, 'a study of the word-classes (*partes orationis*) and syntax of the idealized, perfect language, i.e. Latin,' methodologically presented so that language might be seen as the mirror of that reality which, according to mediaeval metaphysics, grounded the phenomena of the physical world. Those grammarians who wrote treatises on these modes of signifying in the thirteenth and fourteenth centuries were called the *modistae.* Bursill-Hall, *Speculative Grammars of the Middle Ages,* p. 31

16 'Masculinum genus, genus est nominis designans circa rem modum
essendi masculi seu potentiae activae generationis ... Femininum
autem est genus nominis designans circa rem modum essendi
femellae, ratione passivae generationis.' Siger de Courtrai, *Les
oeuvres*, PB, VIII, ed. G. Wallerand (Louvain: Institut Supérieur de
Philosophie de l'Université, 1913), *Summa modorum significandi*, p.
100

17 Propriety was, of course, a principal requirement of classical
rhetoric. See, e.g., Quintilian, *Institutio oratoria*, ed. M.
Winterbottom, SCBO (Oxford: Clarendon Press, 1970), III, Bk. VIII,
ii, pp. 425–427.

18 *Dialogus cui titulus, Ciceronianus, siue, De optimo dicendi genere*, ed.
Pierre Mesnard, *ASD*, 1–2, especially pp. 636–646; *LB*, I,
992C–998F

19 'Ac ne tamen et nobis inconsideratus aliquis calumniam moveat,
tamquam deum quem colimus marem esse credamus, ea scilicet
causa, quod eum cum loquimur pronuntiamus genere masculino,
intellegat non sexum sed usu et familiaritate sermonis appellationem
eius et significantiam promi. Non enim deus mas est, sed nomen
eius generis masculini est.' Arnobius, *Adversus nationes*, (CSLP, LXII),
ed. C. Marchesi (Turin: I.B. Paravia, [1934]), Bk. III, viii, p. 165

20 *De recta latini graecique sermonis pronvnciatione dialogus*, ed. M.
Cytowska, *ASD*, 1–4, pp. 13–103; *LB*, I, 909–968

21 Cicero, *De oratore*, ed. H. Rackham (London: William Heinemann;
Cambridge: Harvard University Press, 1958), Bk. III, vii–xii, pp.
20–38; xlix, 154–156. Quintilian, *Institutio oratoria*, ed.
Winterbottom, Bk. IX, iv, p. 537; I, x, pp. 63–64

22 'Suave autem genus erit dicendi primum elegantia et iucunditate
verborum sonantium et lenium, deinde coniunctione quae neque
asperos habeat concursus neque disiunctos atque hiantes.' Cicero,
De partitione oratoria, ed. and trans. Rackham, vi, 21, pp. 326–327

23 See Chapter 1, n. 79.

24 'Ursus: Scis bonam eruditionis partem esse, scire rerum vocabula.'
De recta pronunciatione, *ASD*, 1–4, p. 43, 983–984; *LB*, I, 930C

25 '... adeo ut nonnumquam vel impudenter addivinantes, vel
sordidissimos consulentes dictionarios ex arbore faciant
quadrupedem, e gemma piscem, e citharoedo fluvium, ex oppido

fruticem, e sidere avem, ex brassica braccam. Abunde doctum videtur istis, si tantum adiecerint: est nomen gemmae, aut: est species arboris, aut: est genus animantis, aut si quid aliud mavis.' *Ratio, H*, p. 185, 12–18; *LB*, v, 79E–F

'Quid profuerit tibi concinnasse syllogismum in celarent aut baroco de crocodilo disputans, si nescias, quod arboris aut animantis genus sit crocodilus?' Ibid., *H*, p. 186, 3–5; *LB*, v, 80A–B. The reference to the crocodile is to the classical puzzle: A crocodile, having seized a woman's son, said that he would restore him if she would tell the truth. She replied, 'You will not restore him.' Was it the crocodile's duty to give him up? Lucian, BIŌN PRASIS, 22 in SUMPOSION Ē LAPITHAI, tr. A.M. Harmon (London: William Heinemann; New York: Macmillan, 1913), II, 490–492, Cf. Quintilian, *Institutio oratoria*, ed. Winterbottom, I, Bk. I, x, 5, p. 59.

Celarent and *baroco* were among the sixty-four combinations of quantities and qualities which comprised the mood of a syllogism. The schoolboy learned them through the mnemonic doggerel:

> Barbara Celarent Darii Ferio: Baralipton
> Celantes Dabitis Fapesmo Frisesomorum:
> Cesare Camestres Festino Baroco: Darapti
> Felapto Disamis Datisi Bocardo Ferison.

A syllogism in *celarent* is in the first figure and has propositions *e* (general negative), *a* (general affirmative), and *e*. A proposition in *baroco* is in the second figure with propositions *a*, *o* (negative particular), and *o*. The doggerel and its explanation are cited from Thomas Gilby, *Barbara Celarent: A Description of Scholastic Logic* (London: Longmans Green, 1949), p. 215, n. 2. According to Grabmann in his edition of William of Sherwood, *Introductiones in logicam* (Munich: Bayerischen Akademie der Wissenschaften, 1937), p. 27, Sherwood may have invented the verse.

26 See Chapter 1, p. 22, n. 69.

27 'In his enim adolescentes vix trimestri studio grammaticae dato, protinus rapiuntur ad sophisticen, dialecticen, suppositiones, ampliationes.' *De recta pronunciatione, ASD*, 1–4, p. 24, 360–362; *LB*, 1 919C. 'Nec huic professioni suus habetur honos, quemadmodum caeteris. Aliis enim honoris causa titulus additur a

baculo, aliis a licentia; alii salutantur magistri artium, doctores medicinae, doctores iuris Caesarei, doctores iuris Pontificii, doctores vtriusque; traduntur insignia, praerogatiuae, dignitas. At grammaticus nihil aliud est quam grammaticus, quemadmodum calcearius nihil est quam calcearius.' Ibid., pp. 25–26, 384–390; *LB*, I, 919F

28 The word etymology 'ab *ethimos*, quod est flos, et *logos*, quod est sermo'; epilogue, 'dicitur ab *epy*, quod est supra, et *logos*, sermo, quasi sermo superiora recapitulans'; tropology, 'dicitur a *tropos*, quod est conversio, et *logos*, quod est sermo, quasi conversio sermonis.' Charles Thurot, *Notices et extraits de divers manuscrits latins pour servir à l'histoire des doctrines grammaticales au moyen age, N et E*, XXII / 2 (Paris: Impériale, 1868), pp. 146, 477, 478

29 *Ratio, H*, p. 186; *LB*, V, 80B–C. 'Atqui non raro ex ipsa rei proprietate pendet intellectus mysterii.' Ibid., *H*, p. 185, 18–19; *LB*, V, 79F

30 '... in his minutulis non minimum esse utilitatis.' *Apologia* to the 1516 edition, Novum Instrumentum, *H*, p. 171, 18; *LB*, VI, **3

31 'Mediocria fortassis eloquentium hominum ingenio commendatur; vt stellarum lumen lucerna quis adiuuet.' To Jean Grolier, *EE*, III, 300 (no. 831, 79–80). Trans., Nichols, II, 364

32 See Chapter 1, n. 68

33 'Caeterum in Nouo Testamento nec ignoro nec inficior permulta incidere minutula; sic enim argumenti ratio postulabat.' To Guillaume Budé, *EE*, II, 254 (no. 421, 93–94). 'De lucubrationibus nostris amo te qui mecum sentias, tantum abest vt sim reclamaturus,' etc. To Budé, *EE*, II, 363 (no. 480, 43–44ff.). 'At quid facias si his minutis sum natus.' Ibid., p. 364, 2. '... nisi quod mihi sane omnia mea nugae videntur; ac saepenumero mecum demiror quid ibid sit quod quidam laudibus vehant.' To Budé, *EE*, 254 (no. 421, 77–78). Trans., Mynors and Thomson, III, 421. '... mihi laus etiam, qui meipsum meo metiens pede mecum habitem et norim quam sit mihi curta supellex ... Mihi cordi est in huiusmodi friuolis philosophari; in quibus et minus video nugacitatis et aliquanto plus fructus quam in magnificis illis, ut ipsis videtur, argumentis.' To Budé, *EE*, II, 364 (no. 480, 60–61, 67–69). 'Denique qui vnum hoc spectat, non vt sese ostentet sed vt prosit,

huic non perinde refert in quam splendidis versetur atque in quam
vtilibus. Non refugiam etiam illo contemptissimo Catunculo
contemptiora, modo sensero ad prouehenda bona studia conducere.'
Ibid., ll. 69–73. 'Atque haec qualiacunque *leptologēmata* grauissimi
theologi amplectuntur, ex his se plurimum hausisse lucis fatentur.'
To Budé, *EE*, II, 255 (no. 421, 99–100). Trans., ibid.

34 See this chapter, n. 29.

35 Erasmus defends Valla's method in a letter To Christopher Fisher,
    EE, I, 407–412 (no. 182).

36 'An dicent non idem esse iruis Vallae grammatico quod Nicolao
    theologo? Vt ne respondeam interim Laurentium a magnis viris
    inter philosophos quoque ac theologos referri, Lyra quum vocem
    excutit, num theologi ac non magis grammatici vices agit? imo
    totum hoc, diuinas vertere scripturas, grammatici videlicet partes
    sunt. Neque vero absurdum si quibusdam in rebus plus sapit Iethro
    quam Moyses. Ac ne ipsa quidem, opinor, disciplinarum omnium
    regina theologia indignum admoueri sibi manus, ac debitum
    exhiberi obsequium a pedissequa grammatica; quae tametsi nonullis
    est dignitate posterior, nullius certe opera magis necessaria.' Ibid.,
    p. 410, 125–135. Trans., Mynors and Thomson, *The Correspondence
    of Erasmus*, II, 94. 'Quod si reclament maiorem esse theologiam
    quam vt grammaticae legibus teneatur, totum interpretandi
    negocium de sacri Spiritus afflatu pendere ... Sed expediant interim
    quid sibi velit, quod Desyderio suo scribit Hieronymus, Aliud est,
    inquiens, esse vatem et aliud interpretem. Ibid Spiritus ventura
    praedicit; hic eruditio et verborum copia quae intelligit transfert.'
    Ibid., p. 410, 137–139, 140–143. 'Tum quorsum attinuerit eundem
    de ratione vertendi diuinas litteras praecipere, si facultas ista diuino
    contigit afflatu?' Ibid., p. 410, 143–145. Trans., Mynors and
    Thomson, II, 94. 'Imo tanto magis nefas est deprauare, tantoque
    attentius corrigendum a doctis quod per inscitiam est adulteratum.'
    Ibid., p. 411, 159–161

37 'Principio duplex omnino videtur cognitio, rerum ac verborum.' *De
    ratione studii*, *ASD*, I–2, p. 113, 4; *LB*, I, 521A. Cf. Cicero, *De
    oratore*, ed. Rackham, II, Bk. III, v, p. 16; Quintilian, *Institutio
    oratoria*, ed. Winterbottom, III, Bk. VIII, prohoemium, p. 420.

38 'Socrates. "Let us suppose that to any extent you please you can

learn things through the medium of names, and suppose that you
can learn them from the things themselves – which is likely to be
the nobler and clearer way; to learn of the image, whether the
image and the truth of which the image is the expression have been
rightly conceived, or to learn of the truth whether the truth and the
image of it have been duly executed?" Cratylus. "I should say that
we must learn of the truth." Soc. " How real existence is to be
studied or discovered is, I suspect, beyond you and me. But we
may admit so much, that the knowledge of things is not to be
derived from names. No, they must be studied and investigated in
themselves." Crat. "Clearly, Socrates." ' Plato, CRATULOS, 439b.
Trans., Jowett, I, 387

39 'Verborum prior, rerum potior.' *De ratione studii, ASD*, 1–2, p.
113, 4–5; *LB*, I, 521A

40 'Sed nonnulli dum *aniptois*, vt aiunt, *posin* ad res discendas festinant,
sermonis curam negligunt, et male affectato compendio in maxima
incidunt dispendia.' Ibid., II, 5–7; *LB*, L, 521A. 'Etenim cum res
non nisi per vocum notas cognoscantur, qui sermonis vim non
calleat, is passim in rerum quoque iudicio caecutiat, hallucinetur,
deliret necesse est.' Ibid., II, 7–9; *LB*, I, 521A. 'Postremo videas
nullos omnium magis vbique de voculis cauillari quam eos qui
iactitant sese verba negligere, rem ipsam spectare.' Ibid., II, 9–11;
LB, I, 521A. 'Quapropter vtroque in genere statim optima, et
quidem ab optimis sunt discenda.' Ibid., ll. 11–13, *LB*, I, 521A

41 'Primum igitur locum grammatica sibi vendicat, eaque protinus
duplex tradenda pueris, graeca videlicet ac latina.' Ibid., p. 114,
2–3; *LB*, I, 521B

The discussion of language in this book is confined to the
trilingual aptitude necessary for theology. For Erasmus' knowledge
and evaluation of the European vernaculars, see: Rachel Giese,
'Erasmus' Knowledge and Estimate of the Vernacular Languages,'
RR, XXVIII (1937), 3–18; L.-E. Halkin, 'Erasme et les langues,'
RLV, XXXV (1969), 566–579; D.F.S Thomson, 'The Latinity of
Erasmus,' in *Erasmus*, ed. T.A. Dorey (Albuquerque: University of
New Mexico, 1970), pp. 129–131.

42 'Sermonis facultas, vt dictum est, citra fastidium vsu comparatur.'
Declamatio de pueris ad virtutem ac literas liberaliter instituendis, ed.

J.–C. Margolin, *ASD*, 1–2, p. 70, 12; *LB*, 1, 511D. 'Quoniam autem
prima puerorum institutio est vt discant explanate emendateque
loqui, hic olim nutrices ac parentes non mediocri erant adiumento.'
Ibid., p. 48, 27–28; *LB*, 1, 501C. 'Linguarum enim inscitia
disciplinas vniuersas aut exstinxit aut deprauauit, atque adeo
theologiam quoque, medicinam et iurisprudentiam.' Ibid., p. 49,
1–3; *LB*, 1, 501D. 'Admirabilis fuit olim Gracchorum eloquentia,
sed quam bona ex parte Corneliae matri debebant, M. Tullii
iudicio. "Apparet," inquit, "filios non tam in gremio educatos quam
in sermone matris": gremium igitur illis maternum erat prima
schola ... Tota domus totaque gens vsque ad nepotes ac pronepotes
saepe retulit maiorum in dicendo elegantiam.' Ibid., ll. 3–6, 10–12;
LB, 1, 501D. Ibid., pp. 49–50, 15–15; *LB*, 1, 501E–502A

43 'Rudolphus Agricola, unicum Germaniae nostrae lumen et
ornamentum, annum egressus quadragesimum Hebraeas litteras
discere nec erubuit, vir in re litteraria tantus, nec desperavit, homo
natu tam grandis.' *Ratio*, H, p. 183, 32–35; *LB*, V, 79A. 'Ipse iam
quinquagesimum tertium ingressus annum ad Hebraicas litteras
olim utcunque degustatas cum licet recurro.' Ibid., H, p. 184, 1–2;
LB, V, 79A. Cf. 'Applicabo me, si patieris, et adiungam lateri tuo,
exhibeboque me tibi discipulum etiam in discendo Graece,
quanquam iam prouectus aetate ex prope senex.' John Colet to
Erasmus, *EE*, II, 258–259 (no. 423, 59–61)

44 'Felicior quidem hac in parte juventus, at interim non desperandi
sunt senes.' *Ratio*, H, pp. 181–184; *LB*, V, 77E–79B

45 'Leo: Ego nullam aetatem ad discendum arbitror immaturam,
praesertim in his quibus discendis statim natura composuit et, vt ita
loquar, finxit hominem. Quorum de numero cum primis sermo est.
Nec enim magno negocio canum foetus discunt adulari aut leporem
cursu petere.' *De recta pronunciatione*, *ASD*, 1–4, p. 14, 53–56; *LB*,
1, 914A

46 'Quae hodie legimus senes, post biduum si denuo legamus noua
videntur.' *De pueris instituendis*, *ASD*, 1–2, p. 50, 7–8; *LB*, 1, 502A

47 'Primum linguarum vsus, qui citra studium omne contingit
infantibus ... Et huc, vt diximus, inuitat infantulos natiua quaedam
imitandi voluptas, cuius vestigium aliquod videmus in sturnis ac
psittacis.' Ibid., p. 66, 15–18; *LB*, 1, 509F

48 'Nam in hoc ipsum infantiae peculiarem quandam, vt modo dicebam, imitandi libidinem addidit, vt quicquid audierint viderintue, gestiant aemulari, gaudeantque si quid sibi videntur assequuti.' Ibid., p. 48, 2–5; *LB*, I, 501A. 'Et videmus in pueris recens natis, velut in psittacis, studium quoddam natiuum, ac voluptatem etiam aemulandi reddendique quod audierint tanta docilitate.' *De recta pronunciatione, ASD*, I–4, p. 14, 64–66; *LB*, I, 914B

49 'Si tibi corpus additum non fuisset, numen eras, si mens ista non fuisset indita, pecus eras.' *Enchiridion, H*, p. 41, 22–24; *LB*, V, 11F–12F. Cf. 'Ratio facit hominem.' *De pueris instituendis, ASD*, I–2, p. 31, 23; *LB*, I, 493C; cf. p. 40, 21–22; *LB*, I, 497E.

In his monograph, *L'Idée de nature dans la pensée d'Erasme*, VASS, VII (Basel and Stuttgart: Helbing and Lichtenhahn, 1967), Jean-Claude Margolin argues that reason (*ratio*), which includes both the natural gift and its exercise through education, constitutes man. He neglects the epistemological thesis adopted by Erasmus in the early pedagogical works that *ratio* is only mediated and known through speech. Margolin also has overlooked Erasmus' developed thesis, which I expose below, that speech (*oratio*) and not reason (*ratio*) makes a human being.

50 'Haec igitur est unica ad beatitudinem via, primum, ut te noris. Deinde, ut ne quid pro affectionibus, sed omnia pro iudicio rationis agas.' *Enchiridion, H*, p. 46 22–24; *LB*, V, 16B. 'Pudet me profecto Christianorum nomine, quorum maxima pars veluti muta pecora servit affectibus suis, adeoque in hac dimicatione non sunt exercitati, ut ne norint quidem rationis atque perturbationum discrimen.' Ibid., *H*, p. 47, 15–18; *LB*, V, 15D–E

51 'Quod philosophi rationem, id Paulus modo spiritum, modo interiorem hominem, modo legem mentis vocat.' Ibid., ll. 28–30; *LB*, V, 15F

52 'Contra in euangelicis litteris Christo dicunt discipuli: Domine, quo ibimus? Verba vitae habes. Cur ita tandem verba vitae? Nempe quod ab ea manarent anima, a qua nunquam vel momento discesserat divinitas, quae et nos vita restituit immortali.' Ibid., *H*, p. 27, 24–28; *LB*, V, 5A

53 '... vnde celebratur illud a Socrate dictum: *Loquere vt te videam*.' *Lingva*, ed. F. Schalk, *ASD*, IV–1, p. 296, 100–101; *LB*, IV, 698C

54 'Nam cum iuxta vocem euangelicam ex abundantia cordis os
loquatur, nimirium viva verba dei loqueretur, si illic adesset vita,
deus.' *Enchiridion*, *H*, p. 27, 21–23; *LB*, v, 5A. Cf. Mt
12:34–35.

55 'Quod illi affectum, hic interim carnem, interim corpus, interim
exteriorem hominem, interim legem membrorum appellat.' Ibid., *H*,
p. 47, 30–32; *LB*, v, 15F

56 'Sepulchrum pectus, guttur et os hiatus sepulchri.' Ibid., *H*, p. 27,
16; *LB*, v, 4F. 'Audis quempiam sermones impios, tumidos,
maledicos, impudicos, obscoenos proferentem, verbis rabiosis in
proximum debacchantem, cave putes isti homini vivam esse
animam. Iacet in sepulchro pectoris putre cadaver, unde eiusmodi
foetores exhalantur et proximum quemque inficiunt.' Ibid., II, 5–10;
LB, v, 4E

57 Isocrates, NIKOKLĒS Ē KUPRIOI, 7. '... for the power to speak
well is taken as the surest index of a sound understanding, and
discourse which is true and lawful and just is the outward image of
a good and faithful soul.' Trans., George Norlin (Cambridge:
Harvard University Press; London: William Heinemann, 1954), I,
81. Erasmus had an edition of Isocrates in his library. To Nikolaus
Bensrott, *EE*, I, 365 (no. 158, 6–7)

58 'Caeterum in hoc est lingua data hominibus, vt hac internuntia
homo hominis mentem et animum cognoscat.' *Lingva ASD*, IV–I, p.
286, 742–743; *LB*, IV, 691B

59 'Eoque dei filius, qui venit in terras, vt per eum cognosceremus
mentem dei, *sermo patris* dici voluit.' Ibid., ll. 745–747, 691C

60 '... mentis illius imago, quae spiritussancti artificio, expressa est
litteris euangelicis ... praesertim in Christo, qui cum esset summa
simplicitas veritasque, nihil omnino poterat esse dissimilitudinis
inter archetypum divini pectoris et inde ductum imaginem
sermonis.' *Enchiridion*, *H*, p. 75, 16–17, 19–22; *LB*, v, 32A. Trans.,
Raymond Himelick, *The Enchiridion of Erasmus* (Bloomington, Ind.:
Indiana University Press, 1963), p. 112

61 'Specula bona fide repraesentant imaginem rei obiectae. Nam quae
mendacia vocantur, in hoc tantum adhibentur, vt risum moueant.
Eloque dei filius, qui venit in terras, ut per eum cognosceremus
mentem dei, *sermo patris* dici voluit, et idem *veritas* dici voluit,

quod turpissimum sit linguam ab animo dissidere.' *Lingua*, *ASD*
IV–I, p. 286, 745–748; *LB*, IV, 691B–C

62 'Spiritum vero, qua divinae naturae similitudinem exprimimus, in
qua conditor optimus de suae mentis archetypo aeternam illam
honesti legem insculpsit digito, hoc est spiritu suo. Hac deo
conglutinamur, unumque cum eo reddimur.' *Enchiridion*, *H*, p. 52,
28–31; *LB*, V, 19B. Trans., Himelick, p. 79

63 'Quod in rebus diuinis est pater ex se progignens filium, hoc in
nobis est mens, fons cogitationum ac sermonis, quod illic est filius
nascens a patre, hoc in nobis est oratio proficiscens ab animo.'
Lingva, *ASD*, IV–I, p. 296, 96–98; *LB*, IV, 698B

64 See Chapter 1, n. 169.

65 'At forma non facit hominem, quam habemus communem cum
statuis. Animo sumus vel homines, vel bestiae ... Quia Galenus me
docuit, hominem a caeteris animantibus, quae vocamus *aloga*,
discerni non ratione, sed oratione.' *De recta pronunciatione*, *ASD*,
I–4, p. 14, 31–32; *LB*, I, 913C–D. Ibid., ll. 33–34; *LB*, I, 913D. The
reference is to Galen, *Exhortatio ad artium liberalium studia*,
translated by Erasmus, *ASD*, I–I, ed. Jan Hendrik Waszink, pp.
637–657.

66 Erasmus' Latin translation was published by Froben in May 1526,
and based on the Aldine *editio princeps* of the Greek, issued in
April–August 1525.

67 'Leo: Quia video complures non humana voce loqui, sed latrare
cum canibus, hinnire cum equis, grunnire cum suibus, mugire cum
bubus, gannire cum vulpibus, stridere cum cicadis, blaterare cum
camelis, barrire cum elephantis, frendere cum apris, fremere cum
pardis, gemere cum vrsis, rudere cum asinis, balare cum ouibus,
strepere cum anseribus, garrire cum picis, conicari cum cornicibus,
crocitare cum coruis, crepitare cum ciconiis, sibilare cum anseribus;
denique quoduis animal referre potius quam humano more loqui.'
De recta pronunciatione, *ASD*, I–4, p. 14, 37–44; *LB*, I, 913D–E

Yet, as Erasmus had observed wryly in the *Querela pacis* of 1516,
the animals manage to preserve concord in their kingdom even
without the civilizing agent of speech; while men, disregarding their
common nature and name, war on their own species: '... unum
animal edidit natura, ratione praeditum, ac divinae mentis capax,

unum benevolentiae concordiaeque genuit, et tamen apud quantumlibet efferas feras, apud quantumvis brutas pecudes, mihi citius locus sit quam apud homines.' *Querela pacis undique gentium ejectae profligataequae, LB,* IV, 626A–B

68 Terrence Heath, 'Logical Grammar, Grammatical Logic, and Humanism in Three German Universities,' *SR,* XVIII (1971), 41. Heath refers to Celtis' letter To the University of Ingolstadt in *Der Briefwechsel des Konrad Celtis,* ed. Hans Rupprich (Munich: C.H. Beck, 1934), p. 56.

69 Christian Dolfen, *Die Stellung des Erasmus zur scholastischen Methode* (Osnabrück: Druck von Meinders & Elstermann, 1936). The section on the *Ratio* is not an analysis of the issue, but a concatenation of quotes on the priority of practical theology over scholastic questions, pp. 51–63.

70 Charles Goerung, *La théologie d'après Erasme et Luther* (Paris: Gabriel Beauchesne, 1913), pp. 47–48

71 'Nam facere, quod apud monachos aliquot fieri videmus, nec aliter ediscere psalmos, quam psittacus ediscit voces humanas, plus habet taedii quam fructus.' *Ratio, H,* p. 293, 22–25; *LB,* V, 132A

72 See, e.g., *Apologia de 'In principio erat sermo,' LB,* IX, 121B; *Ratio, H,* pp. 181, 243, 274, 296; *LB,* V, 77F, 108E, 124E, 133E

73 '*Canina facundia.* Sallustius apud Nonium Marcellum, in dictione Rabula: "Canina, ut ait Appius, facundia exercebatur." Quod quidem Appii dictum apud eruditos scriptores in adagionem cessit in quosdam, qui tantum ad maledicendum eloquentiae studium exercerent, a rixa canum, et oblatratu sumpto epitheto. Siquidem, r, litera, quae in rixando prima est, canina vocatur. Divus Hieronymus in Epistola ad Rusticum monachum: "Pomparum ferculis procedunt in publicum, ut Caninam exerceant facundiam." Idem obretectatores suos subinde *canes* appellat. Sumptum a genere Philosophorum, quos *kunikous,* appellant, sive ob sordidam vitam, sive quod obvios quosque mordent, quum mendicato vivant, more canum.' *Adagia,* II, iii, xxiv; *LB,* II, 534E–F

74 To Andrea Ammonio, *EE,* II, 355 (no. 475, 20–22)

75 'Quonam est iter tam cultis tamque alacribus? Nam inuisitis Louaniensium Academiam?'
'Bona verba.'

'Quamobrem?'

'Quis nunc illic nobis locus, vbi tot porci obgrunniunt, obrudunt asini, obblactiunt cameli, obstrepunt graculi, obgorriunt picae?' 'Epithalamium Petri Aegidii,' *Colloquia*, *ASD*, 1–3, pp. 412–413, 49–54; *LB*, 1, 747B. Trans., Craig R. Thompson, *The Colloquies of Erasmus* (Chicago and London: University of Chicago Press, 1965), p. 226

76 'Procul, inquit, a tergo sequebantur aues aliquot pennis caetera nigris, nisi quod explicatu alarum giluas verius quam candidas plumas ostenderent. Picae, inquit, videri poterant colore et voce, nisi quod singulae duodecim picas aequarent magnitudine corporis, nihilo minores vulturibus, cristam gestantes vertice, rostris et vnguibus aduncis, ventre prominente. Harpyae videri poterant, si tres modo fuissent.' 'Apotheosis Capnionis,' *Colloquia*, *ASD*, 1–3, pp. 269–270, 90–96; *LB*, 1, 690F–691A. Trans., Thompson, p. 83

77 Ibid., p. 270, 104–106, 113–128; *LB*, 1, 691A–C

78 '... balbutiendo ut possumus, excelsa Dei resonamus.' Thomas Aquinas, *ST*, 1,q. 4, art. 1, ad. 1. Aquinas cites here Gregory's *Moralia*, Bk. v, xxvi; see *PL*, LXXV, 715C.

79 'Balbutit nobis divina sapientia et veluti mater quaepiam officiosa ad nostram infantiam voces accommodat ... Tu vero festina adolescere ... Demittet illa sese ad tuam humilitatem, at tu contra ad illius sublimitatem assurge. Monstri simile est semper infantem esse, nimis ignavum ...' *Enchiridion*, H, p. 34, 16–22; *LB*, v, 8F

80 For the Ciceronians as monkeys: 'istos ridiculos simios,' *Ciceronianus*, *ASD*, 1–2, p. 630, 5; *LB*, 1, 988C; 'simiorum formossimus,' ibid., p. 649, 10; *LB*, 1, 1000F. For children learning language as monkeys: 'Simios quosdam esse dicas.' *De pueris instituendis*, *ASD*, 1–2, p. 48, 5; *LB*, 1, 501A

81 For *sermo* see Chapter 1. Concerning the Ciceronians, 'Ista lex seuerior est etiam Draconis legibus, si ob vnam dictiunculam parum ciceronianam, totum volumen damnatur, quamuis alias elegans ac facundum.' *Ciceronianus*, *ASD*, 1–2, p. 611, 31–33; *LB*, 1, 976E

82 '... perinde quasi cum moroso quopiam agas daemone, quem in tuam ipsius perniciem euocaris, si quid te fefellerit in verbis praescriptis, ac non potius cum clementissimo Seruatore ...' To Paul Volz, *EE*, III, 364 (no. 858, 94–96). Trans., Olin, p. 112

83 'Quid autem aliud est Christi philosophia, quam ipse renascentiam
vocat, quam instauratio bene conditae naturae?' *Paraclesis*, *H*, p.
145, 5–7; *LB*, v, 141F

84 'Vides, ut in Christo noventur omnia et rerum vocabula
permutentur.' *Enchiridion*, *H*, p. 96, 4–5; *LB*, v, 43A. Himelick
translates this as, 'You see that in Christ all things are changed and
their names are reversed,' p. 140.

85 The theme of Christ's pedagogical accommodation to his listeners is
prominent in the *Ratio*. See Chapter 3, p. 22

86 See this chapter, n. 79.

87 '... qui sumus ad angelorum consortia, ad divinitatis
communionem destinati.' *Enchridion*, *H*, p. 121, 10–11; *LB*, v, 57A

88 Alain Michel, *Rhétorique et philosophie chez Cicerón, essai sur les
fondements philosophiques de l'art persuader* (Paris: PUF, 1960), pp.
26–27

89 'Uni huic animanti sermo datus, praecipuus necessitudinum
conciliator.' *Querela pacis*, *LB*, IV, 627B

90 'Itaque quum sermo nobis potissimum in hoc datus sit a deo, vt
homini conuictus sit iucundior.' *Lingva*, *ASD*, IV–I, p. 253,
523–524; *LB*, IV, 667E

91 Pedro Laín Entralgo, *The Therapy of the Word in Classical
Antiquity*, ed. and trans. L.J. Rather and John M. Sharp (New
Haven and London: Yale University Press, 1970)

92 'Nec inscite dictum est Graecorum proverbiis: *animi laborantis
medicum esse sermonem.*' *In evangelium Lucae paraphrasis*, praefatio,
LB, VII, 274. Cf. 'Animo aegrotanti medicus est oratio.' *Adagia*, III,
i, xcixc; *LB*, II, 744D–745C. Erasmus cites Plutarch, Aeschylus,
Isocrates, and the Stoics, as well as Scripture, as variants on this
theme. See my 'Erasmus' prescription for Henry VIII: Logotherapy,'
RQ, in press.

93 *In evangelium Lucae paraphrasis*, praefatio, *LB*, VII, 274–276

94 'Quocunque me verto, video mutata omnia, in alio sto proscenio,
aliud conspicio theatrum, imo mundum alium. Quid faciam?
Christiano mihi dicendum est apud Christianos, de religione
Christiana: num vt apte dicam imaginabor me viuere aetate
Ciceronis, et in frequente senatu apud patres conscriptos in arce
Tarpeia dicere, et ex orationibus quas in senatu dixit Cicero,

voculas aliquot, figuras et numeros emendicabo?' *Ciceronianus*,
ASD, 1–2, p. 637, 3–8; *LB*, I, 992E–F. Trans., Izora Scott (Albany,
N.Y.: Brandow for Columbia University Teachers' College, 1908),
p. 62

95 'Haec sententiam: Iesus Christus, verbum et filius aeterni patris,
iuxta prophetias venit in mundum, ac factus homo sponte se in
mortem tradidit ac redemit ecclesiam suam ... sic esseret
Ciceronianus, "Optimi Maximique Iouis interpres ac filius, seruator,
rex, iuxta vatum responsa, ex olympo deuolauit in terras, et hominis
assumpta figura, sese pro salute reipublicae sponte duouit diis
manibus, atque ita concionem siue ciuitatem siue rempublicam
suam asseruit in libertatem."' Ibid., p. 641, 27–29, 32–36; *LB*, I,
995E–F. Trans., Scott, pp. 67–68

96 'Nusquam apud Ciceronem legimus, *Iesu Christi, verbi Dei, spiritus
sancti*, aut *trinitatis* vocabulum,' etc. Ibid., pp. 640–641, 35–7; *LB*,
I, 995B. Trans., Scott, p. 66. Erasmus catalogues many examples of
this type, ibid., p. 641, 9–24; *LB*, I, 995C–D. 'Nosop. Quid igitur?
Num autor eris nobis sic loquendi, quemadmodum scripserunt
Thomas et Scotus? Bul. Si melius dicit qui dicit aptius, sic de rebus
sacris loqui praestiterat, quam in his Ciceronem exprimere.' Ibid.,
p. 642, 12–14; *LB*, I, 996B

97 See this chapter, n. 95.

98 The word *battologia*, preserved in Matt 6:7, was from a bad Greek
poet according to 'Battalogia. Laconismus,' *Adagia*, II, I, xcii; *LB*,
II, 444B–C. Cf. Erasmus' criticism of long-winded prayer by those
'qui adhuc in littera sunt infantes neque ad spiritus maturitatem
adoleverunt.' *Enchiridion*, H, p. 30, 4–5; *LB*, V, 6C

99 'Intolerabilius autem fit, quod cotidie nova conduntur atque his ceu
sacris et *akinētois* Babylonicas turres in caelum usque surgentes
superstruimus.' *Ratio*, H, p. 205, 20–22; *LB*, V, 90B

100 'An non frigidus orator erit, qui ad has materias, veluti pannos
Ciceroni detractos assuat?' *Ciceronianus*, *ASD*, 1–2, p. 637, 15–16;
LB, I, 993A

101 '... nec id sane pristino tuo more mendicatas quasdam
sententiolas, imo (quod turpius est) voces hinc ex Bernardo, illinc
ex Claudiano passim coaceruando, tuisque non aliter quam sibi
cornicula pauonis plumas aptando, imo inepte assuendo: neque

enim id est literas condere sed colligere.' To Servatius Rogerus, *EE*,
I, 89 (no. 15, 34–38). Trans., Mynors and Thomson, I, 20–21

102 'Secutus sum veterem illam M. Tulii regulam, vt in vertendo
sententias modo mihi putarim appendendas, non annumeranda
verba.' To Nicolas le Ruistre, *EE*, I, 393 (no. 177, 95–97)

103 See, e.g., his hermeneutical rule of analysing 'what precedes and
what follows' the pericope under examination, Chapter 3, p. 92, n.
197. Also, 'Audi sermonem divinum, sed totum audi.' *Ratio*, *H*, p.
286, 10–11; *LB*, v, 128c

104 'Bul. Vt autem apte dicamus ita demum fieri, si sermo noster
personis et rebus praesentibus congruat.' *Ciceronianus*, *ASD*, 1–2,
p. 636, 20–21; *LB*, I, 992c. On the development of one's natural
talent: Ibid., pp. 647–648, 35–5; *LB*, I, 1000A–B. Emulation: '... sic
aemularetur, vt praeire contenderet.' Ibid., p. 650, II; *LB*, I, 1001D.
'... aemuleris potius quam sequaris, modo studeas aequalis esse
verius quam similis, modo ne pugnes aduersus genium tuum.' Ibid.,
p. 656, 12–14; *LB*, I, 1005c–D. Cf. ibid., p. 708, 10–12; *LB*, I,
1024E

105 'Vt ne repetam, quod ipsa quoque natura repugnat isti affectationi,
quae voluit orationem esse speculum animi. Porro quum tanta sit
ingeniorum dissimilitudo, quanta vix est formarum, aut vocum,
mendax erit speculum, nisi natiuam mentis imaginem referrat et hoc
ipsum est ... Habet animus faciem quandam suam in oratione velut
in speculo relucentem, quam a natiua specie in diuersam refingere,
quid aliud est, quam in publicum venire personatum?' Ibid., p. 703,
18–21; *LB*, I, 1021E; p. 704, 10–12; *LB*, I, 1022B

106 'Ceterum in probatis viris eatenus unumquodque in exemplum
vocare conveniet, quatenus respondebit cum archetypo Christi.'
Enchiridion, *H*, p. 91, 15–17; *LB*, v, 40c

107 'Homines erant, quaedam ignorabant, in nonnullis halucinati
sunt.' *Ratio*, *H*, p. 295, 22–23; *LB*, v, 133A. Erasmus acknowledges
the fallibility of even Jerome, 'Quamlibet vir pius, quamlibet
eruditus, homo erat et falli potuit, et fallere.' Ibid., *H*, p. 183, 3–4;
LB, v, 78D

108 Erasmus gives examples of changing Christian practice, concerning
ritual abstinence, marriage, slavery, and the sacraments in ibid., *H*,
pp. 200–201, 20–13; *LB*, v, 87E–88A. 'Sunt id genus alia permulta,

quae pro temporum illorum usu instituta post oblitterata sunt aut mutata.' Ibid., p. 201, 7–8; *LB*, v, 87F–88A

109 Most commentary on Erasmus' position on language occurs in the context of hermeneutics and rhetoric rather than philosophy of language as defined strictly in the modern discipline. There is little discussion of the question of signification which engages us here.

'Erasmus indeed has a philosophy of speech of his own, suggested by the *Cratylus*, but very imperfectly worked out, by which the relation of words to the things signified was inherent and fixed.' William H. Woodward, *Desiderius Erasmus concerning the Aim and Method of Education* (Cambridge: Cambridge University Press, 1904), p. 141. 'Erasme, ai-je besoin de la dire, ne pressent pas la science linguistique: il admet trop naïvement, en bon grammarien, l'adequation nécessaire du signifiant au signifié.' Marcel Bataillon, 'La situation présente du message Erasmien,' in *Colloquium Erasmianum* (Mons: Centre Universitaire de l'état, 1968), p. 12. Wilhelm Schenck's version is modified: 'There is then, Erasmus holds, a close connexion between word and thing, *verbum* and *res*.' 'Three Circles: Erasmus on the Clergy, Rulers and Education of the Laity,' *DR*, CCIV (1950), 67. In the concluding pages of *L'Idée de nature dans la pensée d'Erasme* Margolin applies to Erasmus Michel Foucault's thesis of 'the prose of the world' concerning later texts of the sixteenth and seventeenth centuries. Cf. Foucault, *Les mots et les choses* (Paris: Gallimard, 1966), especially pp. 32–59

110 '... verum nihil est necesse rem totam, vt est, voce representari, satis est aliquam similitudinem apparere ... Quum enim sufficiat qualiscunque rei repraesentatio.' *De recta pronuntiatione*, *ASD*, I–4, p.89, 514–515, 524; *LB*, IV, 958E–F

111 Plato, CRATULOS, 430b, 431d, 432b–d, 439

112 'Quod minutum, sermonis est humilitas sub verbis paene sordidis ingentia mysteria claudentis.' *Enchiridion*, *H*, pp. 30–31, 35–1; *LB*, v, 6F–7A. Trans., Himelick, p. 49

113 '... quod est vestis nostro corpori, id est sententiis, elocutio.' *De copia*, *LB*, I, 8A. Trans., Rix and King, p. 18, as 'diction is to the expression of our *thoughts*.' *Italics mine*

114 Trans., Rix and King, title and passim. J.K. Sowards translates

verba and *res* as 'means' and 'ends' in 'Erasmus and the Apologetic Textbook,' *SP*, LV (1958), 128.

115 James F. Larkin translates the phrase as 'things' and 'words' in his unpublished PH D dissertation, Erasmus' *De ratione studii:* Its Relationship to Sixteenth Century English Literature, University of Illinois at Urbana, 1942, p. 271.

116 See Chapter 1, pp. 19–20, nn. 144–151. Erasmus is arguing Augustine's phrase 'cogitando dixit' as evidence against Augustine's own theory of language: 'An non cum ait, "cogitando dixit," satis declarat cogitationem esse sermonem quendam?' *Apologia de* 'In principio erat sermo,' *LB*, IX, 120A. Cf. Chapter 1, n. 147

117 '... si addas allegoriae involucrum.' *Ratio, H*, p. 261, 33–34; *LB*, V, 118B

118 'Me plane reclamante factum est, optime lector, vt Nouum Testamentum a me versum absque Annotationibus excuderetur typis, hoc est nudum et inerme Zoilorum dentibus obiiceretur.' To the Reader, *EE*, IV, 58 (no. 1010, 1–3)

119 See Chapter 1, nn. 170–172.

120 'Sed infelicior erat aetas, quae, me puero modis significandi et quaestiunculis ex qua vi pueros excarnificabat, nec aliud interim docens, quam perperam loqui.' *De pueris instituendis, ASD*, 1–2, p. 77, 3–5; *LB*, I, 514E

121 *Lingua, sive de usu et abusu, ASD*, IV–I, pp. 233–370; *LB*, IV, 657A–754A. This treatise was first published by Froben in 1525. It has not been subjected to modern criticism and is scarcely mentioned in studies of Erasmus' linguistic theories.

122 '... that power which of all the faculties that belong to the nature of man is the source of most of our blessings. For in the other powers which we possess we are in no respect superior to other living creatures; nay, we are inferior to many in swiftness and in strength and in other resources; but, because there has been im-planted in us the power to persuade each other and to make clear to each other whatever we desire, not only have we escaped the life of wild beasts ...' Isocrates, NIKOKLĒS, 5–6. Trans., Norlin, p. 79

123 'And Athens it is that has honoured eloquence, which all men crave and envy in its possessors; for she realised that this is the one endowment of our nature which singles us out from all living

creatures, and that by using this advantage we have risen above them in all other respects as well.' Isocrates, PANĒGURIKOS, 48. Trans., Norlin, pp. 148–149

124 Isocrates, NIKOKLĒS, 9. Trans., Norlin, p. 81. '... because there has been implanted in us the power to persuade each other ... we have come together and founded cities and made laws and invented arts; and, generally speaking, there is no institution devised by man which the power of speech has not helped us to establish.' Ibid., 6–7. Trans., Norlin, pp. 79–80

125 'Hoc enim uno praestamus vel maxime feris, quod colloquimur inter nos, et quod exprimere dicendo sensa possumus. Quam ob rem quis hoc non iure miretur, summeque in eo elaborandum esse arbitretur, ut, quo uno homines maxime bestiis praestent, in hoc hominibus ipsis antecellat? Ut vero iam ad illa summa veniamus; quae vis alia potuit aut dispersos homines unum in locum congregare, aut a fera agrestique vita ad hunc humanum cultum civilemque deducere, aut, iam constitutis civilitatibus, leges, iudicia, iura describere?' Cicero, *De oratore*, ed. Rackham, Bk. I, viii, 32–33. Trans., Sutton, p. 25

126 Quintilian, *Institutio oratoria*, ed. Winterbottom, Bk. II, xvi, pp. 112–114; Bk. III, ii, p. 133; Bk. XII, i, p. 692. 'Ipsam igitur orandi maiestatem, qua nihil di inmortales melius homini dederunt et qua remota muta sunt omnia et luce praesenti ac memoria posteritatis carent.' Ibid., Bk. XII, xi, pp. 746–747. Trans. H.E. Butler (London: William Heinemann; New York: G.P. Putnam's Sons, 1933), p. 513

127 '... linguam Latinam nationibus distribuisse minus erit, optimam frugem, et uere divinam, nec corporis, sed animi cibum. Haec enim gentes illas populosque omnes omnibus artibus, quae liberales uocantur, instituit: haec optimas leges edocuit: haec uiam ad omnem sapientiam miniuit, haec denique praestitit, nec barbari amplius dici possent.' Lorenzo Valla, *Opera omnia* (Basel, 1540, reprinted Turin: Bottega d'Erasmo, 1962), I, *In sex elegantiarum libros*, praef., 3. '... uidentur mihi non modo ditionis nostri homines, uerumetiam linguae propagatione ...' etc. Ibid. 'Magnum ergo Latini sermonis sacramentum est, magnum profecto numen, quod apud peregrinos, apud barbaros, apud hostes, sancte ac

religiose per tot secula custoditur, ut non tam dolendum nobis
Romanis, quam gaudendum sit, atque ipso etiam orbe terrarum
exaudiente gloriandum.' Ibid., 4

128 '... qua uigente quis ignorat studia omnia, disciplinasque uigere,
occidente occidere.' Ibid.

129 See Chapter 3, n. 58; Chapter 4, n. 15.

130 '... sursum deorsum *agontai kai pherontai* ... in hoc.' To Paul Volz,
EE, III, 366 (no. 858, 160, 172). Trans., Olin, p. 115

131 'Quoties me huius rei puduit, quoties vicem populi indolui? Video
simplicem multitudinem hiantem et avidam pendere ab ore
contionantis, exspectare pabulum animi sui cupidam discendi, quo
melior domum redeat, et ibi mihi theologaster quispiam fere
hieroprepei schēmati venerandus e Scoto aut Occam quaestionem
aliquam frigidam ac perplexam ventilat ostentans, quantum in
Sorbona profecerit, et plebis benignitatem hac ostentatione venans.
Interim magna contionis pars domum abit, plane, iuxta Graecorum
proverbium, *lukos chanōn.*' *Ratio, H*, p. 301, 13–21; *LB*, V, 136 A–B

132 Cf. Charles Trinkhaus's definition of Renaissance rhetorical
theology: '... *theologia rhetorica*, the humanist thesis that since
matters of faith cannot be proved by logic, they must be induced by
rhetoric – the word of man in the service of the word of God.' *In
Our Image and Likeness: Humanity and Divinity in Italian Humanist
Thought* (London: Constable, 1970), II, 611. See also, 'The
Religious Thought of the Italian Humanists, and the Reformers:
Anticipation or Autonomy?,' in *The Pursuit of Holiness in Late
Medieval and Renaissance Religion: Papers from the University of
Michigan Conference*, ed. Trinkhaus with Heiko A. Oberman
(Leiden: E.J. Brill, 1974), pp. 339–366. Again, my book is not
devised for the exposition of Erasmus' rhetorical theology in theory
or practice, but for the analysis of how philosophy of language
orders theological methodology.

133 'Hoc philosophiae genus in affectibus situm verius quam in
syllogismis vita magis est quam disputatio, afflatus potius quam
eruditio, transformatio magis quam ratio.' *Paraclesis, H*, pp.
144–145, 35–1; *LB*, V, 141E–F. Trans., Olin, p. 100

134 Erasmus characterizes himself as a theological candidate in a letter
To Thomas Grey, *EE*, I, 190–193 (no. 64); in the *Compendium*

vitae, ibid., p. 50; and describes conditions at the Collège de Montaigu in the colloquy *Ichthuophagia*, *ASD*, I–3, p. 531, 1323 to p. 532, 1377.

135 Because it is necessary first to document the practice of scholasticism in Erasmus' day, particularly as he learned it at Paris, this book will not evaluate the justice of Erasmus' condemnation of it. It will report his opinion and analyse its rationale.

136 Rodolphus Agricola, *De inventione dialectica* (Cologne, 1523, reprinted Frankfurt: Minerva, 1967)

137 'Has contentiones Timotheo scribens *logomachias* appellat, in quas ait quosdam insanire, cum tamen ex his nihil oriatur praeter invidias, contentiones, convicia, suspiciones malas, conflictationes hominum mente corruptorum, veritatis expertium, qui quaestum suum anteponant pietati.' *Ratio*, *H*, p. 303, 19–23; *LB*, V, 136E

138 Athanasius, *Epistola ad Serapionem*, IV, i, *PG*, XXVI, 637B

139 'Neque vero haec eo dixerim, quod damnem ea studia, quae nunc fere videmus in publicis scholis solemnia, modo sobrie casteque tractentur, neque sola tamen.' *Ratio*, *H*, p. 191, 31–33; *LB*, V, 83A. Cf. To Nicolas Bérault, *EE*, IV, 33–34 (no. 1002, 8–18)

140 See Chapter 1, n. 143.

141 '... nec meminimus Paulum ipsum, cui in tercium vsque coelum rapi contigit, libros, qui in membranis essent, per literas petisse.' *Antibarbari*, ed. Kazimierz Kumaniecki, *ASD*, I–I, p. 134, 14–15

142 'Nam (ut omnes ceteras humanas disciplinas negligamus) nulla ratione fieri potest, ut intelligas quod scriptum est, si sermonis, quo scriptum est, fueris ignarus, nisi forte malumus otiosi quicquid hoc est muneris cum apostolis e caelis expectare.' *Ratio*, *H*, p. 182, 14–18; *LB*, V, 78B

143 Jn 1:3

144 'Odit superbam eloquentiam, fateor, at multo magis superciliosam et arrogantem infantiam.' *Apologia* to the 1516 edition, Novum Instrumentum, *H*, p. 173, 31–32; *LB*, VI, **3

THREE: RATIO

1 'Bonae litterae reddunt homines, Philosophia plusquam homines, Theologia reddit divos.' *Querela pacis*, *LB*, IV, 628D

2 *Paraclesis, H,* p. 139, 9; *LB,* V, 137E

3 '... flagitantibus id amicis quibusdam methodum quandam ac
rationem theologici studii curaveram adiciendam, brevem quidem
illam.' *Ratio, H,* p. 177, 4–6; *LB,* V, 75A

4 *Bibliotheca Erasmiana: Bibliographie des oeuvres d'Erasme,* Vol. IX:
Ratio verae theologiae (Gand: C. Vyt, 1914), p. 16. Cf. *Bibliotheca
Erasmiana,* ed. F. Vander Haeghen (Nieuwkoop: B. De Graaf,
1961), 1st series, p. 167, which incorrectly lists the first edition as
Froben's of 1519. The *Ratio* was first issued separately and later
prefaced to the second edition of the New Testament. Erasmus
indicates that it may be studied either way: '... et ita rem
temperabimus, ut, si libeat, praefationis vice possit addi, sin minus,
separatim legi.' *Ratio, H,* p. 177, 10–12; *LB,* V, 75A–B

5 Albert of Brandenburg was archbishop prince-elector of Mainz. For
discussion of the correspondence relating to this dedication see,
Bibliotheca Erasmiana, IX, 13–18.

6 The Latin couplet and Greek adages are added to the printer's
mark, I assume by Erasmus himself. Cf. 'In vino, veritas,' *Adagia,*
I, vii, xvii; *LB,* II, 267B–268C.

This emblem of the sheet-anchor was one of three marks used by
the press of Dirk Martens at Alost, Anvers, and Louvain in the
fifteenth and sixteenth centuries. *Marques typographiques des
imprimeurs et libraires qui ont exercé dans les Pays-Bas, et marques
typographiques des imprimeurs et libraires belges établis à l'étranger*
(Gand: C. Vyt, 1894), I, no pagination

7 See, e.g., Francis M. Nichols, *The Epistles of Erasmus* (New York:
Longmans, Green, 1901–1918), II, 103; John C. Olin, *Christian
Humanism and the Reformation* (New York: Harper and Row, 1965,
p. 115. The translation by R.A.B. Mynors and D.F.S. Thomson
corrects this also, *The Correspondence of Erasmus* (Toronto:
University of Toronto Press, 1975), II, 267.

8 Joannes Amos Comenius, *Orbis sensualium pictus* (3d ed.; London,
1672, reprinted in facsimile by Sidney: University Press, 1967), p.
185

9 '... ad vere sacram ancoram Euangelicae doctrinae.' To Paul Volz,
EE, III, 366 (no. 858, 164). This letter, which shares important

symbols with the *Ratio,* was written in the same year as the *Ratio's* publication.

10 '... illa vere sacra ancora doctrinae euangelicae.' *Ratio, H,* p. 204, 12–13; *LB,* V, 89D

11 Louis Bréhier, *L'art chrétien* (Paris: Renouard, 1928), p. 30

12 'Iam vero eo progressi sumus vt, licet mediis adhuc in fluctibus luctemur, tamen procul portus paulatim sese aperiat; in quem, si Christi aspirauerint aurae, ante quadragesimam appellemus.' To Erard de la Marck, *EE,* III, 194 (no. 757, 26–29). '... atque in fluctibus laboranti e longinquo portus appareat.' To Paschasius Berselius, *EE,* III, 192 (no. 756, 19–20). Cf. To Andrea Ammonio, *EE,* I, 542 (no. 282, 50–51)

13 '... quid vetat imitari nautas quosdam, qui cum ipsi navi ad scopulum elisa nudi vix enatarint, nihilo secius aliis solventibus solent recte consulere, commonstratis periculis ...?' *Ratio, H,* p. 177, 33–35; *LB,* V, 75D

14 'Hos ille formabit quasi eloquentiae parens, et ut uetus gubernator litora et portus et quae tempestatium signa, quid secundis flatibus quid aduersis ratio poscat docebit ... non humanitatis solum communi ductus officio, sed amore quodam operis.' Quintilian, *Institutio oratoria,* ed. M. Winterbottom (Oxford: Clarendon Press, 1970), II, Bk. XII, xi, p. 741. Trans., Butler, p. 499

15 Readers may be referred for another interpretation to Gerhard B. Winkler, *Erasmus von Rotterdam und die Einleitungsschriften zum Neuen Testament: Formale Strukturen und theologischer Sinn* (Münster: Aschendorffsche, 1974) which was not available until after this manuscript was finished.

16 *Apologia, H,* p. 164, 18–23; *LB,* VI, **2; *H,* p. 165ff.; *LB,* VI, **2; *H,* p. 168, 22–24, 29–31; *H,* p. 167, 30–31; *LB,* VI, **2; *H,* p. 173, 27–28; *LB,* VI, **3

17 'Quid autem aliud est Christi philosophia, quam ipse renascentiam vocat, quam instauratio bene conditae naturae?' *Paraclesis, H,* p. 145, 5–7; *LB,* V, 141F. Cf. Jn 3:3.

18 *Bibliotheca Erasmiana,* IX, 95–97

19 Manfred Hoffmann has previously defined the titular terms in *Erkenntnis und Virwirklichung der wahren Theologie nach Erasmus von Rotterdam* (Tübingen: J.C.B. Mohr, 1972), p. 52. In my

judgement his definition of *ratio* is inadequate, and he wrongly contrives a distinct meaning for *methodus* in order to support his thesis that the treatise essentially expresses a relationship between theoretical knowledge and practical application. He understands *ratio* as the plan, the deductive *a priori; methodus* is the technique, the inductive procedure by which it is realised.

20 Plato, PHAIDROS, 265D–277C. See, Rudolph Eucken, *Geschichte der philosophischen Terminologie* (Hildesheim: Georg Olms, 1960; reprint of Leipzig, 1879), p. 17

21 *Topicorum Aristotelis,* trans. Boethius, *PL,* LXIV, 909C, as cited incompletely by Neal W. Gilbert, *Renaissance Concepts of Method* (New York and London: Columbia University Press, 1960), p. 50. Gilbert notes that the authenticity of this translation is disputed and that it may be the work of Jacobus of Venice in the year 1128, ibid., n. 17.

22 Ibid., 49. It is only a scholarly assumption that *via et ratio* translates *methodos* since Cicero himself made no explicit equivalence.

23 Ibid., 50–55. Note that Gilbert's source for determining that Aquinas 'did not have a doctrine of *methodus*' is the reference, *A Lexicon of St. Thomas Aquinas,* ed. Roy J. Deferrari et al. (Washington: Catholic University of America, 1948), which only lists entries from the *Summa* and selected commentaries.

24 On the supremacy of Peter of Spain's *Summulae logicales* in the mediaeval arts course, see Walter J. Ong, *Ramus, Method, and the Decay of Dialogue* (Cambridge: Harvard University Press, 1958), pp. 55–74.

25 '... nam et satis erant grammatici et Petri Hispani Dialecticam magna ex parte didicerant.' To Lambertus Grunnius (pseud.), *EE,* II, 295 (no. 447, 98–99)

26 'Dialectica est ars artium et scientia scientiarum ad omnium methodorum principia viam habens.' Peter of Spain (Joannes XXI), *Summulae logicales,* ed. I.M. Bochenski (Turin: Marietti, 1947), p. 1. In giving the etymology of the term *dialectica,* Peter of Spain translates *logos* as *sermo.*

27 Thomas of Erfurt, *Tractatus de modis significandi sive grammatica speculativa* in *Lexicon Scholasticum Philosophico-Theologicum,* ed.

Mariani Fernandez García (Quaracchi: College of St Bonaventure, 1910), p. 1. Cf. Chapter 2, n. 15.

28 Mario Nizzoli, *Nizolius, sive Thesaurus Ciceronianus* (Basel: 1583), as cited by Gilbert, *Renaissance Concepts of Method,* p. 64. I have verified this in the earlier Aldine edition of 1576, f†† 4.

29 See the list compiled by Gilbert and appended to his book, ibid., 233–235, although he does not enter the earliest Erasmian title containing the term, i.e. the *Methodus* of 1516, but rather the expanded version.

30 '... methodum quandam ac rationem.' *Ratio, H,* p. 177, 4–5; *LB,* V, 75A. '... viam ac methodum.' Ibid., l. 17; *LB,* V, 75B. '... methodi ratio.' Ibid., *H,* p. 263, 29–30; *LB,* V, 119B.

31 See Chapter 1, n. 92.

32 'ratio,' *A Latin Dictionary,* ed. Charleton F. Lewis and Charles Short (Oxford: Clarendon Press, 1879), pp. 1525–1526. For *logos* see Chapter 1, n. 158.

33 'ratio,' *A Latin Dictionary,* ed. Lewis and Short, p. 1527

34 '... quae modo vere sit theologia.' *Ratio, H,* p. 294, 21; *LB,* V, 132D, et passim

35 [In examining the nature of anything] 'ought we not to consider first whether that which we desire to learn and to teach is a simple or multiform thing, and if simple, then to enquire what power it has of acting or being acted upon in relation to other things, and if multiform, then to number the forms.' Plato, PHAIDROS, 270d. Trans., Jowett, I, 274

36 The ubiquitous phrase *philosophia Christi,* or sometimes *christiana philosophia,* which distinguishes Erasmus' religious writings, especially commencing with the *Paraclesis,* is commonly translated by modern scholars as 'philosophy of Christ' and understood to be a kind of Christian *philosophy,* i.e. ethics. In my view the term has two senses, depending upon the context, and neither of them is philosophical. It can mean Christ's own teaching as recorded in the New Testament; or it can mean theology, understood as learned and pious exegesis of that text, as in the patristic usage of *philosophia Christi.* As an example of the first sense, one might reflect upon the title, *Paraclesis, id est, Adhortatio ad Christianae Philosophiae Studium,* a work in which Erasmus urges Christians to

study Christ's own teachings in the NT. For an example of the second sense, see Chapter 1, n. 166.

37 'Simplex est, iuxta tragici sententiam, veritatis oratio; nihil autem Christo neque simplicius, neque verius.' *Ratio, H*, p. 280, 4–5; *LB*, v, 126A

38 '... rudibus ac plebeis venaeque inferioris ingeniis nostra qualicunque industria nitimur subvenire.' Ibid., *H*, p. 178, 17–18; *LB*, v, 75E. 'Itaque quod primo loco praecipiendum erat, id sane perquam facile est.' Ibid., II, 19–20; *LB*, v, 76A. Ibid., II, 7–14; *LB*, v, 75E. Charles Béné had indexed Erasmus' citations in the *Ratio* from *De doctrina christiana* and discussed influences which he considers to be Augustine's in *Erasme et Saint Augustin ou Influence de Saint Augustin sur l'Humanisme d'Erasme*, THR, CIII (Geneva: Droz, 1969), pp. 215–280; 434–436. In this limited context the book can be useful to the reader, although I have reservations about whether the repetition of theological commonplaces proves influence, since Béné does not analyse them in the context of Erasmus' entire programme nor weighed them against citations of other Fathers (a formidable task). Is Erasmus 'Augustinian?' Having read extensively in both literatures, I would not say he is characteristically so, despite citations *ad hoc*. It seems premature to define patristic influence when vast territory is still uncharted, particularly Erasmus' appropriation of the Greek Fathers who were also rhetoricians.

39 'Sed subvereor, ne cui mea tenuitas nota sit, protinus hic reclamet: Tun' viam indicabis, quam ipse nunquam ingressus est aut certe infeliciter ingressus es.' *Ratio, H*, p. 177, 28–30; *LB*, v, 75C. '... certe Mercuriales illa statuas *polukephalous*, quae quondam in compitis poni solitae, suo nonnunquam indicio viatorem eo provehunt, quo nunquam ipsae sint perventurae.' Ibid., *H*, p. 178, 1–3; *LB*, v, 75D. 'Non minima negotii pars est adeundi negotii viam nosse. Et satis festinat, qui nusquam aberrat a via.' Ibid., *H*, p. 177, 20–22; *LB*, v, 75B–C. Cf. To Paul Volz, *EE*, III, 362 (no. 858, 27–28).

40 *Ratio, H*, p. 177; *LB*, v, 75B–C. Cf. *H*, p. 245, 14; *LB*, v, 109E; *H*, p. 259, 30; *LB*, v, 117A.

41 Guillaume Budé, *Annotationes in quatuor et viginti Pandectarum*

libros (Paris, 1535), pp. 37–38. For discussion of later Renaissance etymologies of *methodus,* see Gilbert, *Renaissance Concepts of Method,* pp. 64–66.

42 The terms date to Martinus de Dacia who considered the *antiqui* those grammarians who still were in continuity with Priscian as expositors; the *via antiqua,* therefore, was a treatment of grammatical matters according to Priscian's technique of commentary. Martinus inaugurated a self-supporting treatment of grammatical issues which he called *modi significandi novi* or *moderni.* The *via moderna* is comprised of those who pursue and develop his method. Heinrich Roos, *Die modi significandi des Martinus de Dacia,* BGPTM, XXXVII / 2 (Münster: Westfalen; Copenhagen: Arne Frost-Hansen, 1952), pp. 131–132. Those philosophers and theologians who were influenced by the new grammar adopted the terms to distinguish themselves from those who still proceeded by more traditional methods.

43 Erasmus characteristically calls the Fathers the *antiqui* or *veteres* and the mediaeval theologians the *moderni* or *neoterici.* That the latter category includes the classical scholastics, as well as the nominalists, is evident from his appellation of Thomas Aquinas as 'ipse neotericorum omnium, mea sententia, diligentissimus.' *Ratio,* H, p. 183, 15–16; *LB,* v, 78E. Erasmus was aware, of course, of the factions within scholasticism and sometimes enumerates them in satiric concatenation, e.g. MŌRIAS EGKŌMION, *LB,* IV, 466A.

44 '... sed libuit aliis maiora conaturis viam munire, quo minus offensi salebris ac lamis speciosa illa ac sublimia facilius inueherent.' To Wolfgang, Faber Capito, *EE,* II, 490 (no. 541, 77–79)

45 The term *compendium* occurs in the *Ratio,* H, p. 177, 25; *LB,* v, 75C; H, p. 193, 25; *LB,* v, 84A; H, p. 227, 22; *LB,* v, 100E; H, p. 262, 1; *LB,* v, 118B

46 'Porro qui compendiarium quoque viam indicat, is gemino beneficio iuvat studiosum: primum ut maturius quo tendit pertingat, deinde ut minore labore sumptuque quod sequitur assequatur.' Ibid., H, p. 177, 24–27; *LB,* v, 75C. This recalls the preface to Bk. VIII of the *Institutio oratoria,* ed. Winterbottom, p. 419, in which Quintilian states the necessity of indicating to the student of oratory a simple and brief path to follow.

47 'Proinde quandoquidem in tanta librorum multitudine et in tanta
aetatis fugacitate non vacat evolvere omnia, superest, ut primum
legamus optima.' *Ratio, H*, p. 296, 12–14; *LB*, V, 133C. This was a
recurring theme of Erasmus' pedagogy.

48 Gilbert, *Renaissance Concepts of Method*, p. 56, gives some examples
from John of Salisbury's *Metalogicon* of the mediaeval view on
method as compendious.

49 '... ex tam immensis iisque inter se pugnantibus interpretum
commentariis.' *Paraclesis, H*, p. 141, 25–26; *LB*, V, 139F

50 '... et hac ratione sese compendio liberavit ab omnibus
quaestionibus.' Ibid., *H*, p. 298, 22–23; *LB*, V, 134D. 'Quomodo
autem hoc sit, inquit, noli disquirere, factum est, ut ipse novit.'
Ibid., ll. 12–13; *LB*, V, 134C. Erasmus himself became involved in a
controversy about *hupostasis* when Jacques Lefèvre d'Etaples
attacked his annotation of Heb 2:7. See *Apologia ad Jacobum
Fabrum Stapulensem, LB*, IX, 17A–50E, and related correspondence
to friends about the issue, December 1517.

51 'Incredible, inquit, non est, quod fecit omnipotens dei spiritus.'
Ratio, H, p. 298, 23–24; *LB*, V, 134D

52 *De copia, LB*, I, 109D. 'Nam nihil aeque convenit breviloquentiae,
quam verborum proprietas et elegantia.' Ibid., 110A–B. 'Et cui
placet Homericum illud *paura men*, eidem placeat et hoc quod
protinus sequitur, *alla mala ligeōs*. Et cui probatur *ou polumuthos*,
non praetermittat et hoc quod statim subjicitur *oud' aphamartoepēs.'*
Ibid., 110A. In the fifth chapter of the first book of *De copia*
Erasmus explains that the well-trained artist may speak both
concisely and copiously, as the occasion demands. Ibid., 5B–D

53 It would be impossible to chronicle here the tenacious history of
this misinterpretation of Erasmus. One might read with profit the
recent refutations in *Scrinium Erasmianum*, ed. J. Coppens (Leiden:
E.J. Brill, 1969), II, pp. 77–155, and the excursus on scepticism in
Harry J. McSorley, *Luther: Right or Wrong?* (New York, etc.:
Newman Press; Minneapolis: Augsburg, 1969), pp. 279–282.

54 Near the beginning of the *Ratio* Erasmus distinguishes between
those mysteries which the candidate may approach in colloquy and
those which must be venerated in silence. See this chapter, n. 68.

55 Gilbert writes that emphasis on the usefulness of the arts is Stoic,

expressed in Zeno's *locus classicus*: 'An art, as I heard some wise man say, is a system of grasping (*perceptio*) sense impressions exercised together toward some end useful in life.' Cicero retained this doctrine in his influential grammatical works. But mediaeval versions of the text scrambled *perceptio* into *praeceptio,* thus spawning the idea that an art is a system of precepts or rules. *Renaissance Concepts of Method,* p. 12

56 After attesting to the easiness of theological method, Erasmus continues, 'Ceterum quod ad usum attinet, omnium est longe primum ac maximum.' *Ratio, H,* p. 178, 20–21; *LB,* v, 76A

57 Ibid., *H,* pp. 194, 225, 251, 254, and especially 226; *LB,* v, 84C, 84D, 99E, 112F, 114C, 100B, where he expresses his conviction that '... lenitas haec orbem novit.'

58 '... videbit illic aureum quoddam ire flumen, hic tenues quosdam rivulos, eosque nec puros admodum ne suo fonti respondentes.' Ibid., *H,* p. 189, 31–33; *LB,* v, 82A

59 The primary sense of *pius* in the classical lexicon is 'dutiful,' especially towards the gods, parents, kinsmen, schoolmasters, and country. It includes affection, tenderness, respect, and loyalty. Erasmus discusses piety as filiation in *Querela pacis, LB,* iv, 627E.

60 Erasmus paraphrases Origen's allegorical exegesis of this pericope (Gen 22) early in the *Ratio, H,* pp. 188–189, 8–14; *LB,* v, 81B–E.

61 '... renascimur e supernis, unde et Paulus novam creaturam appellat quisquis in Christo est.' Ibid., *H,* p. 194, 30–32; *LB,* v, 84E.

Erasmus also refers to Christ's command, 'Nicodemum iubet renasci non ex carne sed ex spiritu, non e terra sed e caelo.' Ibid., *H,* p. 257, 21–23; *LB,* v, 115F–116A. Cf. '... veluti renatus esset.' Ibid., *H,* p. 194, 11; *LB,* v, 84C

62 '... tuum ipsius pectus bibliothecam facito Christi.' *Ratio, H,* p. 294, 31; *LB,* v, 132E

63 'Simplex et cuivis paratum est viaticum. Tantum fac afferas pium ac promptum animum et in primis simplici puraque praeditum fide. Tantum esto docilis, et multum in hac philosophia promovisti.' *Paraclesis, H,* p. 141, 28–31; *LB,* v, 140A. Trans., Olin, p. 96

64 '. . . animum afferamus ea dignum, non tantum purum ab omnibus, quoad fieri potest, vitiorum inquinamentis, verumetiam ab omni

cupiditatum tumultu tranquillum ac requietum.' *Ratio, H,* p. 178, 24–27; *LB,* v, 76A. '... velut in amne placido aut speculo levi et exterso, reluceat aeternae illius veritatis imago.' Ibid., *H,* p. 178, 28–29; *LB,* v, 76A. '... si prisci daemonum cultores non recipiebant quemquam ad sua profana mysteria nisi prius multis observationibus repurgatum.' Ibid., *H,* pp. 178–179, 32–1; *LB,* v, 76B

65 Plato, PHAIDROS, 265D–277C

66 'Nam si Hippocrates a suis discipulis exigit mores sanctos et integros.' *Ratio, H,* p. 178, 29–30; *LB,* v, 76A–B

67 '... quanto magis aequum est nos ad huius divinae sapientiae scholam, seu templum verius, purgatissimus animis accedere?' Ibid., p. 179, 1–2; *LB,* v, 76B. Ibid., *H,* ll. 8–14; *LB,* v, 75B–C

68 'At verius et efficacius nobis loquitur deus in arcanis libris quam Mosi de rubo locutus sit, si modo puri accesserimus ad colloquium ... Huic igitur pectus tuum praepares oportet, ut tu quoque verbo prophetico *theodidaktos* vocari merearis. Adsit oculus fidei simplex et columbinus, qui non cernit nisi caelestia. Accedat summus ardor discendi ... Iam hoc sacrum limen adituris, procul absit omnis fastus, procul absit omne supercilium ... Augustum est huius reginae palatium, si penetraris in penetralia, sed vehementer humili ostio patet aditus; cervicem submittas oportet, si velis admitti ... Procul absit illa veri nocentissima pestis, gloriae fames, quae ferocia solet ingenia comitari. Absit rixarum, pertinacia, multo magis caeca temeritas ... Cum loca subis religione veneranda, exoscularis omnia, adoras omnia, et quasi nusquam non adsit numen aliquod, ita nihil non revereris ... Quod datur videre, pronus exosculare; quod non datur, tamen opertum, quicquid est adora simplici fide proculque venerare ... Absit impia curiositas ... Fortassis hoc nos docuit Moses, faciem suam obvelans, ne dominum intueretur e rubo sibi loquentem.' Ibid., *H,* p. 179, 14–15, 19–20, 20–22, 24–25, 29–32; pp. 179–180, 35–2; p. 180, 5, 7–9; *LB,* v, 76C, 75D–E, 76E–77A

69 For *pia curiositas,* see ibid., *H,* p. 213, 27; *LB,* v, 93E.

70 'Sed in eruendis mysteriis non oportet animi tui coniecturas sequi, verum cognoscenda ratio et velut ars quaedam, quam tradit Dionysius quidam in libro de divinis nominibus et divus

H

Augustinus in opere de doctrina Christiana.' *Enchiridion, H*, p. 71, 21–24; *LB*, v, 29E–F. Trans., Himelick, p. 107, with change

71 To Pieter Gillis, *EE*, II, 357 (no. 476, 39–50)

72 '... teneram aetatem recens editam vna et materno lacte et Latinis literis imbui solitam.' To Jacob Canter, *EE*, I, 127 (no. 32, 22)

73 'Hoc enim in homine artifice praestare solet artis ratio, vt tantundem operis quum rectius expeditiusque tum leuius etiam efficiat.' To Christian Northoff, *EE*, I, 173 (no. 56, 36–38). Trans., Mynors and Thomson, I, 114–115

74 *De ratione studii, ASD*, 1–2, 113–151; *LB*, I, 517–530

75 References to the 'sacrosanctae theologiae candidatus,' as e.g., *Ratio, H*, p. 177, 20; *LB*, v, 75B, indicate that the treatise is written for neophytes.

76 'Homines, mihi crede, non nascuntur sed finguntur.' *De pueris institutiendis, ASD*, 1–2, p. 31, 21; *LB*, I, 493B

77 See my article on Erasmus' conviction that baptism confers on all Christians the spiritual gifts for interpreting Scripture. 'Weavers, farmers, tailors, travellers, masons, prostitutes, pimps, Turks, little women and Other Theologians,' *Erasmus in English*, 3 (1971), 1–7

78 'Doctos esse vix paucis contingit, at nulli non licet esse Christianum, nulli non licet esse pium, addam audacter illud: nulli non licet esse theologum.' *Paraclesis, H*, p. 145, 1–3; *LB*, v, 141F. Trans., Olin, p. 100

'... non minus ridicule facturus, quam si caecus caeco dux esse postulet iuxta proverbium euangelicum.' *Ratio, H*, p. 177, 30–31; *LB*, v, 75C. 'Postremo: Caecus uti si monstret iter, tamen aspice.' Ibid., *H*, p. 178, 7; *LB*, v, 75D

79 'The method which proceeds without analysis is like the groping of a blind man.' Plato, PHAIDROS, 270d. Trans., Jowett, I, 274

80 See Chapter 2, n. 39.

81 See Chapter 2, nn. 39–40.

82 'Iam quod ad eas attinet litteras, quarum adminiculo commodius ad haec pertingimus, citra controversiam prima cura debetur perdiscendis tribus linguis, Latinae, Graecae et Hebraicae, quod constet, omnem scripturam mysticam hisce proditam esse.' *Ratio, H*, p. 181, 15–18; *LB*, v, 77E

83 Ibid., *H*, pp. 183–184; *LB*, v, 78F–79A. See Chapter 2, n. 43.

84 '... tamen libro, de doctrina Christiana secundo non dubitat,
harum cognitionem ad sacros codices vel intelligendos vel
restituendos necessariam pronuntiare ... Neque flagitat Aurelius
Augustinus, ut in Hebraeis Graecisque litteris usque ad eloquentiae
miraculum proveharis, quod admodum paucis contingit et in
Romano sermone, satis est, si ad mundiciem et elegantiam, hoc est,
mediocritatem aliquam progrediare, quod sufficiat ad iudicandum.'
Ibid., *H*, p. 181, 20–23, p. 182, 10–14; *LB*, v, 77E, 78A–B

85 '... quemadmodum incognitis elementorum figuris nemo legit quod
scriptum est, ita sine cognitione linguarum nullus intelligit quod
legit.' Ibid., *H*, p. 181, 23–25; *LB*, v, 77E

86 'Inter humanas disciplinas aliae alium habent scopum. Apud
rhetorem hoc spectas, ut copiose, splendideque dicas; apud
dialecticum, ut argute colligas et adversarium illaquees. Hic primus
et unicus tibi sit scopus, hoc votum, hoc unum age, ut muteris, ut
rapiaris, ut affleris, ut transformeris in ea, quae discis.' Ibid., *H*, p.
180, 19–24; *LB*, v, 77B. 'At praecipuus theologorum scopus est
sapienter enarrare divinas litteras, de fide, non de frivolas
quaestionibus rationem reddere, de pietate graviter atque efficaciter
disserere, lacrymas excutere, ad caelestia inflammare animos.' Ibid.,
H, p. 193, 18–22; *LB*, v, 83F–84A

87 '... ut ubique certos habeat scopos, ad quos ea quae legit conferat.'
Ibid., ll. 27–28; *LB*, v, 84A. '... unicum sit centrum, Christus Iesus,
ad cuius simplicissimam puritatem pro sua cuique virili enitendum
est omnibus. Neque enim oportet scopum suo movere loco, quin
potius omnes mortalium actiones ad scopum dirigendae.' Ibid., *H*,
p. 202, 3–7; *LB*, v, 88C

'Ego Christum vobis scopum proposui.' *Paraphrasis in prima
epistola Pauli ad Corinthianos*, 3, *LB*, VII, 868A

88 D.F.S. Thomson, 'The Latinity of Erasmus,' *Erasmus*, ed. T.A.
Dorey (Albuquerque: University of New Mexico, 1970), p. 129, cf.
p. 117

89 Olin translates the word *scopus* in the 'Letter to Paul Volz (August
14, 1518),' in *Christian Humanism and Reform*, p. 118, as 'target.'
No English translation of the *Ratio* is published yet, but a check of
scholarly commentary reveals 'goal' and 'aim' common in partial
citations; *doel* in F. De Maeseneer, *De Methode van de theologie*

volgens Erasmus (Rome: Alfonsiana, 1963), pp. 60–63; *Ziel, Ordnungsprinzip, Richtpunkt,* and *Bezugspunkt* in Hoffmann, *Erkenntnis und Verwirklichung der wahren Theologie nach Erasmus von Rotterdam,* pp. 60ff.; *Ziel* in E.–W. Kohls, *Die Theologie des Erasmus* (Basel: Friedrich Reinhardt, 1966), I, 99. Alfons Auer understands *scopus* in the Pauline sense of the letter to the Philippians, although he does not refer to Erasmus' annotation of it, *Die volkommene Frommigkeit des Christen nach dem 'Enchiridion militis Christiani' des Erasmus von Rotterdam* (Dusseldorf: Patmos, 1954).

90 'scopos,' 'scopus,' *A Latin Dictionary,* ed. Lewis and Short, p. 1646

91 Erasmus himself uses *finis* in this technical sense, as e.g. 'Sunt enim et philosophis quidam fines.' *Enchiridion, H,* p. 64, 5–6; *LB,* V, 25D

   De Maeseneer proposes that Erasmus' choice of *scopus* rather than *finis* shows his preference for the Greek ethicists rather than metaphysicians. This seems to me an artificial distinction since both Plato and Aristotle use the term *skopos.* See this chapter, n. 103, and H. Bonitz, *Index Aristotelicus* (2d ed.; Graz: Akademische Druck–U. Verlagsanstalt, 1955), p. 685.

92 See this chapter, n. 106.

93 'Item et vie nostre finis quidem est regnum Dei. Quid vero sit scopos debet diligenter inquiri ... Finis quidem nostre professionis ut diximus regnum celorem est; destinacio vero scilicet scopos puritas cordis sine qua ad illum finem impossibile est quempiam pervenire.' Florentius Radewijns, *Omnes inquit artes,* f. Ia. Cited by Albert Hyma, *The Christian Renaissance* (2d ed.; Hamden, Conn.: Archon, 1965), p. 367, n. 59

94 In Ficino's translation, 1502, of *De divinis nominibus,* Bk. I, iv, 20, according to *Dionysiaca* (Paris: Desclée de Brouwer, 1937), I, 307

95 'Guillaume Budé has the same word in the same sense.' D.F.S. Thomson, 'The Latinity of Erasmus,' in *Erasmus,* ed. Dorey, p. 129. In response to a letter of inquiry Prof. Thomson writes that 'One example of Budé's use of *scopus* in the sense indicated in my article can be found in the Yale edition of More, vol 4 (Utopia), p. 6 (introductory letter to Lupset), line 1.'

96 'Quare primus nobis labor erit, ut teneamus certum libri scopum,

quid quaerat et quo spectet.' Martin Luther, *Ecclesiastes Salomonis cum annotationibus*, praef., in *Werke* (Weimar: Hermann Böhlaus, 1931), xx, p. 9, 28–29. Published in 1532, this commentary was based on lectures delivered in 1526. In the English translation of Luther's *Works*, ed. Jarislov Pelikan and Hilton C. Oswald (St Louis: Concordia, 1972), xv, 7, *scopus* is rendered as 'aim.'

97 'Itane Scopum nostrum repente e poeta militem esse factum ac pro libris horrida arma tractare?' To Publio Fausto Andrelini, *EE*, I, 238 (no. 103, 1–3). Trans. Mynors and Thomson, I, 193

98 See this chapter, n. 103.

99 '*Scopum attingere. tugchanein tou skopou*, i.e. *Scopum attingere*. Est voti compotem fieri, aut conjectura rem ipsam assequi.' *Adagia*, I, x, xxx; *LB*, II, 376B–C

100 'Nos. Vide quantum aberres a scopo.' *Ciceronianus*, *ASD*, I–2, p. 610, I; *LB*, I, 975C. 'Haud multum aberras a scopo.' *De pronuntiatione*, *ASD*, I–4, p. 18, 149; *LB*, I, 915E

101 'Sed ut certiore cursu queas ad felicitatem contendere, haec tibi quarta sit regula, ut totius vitae tuae Christum velut unicum scopum praefiguras, ad quem unum omnia studia, omnes conatus, omne otium ac negotium conferras ... Simplex ergo sit oculus tuus, et totum corpus tuum lucidum erit ... Ad solum Christum tamquam ad unicum et summum bonum spectet ... Quod si nequam erit oculus tuus et alio quam ad Christum spectaris, etiam si qua recta feceris, infrugifera fuerint aut etiam perniciosa ... Verum quo spectas? ... Nequam est oculus tuus ... Vitiosus est oculus tuus ... Nempe ut tibi vivas, non Christo. Aberrasti a signo, quod Christianum oportet ubique praefixum habere ... Sed ideo valere vis corpore, ut sanctis studiis, sanctis vigiliis sufficias: scopum attigisti ... Alius Christophorum singulis salutat diebus, sed non nisi conspecta eius imagine, quo tandem spectans? ... Ille visit divi Iob simulacra ... Ad hanc regulam si studia et actus omnes tuos excusseris neque usquam constiteris in mediis, donec perveneris usque ad Christum, ne aberrabis unquam a via neque rem ullam in vita aut facies aut patieris, quae tibi non vertatur in materiam pietatis.' *Enchiridion*, *H*, p. 63, 8–11, 16–17, 17–18, 24–27; *LB*, v, 25A–C; *H*, p. 65, 26, 29–30, 31, 34–35; *LB*, v, 26D–E; *H*, pp. 65–66, 36–1; *LB*, v, 26E; *H*, p. 66, 5–6, 11; *LB*, v, 26E–F; *H*, p. 67, 16–20;

LB, v, 27C–D. Trans., Himelick, pp. 94, 95, 98, 100–101. 'Cave quoquam ab exemplari tuo Christo cordis oculos dimoveas. Non errabis veritatis ductum sequens. Non impinges in tenebris post lumen ambulans.' *Enchiridion*, *H*, p. 99, 1–3; *LB*, v, 44D. Trans., Himelick, p. 144

102 'Huc discuntur disciplinae, huc philosophia, huc eloquentia, ut Christum intelligamus, ut Christi gloriam celebremus. Hic est totius eruditionis et eloquentiae scopus.' *Ciceronianus*, *ASD*, 1–2, p. 709, 25–27; *LB*, I, 1026B

103 *skopeō*, *A Greek-English Lexicon*, ed. Henry G. Liddell and Robert Scott, rev. Henry S. Jones and Roderick McKenzie (9th ed. rev.; Oxford: Clarendon Press, 1940), pp. 1613–1614. Werner Jaeger comments on GORGIAS, 507d, 'In this passage Plato introduces the concept of the "aim" – the point toward which we should direct our lives: in Greek it is *skopos*. It is identical with the *telos*, the "end" which in 499e we learnt was the Good.' *Paideia: The Ideals of Greek Culture*, trans. Gilbert Highet (New York: Oxford University Press, 1939), II, 392, n. 116

104 *Cicero, De Attica*, VIII, xi, 2, cited by *A Greek-English Lexicon*, ed. Liddell and Scott, II, 1614

105 Job 16:12; Lam 3:12; Wis 5:12; Jer 6:17; Ezek 3:17, 33:6–7

106 '*kata skopon*,' id est, *secundum scopum* aut *signum praefixum*.' *Annotationes in epistolam ad Philippenses*, 3:14, *LB*, VI, 874C–D, n. 24

107 'Neque tam male vertit interpres quam obscure. Hieronymus admonet Graecam vocem esse significantiorem. Est enim *skopos* proprie signum praefixum sagittantibus. Unde quod animo destinamus ac praefigimus, scopus est. Augustinus cum aliis plerisque locis, tum in Psalmum xxxviii legit, "secundum intentionem," pro *kata skopon*. Cyprianus, *de Clericorum vita*, si modo hoc opus illius videri debet, legit, "ad regulam sequor." Tertullianus libro *de carnis resurrectionis* legit, "secundum scopum persequor ad palmam."' Ibid.

The patristic references are to: Augustine, *Enarrationes in Psalmos* (CCSL, XXXVIII), ed. Eligius Dekkers and Iohannes Fraipont (Turnholt: Brepols, 1956), Ps 38:6, p. 407; a spurious work, *De singularitate clericorum*, *PL*, IV, 911B–948B, possibly written by Pope

Lucius; and Tertullian, *De resurrectione mortuorum* (CCSL, II), ed. A. Gerlo (Turnholt: Brepols, 1954), xxiii, p. 950

108 In the opening paragraph of the *Ratio* Erasmus writes of his NT edition 'iam ad metam decurrentis.' *Ratio, H*, p. 177, 9; *LB*, V, 75A. Cf. 'Nouum Testamentum iam ad metam properat.' To Jakob Wimpfeling, *EE*, III, 187 (no. 385, 2–3). 'Nos in opere Noui Testamenti iam ad metam anhelamus.' To Mark Lauwerijns, *EE*, III, 202 (no. 763, 6). In his later colloquy, 'De lusu,' Erasmus uses *meta* in every case to denote the goals of tennis, shotput, and jumping. 'De lusu,' *LB*, I, 646E, 647B, 647C, 648C–D

109 'praefigo,' *A Latin Dictionary*, ed. Lewis and Short, p. 1419

110 *Annotationes in epistolam ad Philippenses*, 3:14, *LB*, VI, 874B

111 In Erasmus' *Paraphrasis* on this epistle published in 1520 the word *scopus* does not appear. Erasmus explains Paul's intention by appealing to the metaphor of a race. The apostle runs towards the evangelical goal (*meta*) set before him; he gazes at the heavenly prize. 'Neque rursus temere quovis; dispendium enim facit, qui male currit; sed recta tendo ad metam Evangelicam nobis praefixam; et ad praemium coelis spectans conatum nostrum, nos vocat, opitulante Christo Jesu.' *In Epistolam Pauli Apostoli ad Philippenses Paraphrasis, LB*, VII, 1000C

112 'Nec alium scopum sibi praefixerat Paulus in apostolica functione, quam ut gentes omnes sub fidei iugum adduceret.' *Ratio, H*, p. 242, 25–27; *LB*, V, 108C

113 *'skopos,' A Patristic Greek Lexicon*, ed. G.W.H. Lampe (Oxford: Clarendon Press, 1961), II, 1241

114 *'skopos,' A Theological Dictionary of the New Testament*, ed. Gerhard Friedrich, VII, 414

115 tauta ei houtōs kai hoi Christomachoi dienoounto ton te skopon ton ekklēsiastikon hōs agkuran tēs pisteōs epeginōskon, out an enauagēsan peri tēn pistin, oute tousouton ēnaischuntoun, hōs anthistasthai kai tois boulomenois peptōkotas autous egeirai, kai mallon echthrous hēgeisthai tous nouthetountas autous eis eusebeian. KATA ARIANŌN LOGOS PRŌTOS, ed. William Bright (Oxford: Clarendon Press, 1884), III, 58, p. 211. A nineteenth-century translation has *scopus*. *Opera*, ed. A.B. Caillau and M.N.S. Guillon (Paris: Méquinon-Havard, 1830), vol. II:

Adversus Arianos, oratio III, lviii, p. 415

116 *'skopos,'* A Patristic Greek Lexicon, ed. Lampe, II, 1241

117 J.N.D. Kelly, *Early Christian Doctrines* (3d ed.; London: Adam and Charles Black, 1965), p. 47

118 Newman translates the sentence thus: 'Had Christ's enemies thus dwelt on these thoughts, and recognized the ecclesiastical scope as an anchor for the faith, they would not have of the faith made shipwreck.' He comments in his annotation, 'It is remarkable that he [Athanasius] ends as he began, with reference to the ecclesiastical scope, or *Regula fidei.' Select Treatises of S. Athanasius, Archbishop of Alexandria, In Controversy with the Arians,* trans. [John Henry Newman] (Oxford: J.H. Parker; London: J.G.F. and J. Rivington, 1842), p. 482.

119 *Bibliotheca Erasmiana,* ed. Vander Haeghen, 2d series, p. 11. The complete works appeared from the press of Johannes Parvus in Paris. Only the *opuscula* is included in the *LB,* VIII, 330–423. Reuchlin's translation of Athanasius was also shelved in Erasmus' personal library as mentioned in the letter To Jakob Ziegler, *EE,* v, 158 (no. 1330, 61–63).

120 See this chapter, n. 13.

121 '... neque rursum ibi desideat, et velut ad scopulos (vt inquit Gellius) sirenos consenescat.' *De ratione studii, ASD,* 1–2, p. 118, 4–5; *LB,* I, 522C. Erasmus also employs the commonplace with respect to pagan letters, e.g. *Enchiridion, H,* p. 32, 3; *LB,* v, 7D. Cf. 'Herculei labores,' *Adagia,* III, 1, i; *LB,* II, 707C, and Jerome's parable of the shipwrecked soul which Erasmus cites, *De copia, LB,* I, 94D–E.

122 'Absit ut nobis obscuretur illa Cynosura, ne non sit certum aliquod signum, ad quod in tantis errorum undis involuti recto cursui restituamur.' *Ratio, H,* p. 204, 14–16; *LB,* v, 89D–E

The suggestion I develop here (to p. 88) that Erasmus views Christ as the pole star by which the theologian must navigate may have been inspired by Prudentius' 'Hymnus Ephiphaniae' in the *Liber Cathemerinon.* There the poet imagines Christ as the great star which supplants the guiding role of the constellation Cynosura. Erasmus composed a commentary on this hymn, which he dedicated to Margaret Roper in 1524. While even the relevant part of the commentary which identifies the star of Epiphany as Christ is too lengthy to be reproduced here (see *Commentariolus in hymnum Prudentii, de epiphania Jesu nati, LB*, v, 1349A–1350F), vv. 1–24 of the hymn will provide some evidence. The author located this reference only after this book was in press, and therefore has not had the opportunity to study the question of dependence.

> Quicumque Christum quaeritis,
> Oculos in altum tollite
> Illis licebit visere
> Signum perennis gloriae.
> Haec stella, quae Solis rotam
> Vincit decore et lumine,
> Venisse terris nuntiat
> Cum carne terrestri Deum.
> Non illa servit noctibus
> Secuta Lunam menstruam,
> Sed sola coelum possidens
> Cursum dierum temperat.
> Arctoa quamvis sidera
> In se retortis motibus
> Obire nolint, attamen
> Plerumque sub nimbis latent.
> Hoc sidus aeternum manet,
> Haec stella numquam mergitur,
> Nec nubis occursu abdita
> Obumbrat obductam facem.
> Tristis cometa intercidat,
> Et si quod astrum Sirio
> Fervet vapore, jam Dei
> Sub luce destructum cadat.

The text is Erasmus'.

123 For amplification on Cynosura see, William T. Olcott, *Star Lore of All Ages: A Collection of Myths, Legends, and Facts concerning the Constellations of the Northern Hemisphere* (New York and London: G.P. Putnam's Sons, 1911).

124 See, Charles Singer et al., 'Cartography, Survey, and Navigation to 1400,' and E.G.R. Taylor, 'Cartography, Survey, and Navigation

1400–1700,' in *A History of Technology*, ed. Singer et al.' vol. III: *From the Renaissance to the Industrial Revolution, c 1500–c 1700* (Oxford: Clarendon Press, 1957), pp. 501–529; 530–557; or see books on the history of navigation such as W.E. May, *A History of Marine Navigation* (Henly-on-Thames: G.T. Foulis, 1973); Samuel Eliot Morison, *The European Discovery of America: The Northern Voyages A.D. 500–1600* (New York: Oxford University Press, 1971); E.G.R. Taylor, *The Haven-Finding Art: A History of Navigation from Odysseus to Captain Cook* (London: Hollis and Carter, 1956); D.W. Waters, *The Art of Navigation in England in Elizabethan and Early Stuart Times* (New Haven: Yale University Press, 1958).

125 In his article, 'Hermeneutik,' in *PRG*, VII, 728, G. Heinrici comments on Luther's sentence: 'In dieser Richtung ergänzt die Stilerklärung die sprachliche und die geschlichtliche. Für das objective Verständnis liefert die sprachliche die Bausteine, die geschichtliche beschreibt das Haus, wie es dasteht, die stilistiche ermittelt, wie das Haus in seinem Innern nach dem Verhältnis seiner Bestandteile beschaffen ist. In Verfolg dieser Aufgabe untersucht sie die Schrift auf ihre literarische Kategorie,' etc.

126 K. Goldammer, 'Navis ecclesiae: Eine unbekannte altchristliche Darstellung der Schiffsallegorie,' *ZNTW*, XL (1941), 76–86

127 'Pio Lectore,' *LB*, VII, f. 4–5, beginning with the second paragraph

128 'Porro quod est in domo lucerna, quod est oculus in corpore, id est animus in homine. Si lux animi non est vitiata caligine falsarum opinionum, malumque cupiditatum, si mentis oculus non alio diriget aciem, quam ad verum scopum, quicquid agitur in vita gratum Deo est, nihilque non conducit ad cumulum felicitas.' *Paraphrasis in evangelium Matthaei, LB*, VII, 39B

129 Taylor, *The Haven-Finding Art*, p. 100. See, e.g., 'Dicatur similis esse Maria polis.' Alexander Neckham, *De laudibus divinae sapientiae* (RBMAS, XXXIV), ed. Thomas Wright (London: Longman, Green, Longman, Roberts, and Green, 1863), p. 363, 280.

130   'Ave maris stella
      Dei mater alma
      Atque semper virgo
      Felix coeli porta.'

131 John of Garland, *Stella Maris*, ed. Evelyn F. Wilson (Cambridge: Wellesley College and the Medieval Academy of America, 1946)

132 'Deum immortalem quale seculum erat hoc, quum magno apparatu disticha Joannis Garlandini adolescentibus, operosis ac prolixis commentariis enarrabantur! Quum ineptis versiculis, dictandis, repetendis et exigendis magna pars temporis absumebatur!' *De pueris instituendis*, *ASD*, 1–2, p. 77, 11–14; *LB*, I, 514F

133 'Adolphus. Ibi vidisses miseram rerum faciem. Nautae canentes: *Salve regina*, implorabant matrem Virginem, appellantes eam stellam maris, reginam coeli, dominam mundi, portum salutis, aliisque multis titulis ille blandientes, quos nusquam illi tribuunt sacrae literae.

'Antonius. Quid illi cum mari, quae nunquam, opinor nauigauit?

'Adolphus. Olim Venus agebat curam nautarum, quia nata credebatur ex mari. Ea quoniam desiit curare, suffecta est huic matri non virgini Virgo mater.

'Antonius. Ludis.'

'Naufragium,' *Colloquia*, *ASD*, 1–3, p. 327, 71–78

134 Ibid., p. 332, 251–253. Erasmus also satirizes excessive Marian devotion in another colloquy, ICHOUOPHAGIA, *ASD*, 1–3, p. 535, 1458–1466. He did write a Mass, however, in honour of Mary, *Virginis Matris apud Lauretum cultae Liturgia*, published by Froben in November 1523.

135 'Quare capiendae sunt illae de quibus dixi rerum imagines, quas uocari *phantasias* indicauimus, omniaque de quibus dicturi erimus, personae, quaestiones, spes, metus, habenda in oculis, in adfectus recipienda: pectus est enim quod disertos facit, et uis mentis.' Quintilian, *Institutio oratoria*, ed. Winterbottom, Bk. x, vii, p. 617. Trans., Butler, II, 141

136 See this chapter, n. 86.

137 'Quas *phantasias* Graeci uocant (nos sane uisiones appellemus), per quas imagines rerum absentium ita repraesentantur animo ut eas cernere oculis ac praesentes habere uideamur, has quisquis bene ceperit is erit in adfectibus potentissimus.' Quintilian, *Institutio oratoria*, ed. Winterbottom, Bk. vi, ii, p. 335. Trans., Butler, II, p. 435

138 See this chapter, n. 86.

139 'Animum cibus est ita demum utilis non si in memoria ceu
stomacho subsidat, sed si in ipsos affectus et in ipsa mentis viscera
traiciatur.' *Ratio, H*, p. 180, 24–26; *LB*, v, 77B

140 'oculus fidei.' Ibid., *H*, p. 179, 20; *LB*, v, 76D. 'cordis oculos.'
Enchiridion, H, p. 26, 27; *LB*, v, 4D

141 See this chapter, n. 68.

142 'At cur non potius vivam illius et spirantem imaginem in hisce
veneramus libris? ... Quin haec potius auro gemmisque et si quid
his pretiosius insigniuntur, quae tanto praesentius Christum nobis
referunt quam ulla imaguncula?' *Paraclesis, H*, pp. 148–149, 35–37,
5–7; *LB*, v, 144C–D

143 '... qui quod pollicitus est se semper nobiscum fore usque ad
consummationem saeculi, in his litteris praecipue praestat, in
quibus nobis etiamnum vivit, spirat, loquitur, paene dixerim,
efficacius quam cum inter homines versaretur.' Ibid., *H*, p. 146,
22–26; *LB*, v, 142E

144 'Siquidem illa, quid aliud quam corporis figuram exprimit – si
tamen illius quidquam exprimit –, at hae tibi sacrosanctae mentis
illius vivam referunt imaginem ipsumque Christum loquentem,
sanantem, morientem, resurgentem, denique totum ita praesentem
reddunt, ut minus visurus sis, si coram oculis conspicias.' Ibid., *H*,
p. 149, 7–12; *LB*, v, 144D. Trans., Olin, p. 106. Cf. *EE*, II, 185 (no.
384, 46–48), and *Enchiridion, H*, pp. 67–68, 22–23; *LB*, v, 27D–28A.

   Jacques Etienne also notes the force of the text as a living word
for Erasmus: 'L'évangile est moins discours sur le Christ que
discours du Christ; lire les saintes lettres, c'est devenir le disciple
qui écoute, qui entre en contact personnel avec le Seigneur, qui vit
en sa présence agissante et met en pratique son enseignement.' 'La
méditation des Ecritures selon Erasme,' *Scrinium Erasmianum*, ed.
Coppens, II, 4–5

145 'At verius et efficacius nobis loquitur deus in arcanis libris quam
Mosi de rubo locutus sit, si modo puri accesserimus ad colloquium.'
Ratio, H, p. 179, 14–15; *LB*, v, 76C

146 'Sic porro existima nihil tam verum esse eorum, quae vides oculis,
quae manibus contrectas, quam quae ibi legis.' *Enchiridion, H*, p.
33, 25–27; *LB*, v, 8C–D

147 James K. McConica, 'Erasmus and the Grammar of Consent,'

Scrinium Erasmianum, ed. Coppens, II, 92. Georges Chantraine contends with this interpretation in *'Mystère' et 'Philosophie du Christ' selon Erasme*, BN, XLI (Namur: Secrétariat des publications Facultés universitaires; Gembloux: J. Duculot, 1971), p. 365, n. 2, although it is my observation that Chantraine's thesis does not appreciate Erasmus as a humanist.

148 'Cartusianus. Nec interim tamen, quum maxime videor solus, desunt mihi confabulones, longe festiuiores ac suauiores istis vulgaribus congerronibus ... Vides hic codicem Euangelicum. In hoc mecum fabulatur ille, qui olim additus facundus comes in via duobus discipulis proficiscentibus in Emauntem, effecit vt non sentirent itineris laborem, sed sentirent dulcissimum cordis ardorem, inhiantes mellitis illius sermonibus.' 'Cartusianus et miles,' *Colloquia*, *ASD*, 1–3, p. 316, 70–71, 73–76. Trans., Thompson, p. 130

149 The English printer William Caxton (c. 1422–1491) expanded the famous chess manual of Jacobus de Cessolis into an elaborate allegory of the mediaeval estates. The chessmen are the feudal classes who move about on the board of the commonwealth in imitation of their social obligations. *Game and Playe of the Chesse* (1st ed. of 1474 reprinted, London: Elliot Stock, 1883)

150 Nicholas of Cusa, *Concordantiae catholicae* in *Opera omnia* (Paris: In Aedibus Ascensianis, 1514; reprinted, Frankfurt / M.: Minerva, 1962), III, Bk. I, x, f. BBiii and v; Bk. III, i, f. GGiiii

151 'Quemadmodum sunt machinae quaedam tam operosae, vt moram adferant negocio peragendo. Huius generis ferme sunt, quae de arte memoriae, quidam ad quaestum aut ostentationem potius quam ad vtilitatem excogitarunt.' *De pueris instituendis*, *ASD*, 1–2, p. 71, 8–11; *LB*, I, 512A

152 '... adiuuabit non mediocriter, si quorum necessaria quidem, sed subdifficilis erit memoria, veluti locorum quas tradunt cosmographi, pedum metricorum, figurarum grammaticarum, genealogiarum, aut si qua sunt similia, ea quam fieri potest breuissime simul et luculentissime in tabulas depicta, in cubiculi parietibus suspendantur, quo passim et aliud agentibus sint obuia. Item si quaedam breuiter, sed insigniter dicta, velut apophthegmata, prouerbia, sententias in frontibus atque in calcibus singulorum

codicum inscribes, quaedam annulis, aut poculis insculpes, nonnulla pro foribus, et in parietibus, aut vitreis etiam fenestris depinges, quo nusquam non occurat oculis, quod eruditionem adiuuet.' *De ratione studii, ASD,* 1–2, pp. 118–119, 16–5; *LB,* I, 522D

153 '... universum Christi populum in tres circulos dividere, quorum omnium tamen unicum sit centrum, Christus Iesus, ad cuius simplicissimam puritatem pro suo cuique virili enitendum est omnibus.' *Ratio, H,* p. 202, 2–5; *LB,* v, 88c

While there has been occasional reference in the critical literature to this image, there has been no serious attempt to research and interpret it. Chantraine suggests that it probably derives from and profoundly modifies the hierarchies of Pseudo-Dionysius the Areopagite, a suggestion to which I offer my alternatives. I do not see any textual basis for his argument that the literary structure of the *Ratio* is concentric. *'Mystère' et 'Philosophie du Christ' selon Erasme,* pp. 123–124, 155–156

154 'Maneat intactus ille scopus.' *Ratio, H,* p. 204, 11–12; *LB,* v, 89D. 'Neque enim oportet scopum suo movere loco, quin potius omnes mortalium actiones ad scopum dirigendae.' *Ibid., H,* p. 202, 5–7; *LB,* v, 88c

155 'Primum autem circulum teneant, qui, quoniam velut in vices Christi successerunt, Christo proximi sunt, illi semper adhaerentes ac sequentes agnum quocumque ierit, quales sunt sacerdotes, abbates, episcopi, cardinales ac summi pontifices ... in secundum circulum transfundere, qui principes habet profanos, quorum tamen arma legesque suo quodam modo Christi serviunt ... Tertium circulum promiscuo vulgo dare licebit.' *Ibid.,* ll. 7–11, 14–16, 18–19; *LB,* v, 88c–D

156 Ruth Mohl, *The Three Estates in Medieval and Renaissance Literature* (New York: Frederick Ungar, 1933), pp. 6–7. No text by Erasmus is discussed in this book.

157 Ibid., 19

158 'Etenim cum sacerdotes sacrificiis litant deo, cum pabulo sermonis euangelici pascunt populum, cum puris precibus cum deo colloquuntur cumque pro salute gregis interpellant, aut cum domi secretis studiis meditantur, quo populum reddant meliorem ... qui principes habet profanos, quorum tamen arma legesque suo quodam

modo Christo serviunt, sive dum necessariis ac iustis bellis profligant hostem, publicamque tuentur tranquillitatem sive dum legitimis suppliciis coercent facinorosos ... aliter relucet aeternae veritatis fulgor in levi tersoque speculo, aliter in ferro ... Hos oportet quam maxime puros esse a rerum mundanarum contagio, cuiusmodi sunt voluptatum amor, pecuniae studium, ambitio, vitae aviditas ...' Erasmus warns against their tendency 'provocati graviores excitant tragoedias ... infirmorum imbecillitati multa concedunt inviti.' *Ratio, H,* p. 202, 22–26, 15–18; p. 204, 7–8; p. 202, 11–13, 28, 29; *LB,* v, 88D–E

159 Mohl, *The Three Estates in Medieval and Renaissance Literature,* p. 257

160 '... cum baptismus ex aequo communis sit Christianorum omnium, in quo prima Christianae philosophiae professio est.' *Paraclesis, H,* p. 142, 29–31; *LB,* v, 140D, in the context of co-operation in Christ's mystical body of its various members

161 To Paul Volz, *EE,* iii, 368–370 (no. 858, 231–330)

162 Mohl, *The Three Estates in Medieval and Renaissance Literature,* pp. 261, 263–264, 315–316

163 Perhaps the best known discussion of this is Walter J. Ong, *The Presence of the Word: Some Prolegomena for Cultural and Religious History* (New Haven and London: Yale University Press, 1967).

164 Aquinas, *ST,* i, q. 13, is the *locus classicus.*

165 'Religious symbols are distinguished from others by the fact that they are a representation of that which is unconditionally *beyond* the conceptual sphere; they point to the ultimate reality implied in the religious act ... Religious symbols represent the transcendent but do not make the transcendent immanent. They do not make God part of the empirical world.' Paul Tillich, 'The Religious Symbol,' in *Myth and Symbol,* ed. F.W. Dillistone (London: SPCK, 1966), p. 17

166 Frederick J. Streng, 'Problems of Symbolic Structure in Religious Apprehension,' *HR,* iv (1964), 126–153

167 Wolfhart Pannenberg, 'Hermeneutik und universal Geschichte,' *ZThK,* lx (1963), 90–93

168 John Hick, 'Theology and Verification,' *ThT,* xvii (1960), 12–31. Cf. Nels F.S. Ferré, 'Notes by a Theologian on Biblical Hermeneutics,' *JBL,* lxxviii (1959), 112

169 Northrop Frye, *Anatomy of Criticism: Four Essays* (New York: Atheneum, 1969), p. 335

170 Ernst Cassirer, *The Philosophy of Symbolic Forms*, trans. Ralph Mannheim (New Haven: Yale University Press, 1955), II, 86

171 Ong, 'System, Space, and Intellect in Renaissance Symbolism,' *BHR*, XVIII (1956), 228

172 For the history and use of the armillary sphere, as well as photographs of historical models, see, Edward L. Stevenson, *Terrestrial and Celestial Globes* (New Haven: Yale University Press for the Hispanic Society of America, 1921), I.

173 There is a ring dial, composed of three brass rings, one with sighting vanes, in ibid., I, 104, fig. 51.

174 See this chapter, n. 153; cf. nn. 177–181. I wish to correct the model of a flat target with Christ as its bull's-eye which I employed earlier in my article, 'Weavers, farmers, tailors, travellers, masons, prostitutes, pimps, Turks, little women and Other Theologians,' p. 3

175 'Piloto: Porque cuando tomamos el altura del norte llamamos a la cabeza parte de encima y al pie parte de abajo. Como hay en el cielo cabeza y pie? Cosmógrafo: Es de saber que ellas partes del cielo son quatro. Levante poniente medio dia septentrion. Estas quatro partes comparadas al cuerpo de un hombre. Llamandos a la del levante abunque parte mas noble braco izquierdo – y a la de poniente braco derecho y al septentrion cabeza y al medio dia pie.' Pedro de Medina, *Libro de cosmographia* (1538 ed. reprinted in facsimile by Chicago University Press for the Newberry Library, 1972), p. 56. I have transcribed the text into more modern orthography. Trans., Ursula Lamb, p. 169

176 For a history of this idea, see Dietrich Mahnke, *Unendliche Sphäre und Allmittelpunkt* (Halle, 1937), reprinted by Stuttgart and Bad-Canstatt: Friedrich Frommann, 1966).

177 '... et ita tota theologia in circulo posita dicit.' Nicholas of Cusa, *De visione Dei* in *Opera*, I, Bk. I, iii, f. c, niiii

178 '... mirabilem illum orbem et consensum totius Christi fabulae.' *Ratio, H*, p. 209, 2–3; *LB*, V, 91C. Cf. '... totum illum Christi circulum et orbem.' *Methodus, H*, p. 157, 9–10

179 'Totus doctrinae circulus ut secum consentit, ita cum ipsius vita consentit.' *Ratio, H*, p. 210, 4–5; *LB*, V, 91F–92A

180 'Reperies fortassis in Platonis aut Senecae libris, quae non
abhorreant a decretis Christi; reperies in vita Socratis, quae
utcumque cum Christi vita consentiant. At circulum hunc et
omnium rerum inter se congruentium harmoniam in solo Christo
reperies.' Ibid., *H*, pp. 210–211, 33–2; *LB*, v, 92B

181 'Annotandus est apud eundem circulus, in quo fere se volvit,
ubique et societatem et foedus Christianum commendans.
Praesertim capite duodecimo et decimo tertio se declarat idem esse
cum patre, adeo ut qui filium norit, norit et patrem, qui filium
spernat, spernat et patrem; nec separatur ab hac communione
spiritus sanctus.' Ibid., *H*, p. 259, 7–12; *LB*, v, 116E–F

182 'Sic enim legis in epistola: Tres sunt qui testimonium dant in
caelo, pater, sermo, et spiritus; atque hi tres unum sunt.' Ibid., ll.
12–14; *LB*, v, 116F

The occurrence of this verse in the 1519 edition of the *Ratio*
(according to Holborn's redaction) presents a quandary since
Erasmus omitted the so-called *comma Joanneum* from the same
edition of the New Testament text. When Edward Lee and Diego
López Zúñiga (Stunica) incited controversy, Erasmus offered to
insert the verse into a reprint of his text if a Greek MS could be
found which proved the antiquity of the verse. His adversaries did
produce a MS, but a forged one (Trinity College, Dublin, codex
Greg. 61), and Erasmus honoured his promise, but not without
voicing suspicion. *Annotationes in epistola beati Joannis apostoli
prima, LB*, VI, 1080D. See also, *Responsio ad annotationes Eduardi
Lei in Erasmum novas* in *LB*, IX, 277D–278E, and *Apologia respondens
ad ea quae in Novo Testamento taxaverunt Jacobus Lopis Stunica,
LB*, IX, 351F–353E. The question may be raised: what importance
did Erasmus attach to the verse's deletion from the NT since he
quotes it importantly in the methodological preface to the very
edition which omits it? The translation of the verse in the *Ratio*
bears his deliberate hand in the substition of *sermo* for *verbum*.

183 'In idem consortium trahit suos, quos palmites suos appellat,
obsecrans, ut quemadmodum ipse idem erat cum patre, ita et illi
idem essent secum. Impertit iisdem communem patris suumque
spiritum, omnia conciliantem.' *Ratio, H*, p. 259, 14–18; *LB*, v, 116F

184 The term *orbis doctrinae* occurs in the *Ratio, H*, p. 286, 2; *LB*, v,

128B; and *circulus doctrinae*, ibid., *H*, p. 210, 4; *LB*, v, 91F. Cf. '...
orbis ille doctrinae, quem Graeci encyclion paedian uocant.'
Quintilian, *Institutio oratoria*, ed. Winterbottom, I, Bk. I, x, p. 59

185 See Chapter 1, n. 66.

186 Quintilian, *Institutio oratoria*, ed. Winterbottom, Bk. IX, iv, p. 561.
Cf. Cicero, *Orator*, ed. Wilhelm Kroll (Berlin: Weidmannsche,
1958), lxi: '... in totone circuitu illo orationis quam Graeci *periodon*
...' p. 174.

187 Quintilian, ibid.

188 'Nam totius ductus hic est quasi mucro.' Ibid., Bk. IX, iv, p. 540

189 See this chapter, n. 178.

190 See this chapter, nn. 86–87.

191 '... ad unius Christi gloriam referret omnia.' *Ratio, H*, p. 194, 5;
LB, v, 84B. Cf. ibid., *H*, p. 194, 24–25; *LB*, v, 84D

192 Joan Marie Lechner, *Renaissance Concepts of the Commonplaces*
(New York: Pageant, 1962)

193 *De copia, LB*, I, 88E–89E, especially, 'A Theologis, a sacris
voluminibus,' 89D

194 'Saepenumero locorum collatio nodum explicat difficultatis, dum
quod alibi dictum est tectius, alibi dilucidius refertur. Et quoniam
totus ferme Christi sermo figuris ac tropis obliquus est, diligenter
odorabitur theologiae candidatus, quam sustineat personam is, qui
loquitur.' *Ratio, H*, p. 197, 3–7; *LB*, v, 85F. Cf. references to
collatio or *collatio locorum,* ibid., *H*, pp. 283, 291, 295, 304; *LB*, v,
126E, 131B, 132F, 137C.

195 Ibid., *H*, pp. 195–196; *LB*, v, 84E–85E

196 'In disputando servanda sobrietas summaque animi moderatio, ut
collatio, non conflictatio videatur.' Ibid., *H*, p. 180, 30–31; *LB*, v,
77C

197 'Accedet hinc quoque lucis nonnihil ad intelligendum scripturae
sensum, si perpendamus non modo quid dicatur, verum etiam a quo
dicatur, cui dicatur, quibus verbis dicatur, quo tempore, qua
occasione, quid praecedat, quid consequatur.' Ibid., *H*, p. 196,
29–32; *LB*, v, 85E. The rule is repeated, ibid., *H*, p. 204, 25–26;
LB, v, 89F. Ibid., *H*, pp. 196–197, 32–2; *LB*, v, 85E–F.

198 Ibid., *H*, pp. 197–198; *LB*, v, 85F–86E

199 Ibid., *H*, pp. 198–201; *LB*, v, 86F–88C. Erasmus catalogues history

as follows: the time which preceded the age of Christ; the time of advent and the preaching of John the Baptist; the age of miracles and doctrine of Christ, the descent of the Holy Spirit and the birth of the Church; the era of Christian empire; the time of degeneration.

200 Ibid., *H*, p. 201, 8–33; *LB*, v, 88A–B

201 See this chapter, n. 154.

202 Cicero, *De partitione oratoria*, xxxi, 109, trans., H. Rackham (Cambridge: University Press, 1942), p. 395, as cited by Lechner, *Renaissance Concepts of the Commonplaces*

Erasmus discusses commonplaces in *De copia*, *LB*, I, 88F–89E. Cf. Otto Schottenloher, 'Zur Funktion der loci bei Erasmus,' in *Hommages à Marie Delcourt* (Brussels: Latomus, 1970), p. 317–331, which is principally concerned with the propaedeutic role of antiquity.

203 Commonplace has been more usually understood as a popular saying rather than as a collective seat of argumentation.

204 '23 Instaurare/*anakephalaiōsasthai*, id est, *recapitulari*, hoc est, *ut in summam conferrentur*. Nam Oratores vocant *anakephalaiōsin*, id est, *recapitulationem*, cum ea, quae sparsim ac fusius dicta sunt, summatim repetuntur, et simul judici renovantur. Divus Hieronymous legit *recapitulare*, putatque recte verbum hoc a Latinis usurpari posse, et miratur quamobrem in Latinis codicibus magis habeatur *instaurare*, quam *recapitulare*. Sunt, quorum est Theophylactus et Chrysostomus, qui interpretantur *anakephalaiōsin*, ut Christus fieret et Angelorum et hominum et Judaeorum et Gentium caput. Id quod convenit iis quae paulo post sequuntur, *et ipsum dedit caput*. Atque adeo Graeca vox ita sonat, quasi dicas *ad caput revocare*.' *Annotationes in epistola Pauli ad Ephesios*, 1:10, *LB*, VI, 833C–D

205 'Christi autem esse puta, quicquid usquam veri offenderis.' *Enchiridion*, *H*, p. 35, 33–34; *LB*, v, 9D–E

206 'Quod nunc misso Filio patefecit orbi, hoc ab aeterno decretum erat Patri et Filio: verum id certo et inenarrabili consilio secretum et abditum esse voluit, donec impleretur tempus ab ipso praefinitum, huic arcano mortalibus aperiendo: quo jam abolitis superiorum temporum dispendiis, per quae felicitas frustra quaerebatur, aliis per observationem Legis Mosaicae, aliis per

studium Philosophiae, aliis per superstitiosam religionem cultumque
Daemonum, summa cunctorum, quae ad veram innocentiam
veramque beatitudinem pertinent, conferretur in unum Christum
extra quem nihil jam esset cuiquam expetendum, cum ab hoc unico
fonte peti posset, quicquid bonorum vel coelum habet, vel terra.
Hunc enim Pater Deus caput omnium esse voluit, ab hoc uno voluit
omnes pendere, ab hoc sperari, quicquid vere sit expetendum, huic
acceptum ferri, quicquid nobis sua benignitate largitur.' *Paraphrasis
in epistola Pauli ad Ephesios,* 1:10, *LB,* VII, 974A–B

207 'Quarum neque numerus est ullus neque modus neque finis, dum
hydrae in morem pro una recisca sescentae repullulant.' *Ratio, H,* p.
297, 20–22; *LB,* V, 134A

208 'Hoc quod optamus non alia res certius praestet quam ipsa veritas,
cuius quo simplicior, hoc efficacior est oratio.' *Paraclesis, H,* p. 140,
5–7; *LB,* V, 139A. Trans., Olin, p. 94

209 Ibid., *H,* p. 140, 14–25; *LB,* V, 139B–C. 'Affingant illi suae sectae
principibus quantum possunt aut quantum libet. Certe solus hic e
caelo profectus est doctor, solus certa docere potuit, cum sit aeterna
sapientia, solus salutaria docuit unicus humanae salutis auctor,
solus absolute praestitit, quicquid unquam docuit, solus exhibere
potest, quidquid promisit.' Ibid., *H,* pp. 140–141, 34–3; *LB,* V,
139D. Trans., Olin, p. 95

210 Ibid., *H,* p. 141, 18–20; *LB,* V, 139E–F. 'Praesertim cum hoc
sapientiae genus tam eximum, ut semel stultam reddiderit
universam huius mundi sapientiam, ex paucis hisce libris, velut et
limpidissimis fontibus haurire liceat longe minore negotio quam ex
tot voluminibus spinosis, ex tam immensis iisque inter se
pugnantibus interpretum commentariis Aristotelicam doctrinam, ut
ne addam, quanto maiore cum fructu. Nihil enim hic necesse est, ut
tot anxiis disciplinis instructus accedas. Simplex et cuivis paratum
est viaticum.' Ibid., ll. 21–29; *LB,* V, 139F–140A. Trans., Olin, p.
96. *Italics mine.* Ibid., *H,* p. 142, 7–8; *LB,* V, 140B

211 '... ad paucos homines contrahimus rem, qua Christus nihil voluit
esse communius.' Ibid., *H,* p. 144, 33–35; *LB,* V, 141E. Ibid., ll.
8–9; *LB,* V, 141C. Ibid., *H,* pp. 145–146, 35–2; *LB,* V, 142C–D.
Ibid., ll. 6–12; *LB,* V, 142C–D. 'Denique qua, ut sescentas etiam
addas, nulla possit esse sanctior?' Ibid., *H,* p. 147, 7–8; *LB,* V,

143A. Trans., Olin, p. 103. Ibid., *H*, ll. 12–16; *LB*, v, 143A. 'Hunc
auctorem nobis non schola theologorum, sed ipse pater caelestis
divinae vocis testimonio comprovabit, idque bis: primum ad
Iordanem in baptismo, deinde in monte Thabor in transfiguratione.
Hic, inquit, est filius meus dilectus, in quo mihi complacitum est,
ipsum audite.' Ibid., *H*, p. 147, 21–27; *LB*, v, 143B–C. Trans., Olin,
p. 104

212 'Ubi coepit esse minus fide inter Christianos, mox increvit
symbolorum et modus et numerus.' *Ratio, H*, p. 211, 24–26; *LB*, v,
92D

213 '... propositiones, conclusiones et corollaria.' To Maarten
Bartholomeuszoon van Dorp, *EE*, II, 105 (no. 337, 549–550).
Trans., Olin, p. 78. '... ineptias ... rixosas et frigidissimas
quaestiones.' Ibid., p. 95, 151–152. Trans., Ibid. '... friuolas
quaestiunculas.' Ibid., p. 100, 346. Trans., ibid., 70. '... sophisticis
captiunculis.' Ibid., p. 101, 413–414. Trans., ibid., 72. '... spinosas
illas et inextricabileis argutias.' To Paul Volz, *EE*, III, 364 (no. 858,
84). Trans., ibid., 112. '... quaestionum labirynthi.' To Dorp, ibid.,
p. 101, 414–415. Trans., ibid., 72

214 'Tot pene sunt in Sententiarum libros commentarii, quot
theologorum nomina. Quid summulariorum modus aut numerus,
aliud ex alio miscentium ac remiscentium, et pharmacopolarum ritu
ex novis uetera, ex ueteribus nova, e pluribus vnum, ex vno plura
subinde fingentium ac refingentium?' To Paul Volz, *EE*, III, 363
(no. 858, 38–42). Trans., ibid., 110–111. 'Cumque minutatim
excutiant singula ... tamen nec inter se consentiunt.' Ibid., ll. 51–52,
55. Trans., Olin, p. 111

215 '... sed e diuerso permulta sunt quae rectius sit omittere quam
inquirere ... Nunc neque quaestiuncularum vllus est finis.' To Dorp,
EE, II, 101, 102 (no. 337, 418–419, 422–423). Trans., Olin, 72–73

216 See Chapter 2, n. 130.

217 '... et cum sint quouis sue stupidiores ac ne sensu quidem
communi praediti, putant se totius arcem tenere sapientiae. Censent
omnes, damnant, pronunciant, nihil addubitant, nusquam haerent,
nihil nesciunt. Et tamen isti duo tresue magnas saepenumero
commouent trageodias.' To Dorp, *EE*, II, 99 (no. 337, 321–325).
Trans., Olin, p. 69

218 See this chapter, n. 9.

219 '... in futilem quandam ac deformem incidant loquacitatem, dum inani, citraque delectum congesta vocum et sententiarum turba, pariter et rem obscurant, et miseras auditorum aures onerant.' *De copia, LB*, I, 3B. Trans., King and Rix, p. 11. Ibid., 3B–C

220 'Imo contra conniti par est, vt eam quam fieri potest reddamus facillimam et omnibus expositam.' To Paul Volz, *EE*, III, p. 364 (no. 858, 74–75). Trans., Olin, p. 112

221 '... unum illud caput.' Ibid., p. 377, 591. '... in Christo capite nostro ... in capite.' *Enchiridion, H*, p. 28, 9–10, 11; *LB*, V, 6A. '... qui verum est lumen, stultitiae mundanae noctem solus discutiens.' Ibid., *H*, p. 38, 21–22; *LB*, V, 11B. '... ad solum Christum tamquam ad unicum et summum bonum.' '... ad unicum illum bonum.' Ibid., *H*, p. 63, 17–18; p. 65, 11; *LB*, V, 25B, 26B. '... unum omnium esse Dominum Christum Iesum.' Ibid., *H*, p. 105; *LB*, V, 48A. '... unum enim esse tum magistrum, tum dominum, qui et caput omnium nostrum Christus Iesus.' Ibid., *H*, p. 107, 13–14; *LB*, V, 49B. '... unus Christus tibi satis sit, unicus auctor et recte sentiendi, et beate vivendi.' Ibid., *H*, p. 110, 17–18; *LB*, V, 50F. 'Innumerabiles adversum te sed qui pro te stat unus plus potest omnibus.' Ibid., *H*, p. 28, 4–5; *LB*, V, 5B–6A. 'Hoc est enim unicum archetypum.' Ibid., *H*, p. 89, 7–8; *LB*, V, 39B

222 See this chapter, n. 191.

223 '... ut totius vitae tuae Christum velut unicum scopum praefigas, ad quem unum omnia studia, omnes conatus, omne otium ac negotium conferas ... Ad solum Christum tamquam ad unicum et summum bonum spectet, ut nihil ames, nihil mireris, nihil exspectes, nisi aut Christum, aut propter Christum.' *Enchiridion, H*, p. 63, 9–11, 17–19; *LB*, V, 25A–B. Trans., Himelick, pp. 94, 95

224 '... simplex et lucidus ille oculus ex Euangelio.' To Paul Volz, *EE*, III, 367 (no. 858, 223–224). Trans., Olin, p. 117

225 'Hoc est enim unicum archetypum.' *Enchiridion, H*, p. 89, 7–8; *LB*, V, 39B

226 Jn 1:1–3

227 'Debent humanae leges ab hoc archetypo peti.' *Ratio, H*, p. 204, 5–6; *LB*, V, 89D

228 'Hoc est unicum archetypum, unde quisquis vel unguem
discesserit, a recto discedit atque extra viam currit.' *Enchiridion, H*,
p. 89, 7–9; *LB*, v, 39B

229 For an introduction to these patristic texts, see *logos*, in *A Patristic
Greek Lexicon*, ed. Lampe, I, 809, col. 2. For some orientation on
the classical background, see *logos, Realencyclopädie der classischen
Altertumswissenschaft*, ed. Paulys–Georg Wissowa (Stuttgart: Alfred
Druckenmüller, 1926), XIII / 1, 1035–1081, especially the section on
theology.

230 Lechner, *Renaissance Concepts of the Commonplaces*, pp. 4, 26,
121–130

231 Jaeger, *Paideia*, I, 155–159. Cf. Rudolph Allers, 'Microcosmus:
From Anaximandros to Paracelsus,' *Tr*, II (1944), 339

232 Dante Alighieri, *La Divina Commedia* in *Tutte le opera*, ed. Fred
Chiapelli (Milan: U. Mursia, 1965)

233 Erasmus edited the first edition of Ptolemy, which was published
by Froben in 1533.

234 *Enchiridion, H*, pp. 44–45; *LB*, v, 13E–14E

235 Plato, TIMAIOS, 33b. Trans., Francis MacDonald Conford
(London: Routledge and Kegan Paul, 1937), p. 54. Ibid., 33–36,
72–76, 90–91

236 '... novem tibi orbibus vel potius globis conexa sunt omnia,
quorum unus est caelestis, extumus, qui reliquos omnes
complectitur, summus ipse deus arcens et continens ceteros.'
Cicero, *De re publica*, ed. T.E. Page et al (London: William
Heinemann; Cambridge: Harvard University Press, 1948), Bk. VI,
xvii, p. 271. Trans., Keyes, p. 270

237 E. Vernon Arnold, *Roman Stoicism: Being Lectures on the History
of the Stoic Philosophy with Special Reference to Its Development
within the Roman Empire* (New York: Humanities Press, 1958), pp.
161, 222

238 'Omnes enim partes eius undique medium locum capessentes
nituntur aequaliter. Maxime autem corpora inter se iuncta
permanent cum quasi quodam vinculo circumdato colligantur; quod
facit ea natura quae per omnem mundum omnia mente et ratione
conficiens funditur et ad medium rapit et convertit extrema.'
Cicero, *De natura deorum* (London: William Heinemann;

Cambridge: Harvard University Press, 1961), Bk. II, xliv, p. 232

239 Arnold, *Roman Stoicism*, p. 161, cites Cicero on *ratio et oratio* as the bond of the state.

240 'Quocirca si mundus globosus est ob eamque causam omnes eius partes undique aequabiles ipsae per se atque inter se continentur ...' Cicero, *De natura deorum*, II, xlv, p. 232

241 '... nam ea, quae est media et nona, tellus, neque movetur et infima est, et in eam feruntur omnia nuto suo pondera.' Cicero, *De re publica*, ed. Page, Bk. VI, xvii, p. 271. Trans., Keyes, p. 270. Ibid., Bk. VI, xviii, p. 272. For amplification on this ideal, see Leo Spitzer, *Classical and Christian Ideas of World Harmony: Prolegomena to an Interpretation of the Word 'Stimmung,'* ed. Anna G. Hatcher (Baltimore: Johns Hopkins Press, 1963).

242 'Jam tot orbium coelestium, licet nec motus sit idem, nec vis eadem, tamen iis tot jam seculis constant vigentque foedera. Elementorum pugnantes inter se vires, aequabili libramine pacem aeternum tuentur, et in tanta discordia, consensu commercioque mutuo concordiam alunt.' *Querela pacis, LB*, IV, 626B. Trans., Thomas Paynell, ed. William J. Hirten (New York: Scholars Press, 1946), p. 8

243 I do not intend to suggest that for Erasmus the imitation of Christ consists in eloquence rather than piety, for in fact true eloquence springs from human spirit reflecting its divine image. Every student of classical rhetoric knows the traditional equation of the rhetor as *vir bonus*. See, e.g., Quintilian, *Institutio oratoria*, ed. Winterbottom, II, Bk. XII.

Hanna Gray has commented well on the flourishing of this ideal in Renaissance humanism: 'The terms "decorum" and "imitatio," for example, are central in both rhetoric and moral philosophy, and the humanists often appear to fuse their meanings whatever the context. Thus, the imitation of stylistic and of ethical models are spoken of in identical terms; or the idea of always speaking appropriately, of suiting style and manner to subject, aim, and audience is treated as the exact analogue of behaving with *decorum*, of choosing the actions and responses which are best in harmony with and most appropriate to individual character and principles on the one hand, the nature of circumstances on the other.'

'Renaissance Humanism: The Pursuit of Eloquence,' in *Renaissance Essays from the Journal of the History of Ideas*, ed. Paul O. Kristeller and Philip P. Wiener (New York: Harper and Row, 1968), p. 208

244 The comparison of Erasmus with à Kempis is a commonplace of modern scholarship which presupposes that Erasmus was spiritually formed under the tutelage of the Brothers of the Common Life. He was not, as R.R. Post demonstrates in *The Modern Devotion: Confrontation with Reformation and Humanism*, SMRT, III (Leiden: E.J. Brill, 1968), pp. 11–12, 658–660, 673, 675–676. I concur with Post's comment that 'one must not take it for granted that everyone who showed any signs of piety at the end of the Middle Ages, or who assumed to be devout, belonged to the Modern Devotion, or that any pupil from the schools of Deventer or Zwolle who achieved something in later life was a product of the Brothers,' p. 676.

245 '... Erasme, qui avait surement lu et relu à Steyn l'Imitation de Jésus–Christ,' R. Marcel, 'L'Enchiridion Militis Christiani: Sa genèse et sa doctrine, son succès et ses vicissitudes,' *Colloquia Erasmiana Turoniensia*, ed. Margolin (Toronto: University of Toronto Press, 1972), p. 621

246 'Nec inmerito M. Tullius hunc "optimum effectorem ac magistrum dicendi" uocat.' Quintilian, *Institutio oratoria*, ed. Winterbottom, Bk. x, iii, p. 599. Cicero, *De oratore*, ed. Sutton, Bk. II, xxii, p. 264

247 Thomas à Kempis, *Opera omnia*, vol. II: *Admonitiones ad spiritualem vitam utiles* [De imitatione Christi], ed. Michael J. Pohl (Friburg: Herder, 1934), Bk. I, xx, pp. 35–38

248 Richard McKeon separates grammar and rhetoric in his well known article, 'Renaissance and Method in Philosophy,' in *Studies in the History of Ideas* (New York: Columbia University Press, 1935), III, 37–114. Cf. Kristeller's criticism: 'I am not convinced by Keon's [sic] attempt to distinguish within the Renaissance as two separate trends, an emphasis on grammar as represented by Erasmus, and one on rhetoric represented by rhetoric.' 'Humanism and Scholasticism in the Italian Renaissance,' *Byz*, XVII (1945), 354, n. 22a. Also Jerrold E. Seigel's PH D dissertation, Princeton University, p. 329, where he states that 'McKeon's attempt to

distinguish between grammatical and rhetorical method should be rejected.'

249 D.P. Walker, *Spiritual and Demonic Magic from Ficino to Campanella* (London: Warburg Institute, 1958), pp. 38–39

250 Jean Seznec, *La survivance des dieux antiques: Essai sur le role de la tradition mythologique dans l'humanisme et dans l'art de la Renaissance* (London: Warburg Institute, 1940), pp. 64–65. Trans., Barbara F. Sessions (New York: Harper and Row, 1961), p. 66

251 Erasmus refers to the *philosophia Christi* as 'heavenly' in *Ratio*, H, pp. 178, 192, 203, 204; *LB*, V, 76A, 83D, 89B, 89D.

252 Seznec, *La survivance des dieux antiques*, pp. 68–69

253 'Nec minima pars humanarum calamitatum est *Alcumistica*, quae doctis etiam et cordatis viris imponit, adeo morbus hic adlubescit, si quem corripuerit.' 'De utilitatem colloquiorum,' *ASD*, 1–3, p. 746, 201–202

254 'Scoto malim infectum Christum quam istis neniis.' To Wolfgang, Faber Capito, *EE*, III, 253 (no. 798, 22–23)

255 Sibyl Moholy–Nagy, *Matrix of Man: An Illustrated History of Urban Environment* (New York, etc.: Frederick A. Praeger, 1968), p. 43, 44

256 Ibid., 58, 60–61

257 Ibid., 64–65

258 Moholy–Nagy's reference to Augustine's City of God is problematical in this context as it is doubtful that the saint meant an earthly fortified city. Whether the treatise *De civitate Dei* did influence the development of urban plans can only be resolved by scholars knowledgeable in the history of early mediaeval urbanism.

259 Ibid., 66–67. For an illustrated history of urban development in Erasmus' native Holland, see Gerald L. Burke, *The Making of Dutch Towns: A Study in Urban Development from the Tenth to the Seventeenth Centuries* (London: Cleaver–Hume, 1956).

260 Morris Bishop, *The Horizon Book of the Middle Ages* (New York: American Heritage, 1968), p. 168

261 'Le fait essentiel d'urbanisme médiévale est la constitution des villes dont toutes les lignes convergent vers un centre et dont le contour est généralement circulaire: c'est ce que les théoreticiens contemporains appellent le système radio-concentrique.' Pierre

Lavedan, *Historie de l'Urbanisme*, vol. I: *Antiquité–Moyen Age* (Paris: Henri Laurens, 1941), p. 250

262 Lewis Mumford, *The City in History: Its Origens, Its Transformations, and Its Prospects* (New York: Harcourt, Brace and World, 1961), p. 303

263 Ibid., 305–306

264 Rudolf Wittkower, *Architectural Principles in the Age of Humanism* (3d ed. rev.; London: Alec Tiranti, 1962), pp. 1–32

265 Readers interested in the history of hermeneutics might compare the mediaeval use of architectural symbols. See Henri de Lubac, *Exégèse médiévale: Les quatre sens de l'Ecriture* (Paris: Aubier, 1959–1964), IV, 41–60.

266 See this chapter, n. 68.

267 'Ne moveatur haec columna, ut sit, cui innixi adversus huius mundi vim semper in deterius et prolabentis et rapientis obsistamus. Maneat solidum illud et nullis opinionum flatibus aut persecutionum procellis cessurum fundamentum, cui tuto bonus architectus superstruat aurum, argentum et lapides pretiosos.' *Ratio,* *H*, p. 204, 16–21; *LB*, V, 89E. This follows the warning about navigating by Christ rather than by Cynosura. One might imagine this columnar Christ as a tun, like the beacons of timber or stone which marked estuarine channels and ports. The tun was a navigational device in Erasmus' day. See, Waters, *The Art of Navigation in England in Elizabethan and Early Stuart Times*, p. 10.

268 '... quod exustis humanarum commentationum stipulis fenoque.' *Ratio, H*, p. 204, 21–22; *LB*, V, 89E. 'Intolerabilius autem fit, quod cotidie nova conduntur atque his ceu sacris et *akinētois* Babylonicas turres in caelum usque surgentes substruimus.' Ibid., *H*, p. 205, 20–22; *LB*, V, 90B

269 'Illic solidis scripturarum fundamentis innixum aedificium surgit in altum, hic futilibus hominum argutiis aut etiam adulationibus non minus inanis quam immanis superstructa machina tollitur in immensum.' Ibid., *H*, p. 190, 3–7; *LB*, V, 82B

270 'Templum Deo sacrum dicitur aedificium pontificum verbis et unctione dicatum, intus templum vere sacrum est animus dei simulacrum referens nec ullum turpitudinis idolum admittens.' Ibid., *H*, p. 265, 14–17; *LB*, V, 120A. '... divinae sapientiae

scholam, seu templum verius.' Ibid., *H*, p. 179, 1–2; *LB*, v, 76B.
Ibid., *H*, pp. 221, 7–10; 258, 30–31; 264, 7; cf. 209, 30–31; 257,
18–19; *LB*, v, 97C, 116D, 119C; cf. 91E, 115F.

271 '... hi se faciunt Christianae religionis columnas.' Ibid., *H*, p. 305,
21–22; *LB*, v, 138C

272 'A studio theologiae abhorrebat, quod sentiret animum non
propensum vt omnia illorum fundamenta subuerteret, deinde
futurum vt haeretici nomen inureretur.' *Compendium vitae, EE*, I, p.
50, 111–113

273 Joseph Lortz, *The Reformation in Germany*, trans. Ronald Walls
(London: Darton, Longman and Todd; New York: Herder and
Herder, 1968), I, 139

274 Mahnke, *Unendliche Sphäre und Allmittelpunkt*, pp. 43–144

275 'Circularis, imo circulus perfectissimus, est ipse Christus, in quo
duae extremitates linae velut in puncto uniuntur.' Bonaventure,
Opera omnia, ed. A.C. Peltier (Paris: Ludovicus Vivès, 1866), vol.
VII: *De ecclesiastica hierarchia*, IV, vi, p. 490. For an interpretation of
Bonaventure's christocentricity, see Ewart H. Cousins, 'The Two
Poles of St. Bonaventure's Theology,' in *S. Bonaventura
1274–1974*, vol. IV: *Theologica* (Rome: College of St Bonaventure,
1974), pp. 153–176.

276 Nicholas of Cusa, *De docta ignorancia* in *Opera*, I, Bk. III, viii, f.
d v

277 *New Testament Apocrypha*, ed. E. Hennecke, ed. W.
Schneemelcher (London: Lutterworth, 1965), II, pp. 227–228.
Trans., Ernest Best et al

278 Plotinus, *Opera*, vol. III: ENNEAS, ed. Paul Henry and
Hans–Rudolf Schwyzer (Paris: Desclée de Brouwer, 1951), Bk. VI,
ix, 8, pp. 321–322

279 'Is filius Dei, qui solus novit Patrem, docuit imitationem patris, et
jussit sui perfecti essent, sicuti Pater in celis. Cujusmodi autem
perfectio illa celestis in hominibus sit, docuit ipse Jesus homo
celestis sua ipsa vita, quasi loquens expressius et instruens
homines. Quam profecto est omnium totis conatibus imitari, qui
illius tam re quam nomine haberi volunt, et tanquam ad commune
signum, propositum omnibus, illuc dirigere vitam, ut prope quasi
sagittantes ad vitam, ipsam vitam lucrentur, qua mensurabuntur

omnia.' John Colet, *Opera*, vol. II: *Enarratio in epistolam primam S. Pauli ad Corinthios*, ed. and trans., J.H. Luption (London: Bell and Daldy, 1867–1876; reprinted Ridgewood, N.J.: Gregg, 1965–1966), pp. 208–209. Trans., p. 70

Chantraine also mentions that Erasmus may have been influenced by this passage, *'Mystère'* et *'Philosophie du Christ'* selon Erasme, p. 123.

280 Colet, *Enarratio in epistolam primam S. Pauli ad Corinthios*, ed. Luption, p. 70, n. 1

281 Erasmus does employ *scopus* as the mark towards which an athlete runs in 'Aliptae futurum athletam iam tum a puero delectum fingunt ac formant in futura certamina et ad scopum suum omnia destinant.' *Ratio, H*, p. 193, 16–18; *LB*, V, 83F. In *De pueris instituendis* he uses *scopus* to designate a target in the pedagogical example of the boy who aimed with bow and arrow at a target painted with Greek or Roman letters and was rewarded by his father with a cherry for every hit: 'Quidam itaque solertis ingenii pater, animaduertens in filio miram iaculandi voluptatem, bellissimum acrum ac sagittas perpulchras parauit, in omnibus tum arcu, tum sagittis erant depictae literae. Deinde scoporum vice, graecarum primum, deinde latinarum literarum figuras proposuit.' *ASD*, 1–2, p. 70, 23–26; *LB*, I, 511F

282 Colet, *Enarratio in epistolarm primam S. Pauli ad Corinthios*, ed. Luption, p. 70, n. 1

283 'Tout microcosme, toute région habitée, a ce qu'on pourrait appeler un "Centre" c'est-à-dire un lieu sacré par excellence. C'est là, dans ce Centre, que le sacré se manifest d'une manière totale.' Mircea Eliade, *Images et symboles: essais sur le symbolisme magico-religieux* (Paris: Gallimard, 1952), p. 49. Trans., Philip Mairet (London: Harvill, 1961), p. 39. Ibid., 49–52

284 See Pseudo-Dionysius the Areopagite as the determinant of mediaeval hierarchical conceptions.

285 1 Cor 12:12–26; Eph 1:22–23, 4:12, 15–16; Col 1:18–24. Cf. '... corpus universum ecclesiae.' *Ratio, H*, p. 206, 20; *LB*, V, 90F. '... ecclesiam quae Christi corpus est.' Ibid., *H*, p. 285, 17–18; *LB*, V, 127F

286 Ernst H. Kantorowicz, *The King's Two Bodies: A Study in*

Mediaeval Political Theology (Princeton: Princeton University Press, 1957), pp. 193–232; Otto Gierke, *Political Theories of the Middle Ages*, trans. Frederic W. Maitland (Cambridge: Cambridge University Press, 1927), pp. 22–30

287 Plato, PHAIDROS, 264c. Trans., Jowett, I, 268

288 See this chapter, n. 86.

289 *Ratio*, H, pp. 202–203, 32–5; *LB*, V, 88F–89A

290 'Sic et Christus ad discipulorum imbecillitatem sese frequenter accommodabat. Sic Paulus multa indulgebat Corinthiis.' Ibid., H, p. 203, 6–8; *LB*, V, 89A

291 'Ideo venit tantus legatus, ut ingens amoris incendium excitaret, et ob id ignem vocat. Magna est naturae caritas; at haec prae Christi caritate glacies est.' Ibid., H, p. 239, 1–3; *LB*, V, 106D

292 See this chapter, nn. 237–240.

293 Aristotle, OURANOU, 293b

294 '... in his, qui vere sapiunt Christum, qui ardent, qui vivunt aguntque, qui veram pietatem et docent et praestant.' *Ratio*, H, pp. 296–297, 34–4; *LB*, V, 133E. Erasmus discourses on Paul's *ignea lingua,* ibid., H, p. 243, 3–13; *LB*, V, 108E.

295 Ibid., H, pp. 203–204; *LB*, V, 89A–D

296 Cf. the verbs *rapere, transformare, vertere* in Erasmus' description of nature's elemental activity (ibid., H, pp. 202–203; *LB*, V, 88F–89A) with the verbs used to describe the goal of true theology, *mutare, rapere, transformare,* this chapter, n. 86.

297 Mohl, *The Three Estates in Medieval and Renaissance Literature,* pp. 332–340

298 Gal 3:28

299 *Inquisitio de fide*, ed. Craig R. Thompson (New Haven: Yale University Press, 1950), pp. 70–71, 307–340

300 Pico deila Mirandola, *De hominis dignitate* in *Opera omnia*, ed. Eugenio Garin (Basel, 1572; reprinted Turin: Bottega d'Erasmo, 1971), I, 314–315

301 See this chapter, n. 161.

302 '... episcopus, qui totus inuigilat gregi dominico.' 'De rebus et vocabulis,' *Colloquia, ASD*, 1–3, p. 567, 37. This phrase occurs in a series of definitions of the social classes. Cf. *LB*, IV, 482A

303 *Ratio*, H, p. 198, 10; *LB*, V, 86C–D

304 '... nec usquam spectanti nisi ad huius gloriam.' Ibid., *H*, p. 198,
12; *LB*, v, 86D

305 'Nam in hoc corpore qui modo pes erat, oculus fieri potest.' To
Paul Volz, *EE*, III, 369 (no. 858, 297)

306 See this chapter, n. 86.

307 Howard R. Patch, *The Tradition of the Goddess Fortuna in Roman
Literature and in the Transitional Period* (Northampton, Mass.:
Smith College, 1922), pp. 138, 135, 154, 142, 152–153, 149, 156,
145

308 '... a corpore ad spiritum, a mundo visibili ad invisibilem, a
littera ad mysterium, a sensibilibus ad intelligibilia, ad compositis
ad simplicia.' *Enchiridion, H*, p. 88, 25–28; *LB*, v, 38F–39A

309 *Silenoi Alkibiadou*, i.e. *Sileni Alcibiadis*, apud eruditos in
proverbium abiisse videntur, certe in Collectaneis Graecorum
proverbii vice referuntur, quo licebit uit, vel de re, quae cum in
speciem, et prima, quod ajunt, fronte vilis ac ridicula videatur,
tamen interius ac propius contemplanti, sit admirabilis: vel de
homine, qui habitu vultuque longe minus prae se ferat, quam in
animo claudat. Ajunt enim Silenos imagunculas quaspiam fuisse
sectiles, et ita factas, ut diduci et explicari possent, et quae clausae
ridiculam ac monstrosam tibicinis speciem habebant, apertae subito
Numen ostendebant, ut artem scalptoris gratiorem jocosus faceret
error.' *Adagia*, III, iii, 1; *LB*, II, 770C–D. Trans., Margaret Mann
Phillips, *The 'Adages' of Erasmus: A Study with Translations*
(Cambridge: University Press, 1964), p. 269

310 Ibid., 770D–771D. 'An non mirisicus Silenus fuit Christus?' Ibid.,
771D. Trans., Mann Phillips, p. 271. Ibid., 772A–D, 773C–D. '... hic
e diverso, quae minime cernuntur oculis, quaeque longissimae
recesserunt a natura corporum, ea sola sectatur, caeteris aut
praeteritis, aut contemptius adhibitis ab intimis illis omne rerum
judicium ducens.' Ibid., 774C–D. Trans., Mann Phillips, p. 278

311 The hermetic cryptogram V.I.T.R.I.O.L.: 'Visita interiora terrae;
rectificando invenies occultum lapidem.'

312 See this chapter, n. 214.

313 John W. Aldridge, *The Hermeneutic of Erasmus*, BST, II (Zürich:
EVZ, 1966)

314 J. Huizinga, *Erasmus of Rotterdam*, trans. F. Hopman (London:

Phaidon, 1952), p. 101. For fresh evaluation of Erasmus' use of symbol, figure, and allegory, see, Sister Geraldine Thompson, *Under Pretext of Praise: Satiric Mode in Erasmus' Fiction* (Toronto: University of Toronto Press, 1973).

315 De Lubac, *Exégèse médiévale*, IV, 440–453; John B. Payne, 'Toward the Hermeneutics of Erasmus,' *Scrinium Erasmianum*, ed. Coppens, II, 35–47; Chantraine, *'Mystère' et 'Philosophie du Christ' selon Erasme*, pp. 316–362. I have only capsulized here the scholarship of these authors which deserves more detailed examination by readers interested in Erasmus' hermeneutics.

316 'Christus aliquoties fallit suos ad tempus allegoriarum aenigmatibus.' *Ratio*, H, p. 263, 30–31; *LB*, V, 119B. Examples: *H*, pp. 263–264; *LB*, V, 119B–C. Ibid., *H*, pp. 262–263, 12–28; *LB*, V, 118C–119A. Ibid., *H*, p. 284, 23–24; *LB*, V, 127D; *H*, pp. 188–189, 8–14; *LB*, V, 81B–E

317 '... litterarum omnium principem.' To John Colet, *EE*, I, 247 (no. 108, 49)

318 *De copia*, *LB*, I, 6E–7A. '... atque in his vigilantibus oculis figuras omneis observemus, observatas memoria recondamus, reconditas imitemur, crebraque usurpatione consuescamus habere in promptu.' Ibid., 7A. Trans., King and Rix, pp. 17–18

319 'Horum igitur commentationes te malo evolvere, utpote qui non ad scholasticam concertationem, sed ad bonam mentem te instituam.' *Enchiridion*, H, p. 72, 8–10; *LB*, V, 30B

320 'A divinis oraculis nomen habet theologus, non ab humanis opinionibus.' *Ratio*, H, p. 305, 14–15; *LB*, V, 138B

321 '... ut in oratione cuiusque relucet imago mentis praesertim in Christo, qui cum esset summa simplicitas veritasque, nihil omnino poterat esse dissimilitudinis inter archetypum divini pectoris et inde ductam imaginem sermonis. Ut nihil patri similius quam filius patris verbum ex intimo illius corde promanans, ita Christo nihil similius quam Christi verbum de pectoris illius sanctissimi adytis redditum.' *Enchiridion*, H, p. 75, 18–24; *LB*, V, 32A. Trans., Himelick, p. 112. Cf. Augustine who characterizes Christ as the utterance of the Father's heart in *Enarratio in psalmum*, ed. Dekkers and Fraipont, XLIV, 5, p. 497.

322 See this chapter, n. 70.

323 *Ratio, H*, pp. 188–189, 8–14; *LB*, v, 81B–E

324 '... quomodo iuxta allegoricum, qui capitis ac totius corporis mystici tractat arcana.' Ibid., *H*, p. 284, 5–6; *LB*, v, 127B

325 Aristotle, POIĒTIKĒS, 1448b. *The Basic Works of Aristotle*, ed. Richard McKeon and trans. Ingram Bywater (New York: Random House, 1941), p. 1457. Ibid.

326 '... sive hace difficultate segnitiem nostram exercere voluit.' *Ratio, H*, p. 260, 1–2; *LB*, v, 117B. Erasmus lists other motives for allegory, ibid., ll. 3–5; *LB*, v, 117B. '... ut postea gratior esset fructus.' Ibid., l. 2; *LB*, v, 117B. 'Neque vero tantum ad docendum ac persuadendum efficax est parabola.' Ibid., ll. 10–11; *LB*, v, 117C

327 '... verum etiam ad commovendos affectus, ad delectandum.' *Ratio, H*, p. 260, 11–12; *LB*, v, 117C

328 '... studiorum profectum mutua animorum benevolentia potissimum constare, unde et humanitatis literas appellavere prisci.' *De pueris instituendis, ASD*, 1–2, p. 69, 5–7; *LB*, I, 511A. Trans., William H. Woodward, *Desiderius Erasmus concerning the Aim and Method of Education* (Cambridge: University Press, 1904), p. 214

329 'Nihil autem vetat quo minus voluptati comes sit utilitas, et iucunditati iuncta sit honestas.' Ibid., ll. 8–9; *LB*, I, 511A. 'Tum autem sunt quaedam et cognitu iucunda et puerilibus ingeniis quasi cognata, quae discere ludus est potius quam labor.' Ibid., p. 24, 14–15; *LB*, I, 489C. Cf. ibid., p. 53, 17–18; *LB*, I, 503E. *De ratione studii, ASD*, 1–2, p. 125, 4–5; *LB*, I, 523F

330 *Ratio, H*, p. 260, 27–31; *LB*, v, 117C. Ibid., *H*, p. 261, 6–9; *LB*, v, 117E

331 See chapter 2, n. 117.

332 'Sic gratior est veritas deprehensa, quae nos prius torserit aenigmatis involucro.' *Ratio, H*, p. 262, 5–6; *LB*, v, 118C

333 Jean Leclercq, *L'Amour des lettres et le désir de Dieu: initiation aux auteurs monastiques du moyen age* (Paris: Cerf, 1957)

334 *De contemptu mundi epistola*, xi, *LB*, v, 1257B

335 Chapter 4

336 *Ratio, H*, p. 274, 24–32; *LB*, v, 124E–125A

337 Ibid., *H*, pp. 188, 190, 191; *LB*, v, 81B, 82B, 82F. 'Sunt, qui ludant verbis scripturae divinae, ac veluti fit in centonibus poetarum, ad alienum sensum ceu per iocum abutuntur.' Ibid., *H*,

p. 287, 19–21; *LB*, v, 129A. Erasmus frequently uses *torquere* to describe the scholastic abuse of language, e.g., ibid., *H*, pp. 279, 282, 284, 291, 297; *LB*, v, 125D, 125F, 126D, 127D–E, 130F, and especially 134A where he catalogues examples of the distortion of Scripture by logic. 'Nam quod hodie quidam, si quando festivi student videri, verba mystica depravant ad iocos scurriles, non solum indoctum est verum etiam impium et supplicio dignum.' Ibid., *H*, p. 287, 24–26; *LB*, v, 129A. 'Quid enim tam dispar ac discrepans a stilo prophetarum, Christi et apostolorum quam hoc, quo qui Thomam ac Scotum sequuntur, nunc de rebus divinis disputant?' Ibid., *H*, p. 191, 24–26; *LB*, v, 83A

338 Ibid., *H*, pp. 266–272; *LB*, v, 120C–123C

339 'Si in ieiunis, in frigidis, in fucatis, in spinosis ac rixosis scriptoribus assidui simis, tales evadamus oportet; sin in his qui vere sapiunt Christum, qui ardent, qui vivunt aguntque, qui veram pietatem et docent et praestant.' Ibid., *H*, pp. 296–297, 34–4; *LB*, v, 133E; cf. ibid., *H*, p. 243, 3–13; LB, v, 108E. 'Ideo venit tantus legatus, ut ingens amoris incendium excitaret, et ob id ignem vocat. Magna est naturae caritas; at haec prae Christi caritate glacies est.' Ibid., *H*, p. 239, 1–3; *LB*, v, 106D

340 'Atque ideo res in oratore praecipua consilium est, quia uarie et ad rem momenta conuertitur.' Quintilian, *Institutio oratoria*, ed. Winterbottom, I, Bk. II, xiii, p. 101

341 *Ratio, H*, pp. 211–215; *LB*, v, 92E–94C, 105D–E. 'Adeo cum nostro Christo nihil sit simplicius, tamen arcano quodam consilio Proteum quemdam representat varietate vitae atque doctrinae.' Ibid., *H*, p. 214, 31–33; *LB*, v, 94B

342 'Haec omnibus ex aequo sese accommodat, submittit se parvulis, ad illorum modulum sese attemperat, lacte illos alens, ferens, confovens, sustinens, omnia faciens, donec grandescamus in Christo.' *Paraclesis, H*, p. 141–142, 35–2; *LB*, v, 140A. Trans., Olin, p. 96

343 'Iam paucis, si libet, conferamus, quemadmodum ad magistri formam apostolorum vita doctrinaque respondeat.' *Ratio, H*, p. 223, 32–33; *LB*, v, 98F. Paul as *chamaeleonta*, ibid., *H*, l. 34; *LB*, v, 98F; as *polypus*, ibid., *H*, p. 248, 31; *LB*, v, 111D

344 'Quod si nunc labor hic interrumperetur, nunquam animo meo

queam imperare vt rursum sese in huiusmodi pistrinum immittat.
Nunc dum captus est Proteus, stringenda sunt vincula, donec in se
reuersus oraculum absoluat.' To Paschasius Berselius, *EE*, III, 192
(no. 756, 21–24)

345 Of many books on allegory, the most helpful for orienting this
analysis has been Angus Fletcher, *Allegory: The Theory of a
Symbolic Mode* (Ithaca, N.Y.: Cornell University Press, 1965).

346 See the discussion of *kosmos* as 'ornament,' ibid., 108–120.

347 Maurice Merleau–Ponty, 'Le langage indirect et les voix du
silence,' in *Signes* (Paris: Gallimard, 1960), pp. 49–104

348 'Neque vero confundit hanc harmoniam Christi varietas; immo
sicut e diversis vocibus apte compositis concentur suavissimus
redditur, ita Christi varietas pleniorem efficit concentum.' *Ratio, H*,
p. 211, 28–30; *LB*, V, 92E

349 'In his haec quoque servanda regula, ut sensus, quem ex obscuris
verbis elicimus, respondeat ad orbem illum doctrinae Christianae,
respondeat ad illius vitam, denique respondeat ad aequitatem
naturalem.' Ibid., *H*, p. 286, 1–4; *LB*, V, 128B

350 See Chapter I, n. 66.

351 Plato, CRATULOS, 421d–427d

352 Ibid., 394a–422b, 426c–427, 437a–c. Ibid., 389a, 390d. Ibid.,
394a–422b, 426c–427d, 437a–c

353 Plato, PHAIDROS, 229e. Trans., Jowett, I, 235. Ibid., 229d.
Trans., ibid., Ibid., 229e–230a. Trans., ibid., 235–236

354 '... semper sub paedagogis agentes, semper sub iugo, nec unquam
ad libertatem spiritus aspirantes, nunquam ad amplitudinem
caritatis crescentes.' *Enchiridion, H*, p. 81, 23–26; *LB*, V, 35B

355 'Accommodavit sese his, quos ad sese trahere studebat.' *Ratio, H*,
p. 222, 7–8; *LB*, V, 97F

356 Chantraine, *'Mystère' et 'Philosophie du Christ' selon Erasme*. He
argues 'la motivation profonde, qui est l'idée de mystère,' p. 45.
Erasmus' *Ratio* is the flowering of a mysterious sacral relationship
between good letters and friendship, as revealed in his early
monastic correspondence. The *Ratio* resolves the personal quandry:
'Le christianisme est source de beauté: comment peut-on etre un
poète chrétien et ne pas s'y abreuver?' p. 49. Charmed by poetic
beauty, Erasmus divines its source in sacred mystery and aims in

the *Ratio* to restore the purity of that mystery, p. 56. Theology is defined for Erasmus by Chantraine as 'initiation aux mystères. Elle est comme une liturgie qui après la procession d'entrée, se déploi dans le Temple et en découvre le mystère,' p. 364.

It is not possible here to argue and to detail the differences in research and interpretation between my book and those of other scholars who have commented on the *Ratio*. If one example might be given, however, it can be noted that I have attempted to read Erasmus' theology in the context of Renaissance humanism and the classical currents which fed it. Chantraine only reads Erasmus 'par rapport à la théologie patristique, à la "théologie monastique," et à la théologie luthérienne,' p. 263. One result is that his first conclusion, i.e. that the words *harmonia, varietas, concentus, orbis, circulus, consensus, fabula,* and *accomodatio* 'appartiennent au vocabulaire de *mysterium*,' p. 363, overlooks the fact that these are terms of classical rhetoric. But this only a sample of what I understand to be broader differences between the readings of Erasmus other theologians have offered and mine.

357 Hoffmann, *Erkenntnis und Verwirklichung der wahren Theologie nach Erasmus von Rotterdam.* This scholar deploys the *Ratio* as a heuristic for determining the 'Einheit und Ordnung im Erasmischen Denken,' p. 221. Assuming that Erasmus has evolved a theological system (pp. 27ff.), an idea that appears popular with German scholars since Kohls, Hoffmann decides that the epistemological and ontological pivot of that system is a kind of dialectic, especially between theological knowledge and its practical application, p. 52.

358 'The starting point for Erasmus' hermeneutics, as indeed for his whole theology, is the neo-Platonic conception of the contrast between flesh and spirit, which is grounded in the nature of the world and of man.' Payne, 'Toward the Hermeneutic of Erasmus,' *Scrinium Erasmianum*, ed. Coppens, II, 17

359 'For Erasmus theology did not begin with true propositions but with the life experiences of persons.' Albert Rabil, Jr., *Erasmus and the New Testament* (San Antonio: Trinity University Press, 1972), p. 141

360 Mc Conica, 'Erasmus and the Grammar of Consent,' *Scrinium Erasmianum*, ed. Coppens, II, 78–79

361 Cf. Kohls' claim for 'das universale christozentrische System,' *Die Theologie des Erasmus*, I, 175–177

362 *logos* is occasionally asserted as an inspiration for Erasmus, although that claim has been neither researched nor developed prior to this book. Oskar Linkenheil proposed that the discernment of the *logos* in the labours of ancient and modern man, a counterpart to the birth of Jesus of Nazareth, transformed Erasmus' life and was the source of his interior rebirth. 'Terminus,' *Ethik*, XIII (1936), 23–24. Kohls mentions the influence of the Alexandrian *logos* theology, especially Origen's, as does André Godin. See my disagreement, pp. 24–25. Lewis Spitz claims the influence of Justin Martyr's theory of the spermatic *logos*. See Chapter 1, n. 180. Hoffmann states that 'Für Erasmus ist der wahre, eigentliche Logos jedoch mit dem scopus oder archetypus Christus gleich,' *Erkenntnis und Virwirklichung der wahren Theologie nach Erasmus von Rotterdam*, p. 197. Sister Geraldine Thompson concludes her book, *Under Pretext of Praise*, with the comment that for Erasmus the human production of the right word aligns man with the *logos*, pp. 179–180. My own interpretation was conceived and executed independently of this literature.

FOUR: CONFABULATIO

1 See Chapter 2, p. 37.

2 'Proteus enim est proprie sermo Dei, omnia transformans sese in miracula rerum. Quem Sermonem si fide tenere, si studio colere, si amore complecti institerimus, docebit nos ille omnia quae sint, quae fuerint, quae mox uentura trahentur.' Guillaume Budé, *De transitu Hellenismi ad Christianismum* in *Opera omnia* (Basel: N. Episcopius Jr., 1557, reprinted Westmead: Gregg 1966), I, Bk. III, f. 239B.

3 'Ex his sint omnia Christianorum omnium colloquia. Tales enim ferme sumus, quales sunt cotidiane nostrae confabulationes. Assequatur quisque quod potest, exprimat quisque quod potest.' *Paraclesis, H*, p. 142, 23–26; *LB*, V, 140C. Trans., Olin, p. 97

4 'Confabulatio pia,' in *Colloquia, ASD*, I–3, pp. 171–181; *LB*, I, 648–653

5 'Utinam hinc ad stivam aliquid decantet agricola, hinc nonnihil ad

radios suos moduletur textor, huismodi fabulis itineris taedium lenet viator.' *Paraclesis, H,* p. 142, 21–23; *LB,* v, 140C

6 'Huic simillimum est lemma: "Si populo fas sit tractare Sacros Libros, periculum esse, ne quando veniant in locum parum honestum, et contrectentur manibus corio aut sebo unctis." O graves rationes! quasi Sacri Libri non dignentur jacere, nisi inter pulvillos sericos, neque contractari manibus, nisi balsamo unctis.' *Apologia adversus debacchationes Petri Sutoris, LB,* IX, 786B–C. Cf. the paraphrase by Roland Bainton, *Erasmus of Christendom* (New York: Scribners, 1969), p. 141, as 'Do you think that the Scriptures are fit only for the perfumed?', which misses the force of Erasmus' thrust at priests, who are anointed at ordination.

7 'Doctos esse vix paucis contingit, at nulli non licet esse Christianum, nulli non licet esse pium, addam audactur illud: nulli non licet esse theologum.' *Paraclesis, H,* p. 145, 1–3; *LB,* v, 141F. Trans., Olin, p. 100

8 'Socrates philosophiam e coelo deduxit in terras, ego philosophiam etiam in lusus, confabulationes et compotationes deduxi.' 'De vtilitate colloquiorum,' in *Colloquia, ASD,* 1–3, p. 746, 179–180; *LB,* I, 905B. Trans., Craig R. Thompson, *The Colloquies of Erasmus* (Chicago: University of Chicago Press, 1965), p. 630

9 Cf. '... sed quod negari non potest, ad paucos homines contrahimus rem, qua Christus nihil voluit esse communius.' *Paraclesis, H,* p. 144, 33–35; *LB,* v, 141E

10 Cf. 'Cur sic arctamus Christi professionem quam ille latissime voluit patere? Si magnificis vocabulis commouemur, quaeso te, quid aliud est ciuitas quam magnum monasterium?' To Paul Volz, *EE,* III, 376 (no. 858, 559–61)

11 'Conuiuium religiosum,' in *Colloquia, ASD,* 1–3, pp. 231–266; *LB,* I, 672C–689E. This is one of six colloquies which are 'feasts.'

Other scholars have defined the 'Conuiuium religiosum' as an exemplar of 'Christian humanism': 'More than any, perhaps, the Godly Feast (*Convivium religiosum*) embodies the blend of classical and Christian idealism,' Margaret Mann Phillips, 'Erasmus and the Classics' in *Erasmus,* ed. T.A. Dorey (Albuquerque: University of New Mexico Press, 1970), p. 27; '... this colloquy provides the key to his special kind of Christian humanism. It embodies Erasmus' dream of a life lived in harmonious intercourse with friends, simple yet civilised, beautiful yet devout,' Wilhelm Schenck, 'The Erasmian Ideal,' *HJ*, XLVII (1950), 262; 'Few dialogues of the same scope, whether in Latin or English, furnish better examples of what is embraced by so called Christian humanism,' Thompson, *The Colloquies of Erasmus*, p. 114

12 'Nos philosophi sumus.' 'Conuiuium religiosum,' *ASD*, 1–3, p. 231, 15; *LB*, I, 672D

13 'Gardens and country houses were so common as settings for dialogues in the Renaissance, as in classical, literature, that we may be sure Erasmus was deliberately following literary tradition in describing Eusebius' house and grounds.' Thompson, *The Colloquies of Erasmus*, p. 46

14 'Itaque studiosus ille velut apicula diligens, per omnes auctorum hortos volitabit, flosculis omnibus adsultabit, undique succi nonnihil colligens, quod in suum deferat alvearium.' *De copia*, *LB*, I, 102A. Trans., King and Rix, p. 90

15 'Illic velut in felicissmis hortis affatim tum oblectaberis tum expleberis, dum hic inter spineta sterilia dilaceraris ac torqueris.' *Ratio*, *H*, p. 190, 7–9; *LB*, V, 82B. Erasmus often characterizes scholastic disputation as 'thorny,' e.g., ibid., *H*, p. 189, 19; p. 297, 1; *LB*, V, 81F, 133E.

'Horres contagium pestis corporalis multo magis vitanda morum pestilentium contagio. Res elegans tibi videtur hortus omni florum et arborum genere vernans; quale spectaculum animus innocentia virens ac virtutum omni genere exuberans.' Ibid., *H*, p. 283, 14–17; *LB*, V, 126F. This occurs in the context of comparison between the philosophy of Christ and Scotist augmentation.

16 'Conuiuium religiosum,' *ASD*, 1–3, p. 233, 65–79; p. 234, 80–84; *LB*, I, 673B–C. Trans., Thompson, pp. 49–50

17 *Dialogus, Julius Exclusis e coelis* in *Erasmi Opuscula: A Supplement to the Opera Omnia*, ed. Wallace K. Ferguson (The Hague: Martinus Nijhoff, 1933), pp. 65–124

18 'In altari Iesus Christus suspiciens in coelum ad Patrem et Spiritum Sanctum illinc prospicientes atque eodem dextram porrigens leua velut inuitat et allectat praetereuntem.' 'Conuiuium religiosum,' *ASD*, 1–3, p. 234, 86–88; *LB*, I, 673C–D. Trans., Thompson, p. 50.

Ibid., ll. 89–91; *LB*, 1, 673D. '... per se trahat nos ad se.' Ibid., l. 97; *LB*, 1, 673D. Trans., Thompson, p. 50

19 '... repraesentans vnicum illum fontem, qui coelesti latice refocillat omnes laborantes et oneratos, et ad quem anhelat anima delassata malis huius mundi, non aliter quam, iuxta psalmistam, ceruus aestuans siti.' Ibid., ll. 103–106; *LB*, 1, 673E. Trans., Thompson, p. 51. Cf. Jn 4: 13–14.

20 See Chapter 3, n. 58.

21 'Balbinus. Ego affatim hausi e fonte Scoti.
'Alypius. Non ille fons est Musarum, sed lacus ranarum.'
'Epithalamium Petri Aegidii,' *Colloquia*, *ASD*, 1–3, p. 412, 24–25; *LB*, 1, 746F

22 'Conuiuium religiosum,' *ASD*, 1–3, pp. 234–235, 106–112; *LB*, 1, 673E–674A. 'Totus hic locus voluptati dicatus est, sed honestae, pascendis oculis, recreandis naribus, reficiendis animis.' Ibid., ll. 113–114; *LB*, 1, 674A. Trans., Thompson, p. 51

23 See Chapter 3, nn. 328–329.

24 '... alii domos habent opulentas, ego loquacissimam habeo.'
'Conuiuium religiosum,' *ASD*, 1–3, p. 235, 118; *LB*, 1, 674A. Trans., Thompson, p. 51

25 Ibid., ll. 114–117, 123–124; *LB*, 1, 674A–B. Ibid., p. 237, 185; *LB*, 1, 675A. Trans., Thompson, p. 53. Ibid., pp. 263–264, 1112–1028; *LB*, 1, 688C–E. Ibid., p. 264, 1034–1039; *LB*, 1, 688F. Ibid., pp. 264–265, 1052–1058; *LB*, 1, 689A. Ibid., p. 265, 1058–1064; *LB*, 1, 689B. 'Mira varietas. Nec quicquam est ociosum. Nihil est, quod non aut agat aut loquatur aliquid.' Ibid., p. 237, 183–184; *LB*, 1, 675A. Trans., Thompson, p. 53
On the emblematic character of the dinner service, ibid., p. 248, 520ff.; *LB*, 1, 680C; on the emblematic gifts, ibid., pp. 262–263, 958–1004; *LB*, 1, 687D–688B; and on the emblematic names, see this chapter, p. 140. Ibid., p. 235, 125–139; *LB*, 1, 674B–C

26 See Chapter 3, n. 144.

27 'Praeterea bis delectamur, quum pictum florem cum viuo decertantem videmus, et in altero miramur artificium naturae, in altero pictoris ingenium. In vtroque benignitatem Dei, qui in vsum nostrum largitur haec omnia, nulla in re non mirabilis, pariter et

amabilis.' 'Conuiuium religiosum,' *ASD*, 1–3, p. 236, 158–162; *LB*,
I, 674E. Trans., Thompson, p. 52

28 'Agnoscitis herbae figuram?' Ibid., p. 237, 191; *LB*, I, 675A. 'At non
agnoscis herbam in cuius folium incidit?' Ibid., p. 238, 215; *LB*, I,
675C. Trans., Thompson, pp. 53–54

29 See Chapter 2, n. 29.

30 Ibid.

31 'Haec pascunt oculos et ventrem non explent: properemus ad
reliqua.' 'Conuiuium religiosum,' *ASD*, 1–3, p. 239, 251–252; *LB*,
I, 675F. Trans., Thompson, p. 55

32 See Chapter 3, n. 139.

33 'Lautissimae epulae sunt studium sanctarum scripturarum.'
Enchiridion, H, p. 94, 34–35; *LB*, V, 42C. Trans., Himelick, p. 138.
'Non tam panis cibus est corporis quam animae cibus verbum dei.'
Ibid., H, p. 26, 16–17; *LB*, V, 4C. Trans., Himelick, p. 43. Ibid., H,
pp. 30–31, 35–12; *LB*, V, 6F–7A. Ibid., H, p. 26, 17–21; *LB*, V,
4C

34 'Conuiuium religiosum,' *ASD*, 1–3, p. 241, 316; *LB*, I, 677A.
'Etenim si ethnicis quoque religiosa erat mensa, quanto magis
oportet esse sacram Christianis, quibus habet imaginem quandam
illius sacrosancti conuiuii, quod Dominus Iesus postremum egit
cum suis discipulis.' Ibid., p. 240, 276–279; *LB*, I, 676C

35 'Quid illa sacrosancti panis, et calicis philotesii communio, nisi
novam quamdam et indissolubilem concordiam sanxit?' *Querela
pacis*, *LB*, IV, 631C. '... et Christianos coelestis ille panis, ac
mysticus ille calix non continet in amicitia, quam ipse sanxit
Christus, quam illi quotidie renovant, ac repraesentant sacrificiis?'
Ibid., 632D

36 'Hoc autem symbolum arcanum duabus rebus consecravit, quibus
inter homines olim solet amicitia conciliari: ut ea caritas, qua
Christus seipsum impendit suis, nos quoque copularet.' *Paraphrasis
in evangelium secundum Matthaeum*, *LB*, VII, 133F

37 'Lauemus, amici, vt puris manibus et animis ad mensam
accedamus.' 'Conuiuium religiosum,' *ASD*, 1–3, p. 240, 275–276;
LB, I, 676C. Trans., Thompson, p. 55

38 See Chapter 3, n. 64.

39 '... atque ad divinarum scripturarum cognitionem mire praeparant,

ad quas ilico pedibus manibusque illotis irrumpere paene sacrilegii genus est.' *Enchiridion*, *H*, p. 13–15; *LB*, v, 7E

40 'Aut si Divinas Literas interpretari conetur, Graecae, Latinae, et Hebraicae linguae, denique et omnis antiquitatis rudis et imperitus, sine quibus non stultum modo, verum etiam impium est, Theologiae mysteria tractanda suscipere.' 'Illotis manibus,' *Adagia*, I, ix, 55; *LB*, II, 355A

41 See Chapter 3, n. 64.

42 '... cum baptismus ex aequo communis sit Christianorum omnium, in quo prima Christianae philosophiae professio est.' *Paraclesis*, *H*, p. 142, 29–31; *LB*, v, 140D.

43 'Conuiuium religiosum,' *ASD*, I–3, p. 240, 284–295; *LB*, I, 676C–D

44 'Lectionem subinde interrumpat praecatio.' *Ratio*, *H*, p. 180, 32; *LB*, v, 77C

45 'Id quo magis dignetur et nos tanti hospitis reddamur capaciores, si molestum non est, auscultabitis paululum e sacra lectione.' 'Conuiuium religiosum,' *ASD*, I–3, p. 241, 312–314; *LB*, I, 676F–677A

46 See Chapter 3, n. 144.

47 'Conuiuium religiosum,' *ASD*, I–3, pp. 241–242, 317–339; *LB*, I, 677A–C. Trans., Thompson, pp. 56–57

48 *Enchiridion*, *H*, p. 55, 19–22; p. 22, 6; p. 135, 5; *LB*, v, 19E–20E, 1B, 66C

49 '... aut quis possit secum Aquinatis Secundae secundam circumferre?' To Paul Volz, *EE*, III, 363 (no. 858, 59–60). Trans., Olin, p. 111, with my correction

50 See this chapter, n. 5.

51 'Atque vtinam adesset aliquis vere theologus, qui ista non intellegeret solum, verum etiam saperet. Nobis idiotis nescio an fas sit hisce de rebus confabulari ... Ego vero puto vel nautis esse fas, modo absit definiendi temeritas. Fortasse et Christus, qui pollicitus est sese adfuturum vbicunque duo conuenerint de ipso tractantes, aspirabit nobis tam multis.' 'Conuiuium religiosum,' *ASD*, I–3, pp. 242, 345–349; *LB*, I, 677C. Trans., Thompson, p. 57. Cf. Mt 18:20.

52 Ibid., p. 242, 350; *LB*, I, 677D

53 Ibid., pp. 242–243, 353–383; *LB*, I, 677D–678A. Ibid., p. 244, 389–390; *LB*, I, 678B. Ibid., ll. 392–400; *LB*, I, 678B–C. Ibid., pp.

244–245, 415–424; *LB*, I, 678D–E. Ibid., p. 246, 455–468; *LB*, I, 679C–680A. Ibid., pp. 246–247, 469–505; *LB*, I, 679C–680A. Ibid., pp. 248–251, 535–604; *LB*, I, 680D–681E. Ibid., p. 243, 384–385; *LB*, I, 678A. Ibid., p. 244, 412–414; *LB*, I, 678D. Cf. I Cor 13:12. Trans., Thompson, p. 58

54 Ibid., p. 251, 619; *LB*, I, 682A. Ibid., ll. 614–623; *LB*, I, 681F–682A. Ibid., pp. 251–252, 623–630; *LB*, I, 682A. Ibid., pp. 252–253; 631–666; *LB*, I, 682B–E

55 Ibid., pp. 253–254, 667–710; *LB*, I, 682E–683D. Ibid., pp. 254–258, 713–844; *LB*, I, 683E–685E. Ibid., pp. 258–259, 850–855; *LB*, I, 685F–686A. Ibid., p. 261, 931–938; *LB*, I, 687B–C. Ibid., pp. 265–266, 1086–1094; *LB*, I, 689D–E

56 'Dominus Iesus te feliciter deducat ac reducat.' Ibid., p. 266, 1101; *LB*, I, 689E. Trans., Thompson, p. 77

57 Compare *eusebeia*, *Patristic Greek Lexicon*, ed. G.W.H. Lampe (Oxford: Clarendon Press, 1961), I, 575, and *orthodoxia*, ibid., II, 971. Erasmus appeals to *eusebeia*, for example, in justifying *sermo* when he reminds his readers that Cyprian was not only a learned and eloquent thinker but also a martyr. See Chapter I, n. 101.

For conjecture on the historical identity of these interlocuters see, Preserved Smith, *A Key to the Colloquies of Erasmus* (Cambridge: Harvard University Press, 1927), p. 11

58 Lucian, SUMPOSION Ē LAPITHAI, trans. A.M. Harmon (London: William Heinemann; New York: Macmillan, 1913), I

59 '... colloquia quam frigida, quam inepta, quam non sapientia Christum, conuiuia quam laica.' To Servatius Rogerus, *EE*, I, 567 (no. 296, 57–58). Trans., Mynors and Thomson, I, 296

60 See this chapter, n. 34.

61 'Conuiuium religiosum,' *ASD*, I-3, p. 232, 36–37; *LB*, I, 672F

62 '... qui in apostolorum vices succedunt.' *Ratio*, H, p. 236, 32–33; *LB*, V, 105C

63 See this chapter, n. 51, and 'Conuiuium religiosum,' *ASD*, I-3, p. 265, 1077.

64 'Negant huius disciplinae mysteria percipi posse ab eo cui quicquam omnino commercii sit cum Musis aut cum Gratiis.' To Thomas Grey, *EE*, I, 192 (no. 64, 77–78)

65 'Conuiuium religiosum,' *ASD*, I-3, p. 234, 86–88 (see this chapter,

n. 18; and p. 264, 1037–1039: 'Christus primum habet locum, porrecta manu sedens in monte. Capiti imminet pater dicens: *Ipsum audite*. Spiritus Sanctus expansis alis multa luce complectitur illum.'

66 See this chapter, n. 18.

✄ Bibliography ✄

THIS IS A LIST OF TEXTS CITED *ad fontes*. Full reference to
secondary literature is given in the notes.

I

Vetus Latina. Edited by Bonifatius Fischer. 6 vols. Freiburg:
   Herder, 1949–
Novum Testamentum. Edited and translated by Jerome. Edited
   by John Wordsworth and Henry J. White. Oxford:
   Clarendon Press, 1889–1919
Novum Testamentum. Edited by Desiderius Erasmus of
   Rotterdam. *LB*, VI
New Testament Apocrypha. Edited by E. Hennecke. Edited and
   translated by W. Schneemelcher. 2 vols. London:
   Lutterworth, 1965
Concilium Tridentium. Edited by Societas Goerresiana. 13 vols.
   2d ed. Freiburg: Herder, 1961
Sacrosanctum Oecumenicum Concilium Vaticanum II.
   Constitutiones Decreta Declarationes. Vatican: Polyglot
   Vatican, 1966.

II

Desiderius Erasmus of Rotterdam. *Opera omnia*. Edited by J.
   Clericus. 11 vols. Leiden, 1703–6
– *Opera omnia*. 6 vols. Amsterdam: North Holland, 1971–

- *Erasmi Opuscula: A Supplement to the Opera omnia.* Edited by Wallace K. Ferguson. The Hague: Martinus Nijhoff, 1953
- *Erasmi Epistolae.* Edited by P.S. Allen et al. 12 vols. Oxford: Clarendon Press, 1906–58
- *Ausgewählte Werke.* Edited by Hajo Holborn and Annemarie Holborn. Munich: C.H. Beck, 1964
- *Apologia Erasmi Roterodami palam refellens quorundam seditiosos clamores apud Populum ac Magnates, quibus ut impie factum iactitant, quod in evangelio Ioannis verterit, in principio erat sermo.* [Nürnberg: Friedrich Peypus, c. 1520]
- *Inquisitio de fide.* Edited by Craig R. Thompson. New Haven: Yale University Press, 1950

References to Erasmus' editions of classical and patristic texts are entered below under the author's name.

III

Agricola, Rodolphus. *De inventione dialectica libri omnes.* Cologne, 1523. Reprinted, Frankfurt/M.: Minerva, 1967

Alexander de Villa-Dei. *Doctrinale.* Edited by Dietrich Reichling. MGP, XII. Berlin: A. Hofmann, 1893

Ambrose. *Omnia quotquot extant Divi Ambrosii opera.* Edited by Erasmus et al. 5 vols. in 2. Basel: Froben, 1538
- *Opera.* Edited by Carolus Schenkl et al. CSEL, XXXII, LXII, LXIV, LXXIII, LXXVIII, LXXIX, LXXXII. 7 vols. Vienna: F. Tempsky, 1897
- *Opera.* Edited by M. Adriaen. CCSL, XXVI. Turnholt: Brepols, 1957
- *Tractatus in evangelio secundum Lucam.* Edited by Gabriel Tissot. SC, XXI. 2 vols. Paris: Cerf, 1956

Anselm of Canterbury. *Opera omnia.* Edited by Franciscus Salesius Schmitt. 6 vols. Segovia: Abbey Press, 1938–40 and Edinburgh: T. Nelson, 1946–61

Anselm of Laon et al. *Glossa ordinaria. PL,* CXIV

Aristotle. *Opera.* 2 vols. Darmstadt: Wissenschaftliche
Buchgesellschaft, 1960

Arnobius. *Adversus nationes.* Edited by C. Marchesi. CSLP, LXII.
Turin: I.B. Paravia [1934]

Athanasius. *Opera.* Edited by A.B. Caillau and M.N.S. Guillon.
4 vols. Paris: Méquinon-Harvard, 1830

– KATA ARIANOS LOGOS PROS. Edited by William
Bright. 3 vols. Oxford: Clarendon Press, 1884

– *Select Treatises of S. Athanasius, Archbishop of Alexandria. In
Controversy with the Arians.* Translated by John Henry
Newman. Oxford: J.H. Parker; London: J.G.F. and J.
Rivington, 1842

Augustine. *Opera.* CCSL. 19 vols. Turnholt: Brepols,
1958–

– *Opera. PL,* XXXII–XLVII

– *De trinitate.* Venice: Paganinus de Paganinis, 1489

Balbus, Joannes. *Catholicon.* Mainz, 1460. Reprinted,
Westmead: Gregg, 1971

Boethius, trans. *Topicorum Aristotelis. PL,* LXIV

Bonaventure. *Opera omnia.* Edited by A.C. Peltier. 15 vols.
Paris: Ludovicus Vivès, 1866

Budé, Guillaume. *Opera omnia.* Basel: N. Episcopius, Jr., 1557.
Reprinted, Westmead: Gregg, 1966. 4 vols.

Caxton, William. *Game and Playe of the Chesse.* 1474 ed.
Reprinted, London: Elliot Stock, 1883

Celtis, Konrad. *Der Briefwechsel.* Edited by Hans Rupprich.
Munich: C.H. Beck, 1934

Cicero. *De natura deorum.* Cambridge: Harvard University
Press; London: William Heinemann, 1961

– *De oratore.* Edited and translated by H. Rackham. London:
William Heinemann; Cambridge: University Press, 1942

– *De partitione oratoria.* Edited and translated by H. Rackham.
Cambridge: University Press, 1942

– *De re publica.* Edited and translated by T.E. Page et al.
London: William Heinemann; Cambridge: Harvard
University Press, 1948

– *Orator*. Edited by Wilhelm Kroll. Berlin: Weidmannsche, 1958

Colet, John. *Opera*. Edited and translated by J.H. Luption. 4 vols. London: Bell and Daldy, 1867–76. Reprinted, Ridgewood, N.J.: Gregg, 1965–6

– Epistolae in *EE*

Comenius, Joannes Amos. *Orbis sensualium pictus*. 3d ed. London, 1672. Reprinted, Sidney; University Press, 1967

Cyprian. *Opera omnia*. Edited by Guilelmus Hartel. 3 vols. Vienna: C. Geroldi, 1871

– *PL*, III–IV

– *Opera*. Edited by R. Weber and M. Bénevot. CSSL, III. Turnholt: Brepols, 1972

Dante Alighieri. *Tutte le opera*. Edited by Fred Chiapelli. Milan: U. Mursia [1965]

Durand of Saint-Pourçain. *In Petri Lombardi Sententias Theologicas Commentariorum libri IIII*. Venice: Guerraea, 1571. Reprinted, Ridgewood, N.J.: Gregg, 1964. 2 vols.

Eberhard Bethuniensis. *Graecismus*. Edited by Iohannes Wrobel. CGMA, I. Bratislava: G. Koebner, 1887

Eusebius Vercellensis. *Opera*. Edited by Vincent Bulhart. CCSL, IX. Turnholt: Brepols, 1957

Galen. *Exhortatio ad artium liberalium studia*. Translated by Erasmus. *ASD*, I–1. Edited by Jan Hendrik Waszink

Grammatici Latini. Edited by Henric Keil and Martin Hertz. 8 vols. Hildesheim: Georg Olms, 1961

Gregory the Great. *Opera*. *PL*, LXXV–LXXVIII

Gregory Nazianzen. *Opera omnia*. Edited by A.B. Caillau and M.N.S. Guillon. CSEP, XLIX–LII. Paris: Parent-Desbarres, 1835–43

Hilary. *Lucubrationes quotquot extant*. Edited by Erasmus. Basel: Eusebius Episcopius and Nicolas Frater, 1570

– *Opera*. Edited by A.B. Caillau and M.N.S. Guillon. CSEP, XXVI–XXIX. Paris: Méquignon-Havard, 1830

– *De Trinitate, contra Arianos*. [Venice: Paganinus de Paganinis, 1489]

– *De Trinitate*. Edited by Joseph L. Perugi. Turin: Marietti, 1930

Hugh of St Cher. *Opera omnia in universum vetus, et novum testamentum.* 8 vols. Venice: Nicolaus Pezzana, 1732

Ignatius of Antioch. EPISTOLAI. Edited by Th. Camelot. Paris: Cerf, 1951

Isaac Judaeus. *Opera.* Edited by A. Hoste. CCSL, IX. Turnholt: Brepols, 1957

Isidore of Seville. *Etymologiarum sive originum.* Edited by W.M. Lindsay. Oxford: Clarendon Press, 1911

Isocrates. [Works]. Translated by George Norlin and Larue Van Hook. 3 vols. London: William Heinemann; Cambridge: Harvard University Press, 1954

Irenaeus. *Contra haereses.* Edited and translated by F. Sagnard. SC, XXXIV. Paris: Cerf, 1952

Jerome. *Omnes quae extant stridonensis lucubrationes.* Edited by Erasmus. 9 vols. in 5. Basel: Froben, 1537
– *Homilia in Ioannem Evangelistam* in *PLS,* II

John Chrysostom. *Omnia quae extant opera juxta Benedictionorum versionem.* Edited by A.B. Caillau and M.N.S. Guillon. CSEP, I–XXV. Paris: Mellier, 1835–43

John of Garland. *Stella Maris.* Edited by Evelyn F. Wilson. Cambridge: Wellesley College and the Medieval Academy of America, 1946

Justin Martyr. PROS TRUPHŌNA IOUDAION DIALOGOS. *PG,* VI.

Lactantius. *Opera. PL,* VI

Lucian. *Icaromenippus sive Hypernephelus.* Translated by Erasmus. *ASD,* I–I. Edited by Christopher Robinson
– SUMPOSION ĒLAPITHAE. Translated by A.M. Harmon. London: William Heinemann; New York: Macmillan, 1913

Lucius, *pope.?* *De singularitate clericorum. PL,* IV

Luther, Martin. *Werke.* 58 vols. Weimar: Hermann Böhlaus, 1931

Marchesinus, Johannes. *Mammotrectus super Bibliam.* Venice: Nicolaus Jenson, 1479

Marius Victorinus. *Opera. PL,* VIII

Maximus. *Opera.* Edited by Almut Mutzenberger. CCSL, XXIII. Turnholt: Brepols, 1962

Medina, Pedro de. *Libro de Cosmographia.* Edited by David
Woodward and translated by Ursula Lamb. 1538 ed.
Reprinted, Chicago: University of Chicago Press, for the
Newberry Library, 1972

More, *Sir* Thomas. *The Correspondence of Sir Thomas More.*
Edited by Elizabeth F. Rogers. Princeton: Princeton
University Press, 1947

Neckham. Alexander. *Opera.* Edited by Thomas Wright. RBMAS,
XXXIV. London: Longman, Green, Longman, Roberts, and
Green, 1863

Nicholas of Cusa. *Opera.* 3 vols. Paris: In Aedibus Ascensianis,
1514. Reprinted, Frankfurt/M.: Minerva, 1962

Nicolas of Lyra. *Biblia sacra cum glossa ordinaria.* Edited by
Strabo Fuldensis. 7 vols. Paris: Franciscus Fevardentium,
1590

Nizzoli, Mario. *Nizolius, sive Thesaurus Ciceronianus.* Venice:
Aldus, 1576

*Notices et extraits de divers manuscrits latins pour servir à
l'histoire des doctrines grammaticales au moyen age.* Edited by
Charles Thurot. *N et E,* XXIII/2. Paris: Impériale, 1868

Novatian. *Opera.* Edited by G.F. Diercks. CCSL, IV. Turnholt:
Brepols, 1972

Origen. TO KATA IŌANNEN EUAGGELION
EXĒGĒTIKON. Edited by Cécile Blanc. Paris: Cerf, 1966

Perotti, Niccolò. *Rudimenta grammatices.* [Bologna]: Johannes
Schriber de Annunciata, 1468 or 1478

Petrarch. *Operum.* Basel: Henrichus Petri, n.d.

Petrus Hispanus. (Johannes XXI, *pope*). *Summulae logicales quas e
codice manu scripto Reg. Lat. 1205.* Edited by I.M.
Bocheński. Turin: Marietti, 1947

Pico deila Mirandola, Giovanni. *De hominis dignitate, Heptaplus
et De Ente et uno.* Edited by Eugenio Garin. Florence:
Vallecchi, 1942

Plato. *Opera.* Edited by John Burnet. SCBO. 5 vols. Oxford:
Clarendon Press, [1902–6]

Plotinus. *Opera.* Edited by Paul Henry and Hans-Rudolph
Schwyzer. 3 vols. Paris: Desclée de Brouwer, 1951

Prudentius Clemens, Aurelius. *Carmina*. Edited by Maurice P. Cunningham. CCSL, CXXVI. Turnholt: Brepols, 1966

Pseudo Dionysius the Areopagite. *Opera*. Translated by Marsilio Ficino. Strasburg, 1502

– *Opera*. PL, IV

Quintilian. *Institutiones oratoriae libri duodecim*. Edited by M. Winterbottom. SCBO. 4 vols. Oxford: Clarendon Press, 1970

Remigius of Auxerre. *Opera*. PL, CXVII

Siger de Courtrai. *Les oeuvres*. Edited by G. Wallerand. PB, VIII. Louvain: Institut Supérieur de Philosophie de l'Université, 1913

Stoicorum veterum fragmenta. Edited by Hans von Arnim. 4. vols. Leipzig: B.G. Teubner, 1903–24

Tatwin. *Ars*. Edited by Maria de Marco. CCSL, CXXX/I. Turnholt: Brepols, 1968

Tertullian. *Opera*. Edited by Aem. Kroymann et al. CCSL, I–II. Turnholt: Brepols, 1954

Thomas à Kempis. *Opera omnia*. 26 vols. New York: Musurgia, 1949

Thomas Aquinas. *Opera omnia*. 16 vols. Rome: Polyglota S.C. De Propaganda Fide, 1882–1948

Thomas of Erfurt. *Tractatus de modis significandi sive grammatica speculativa* in *Lexicon Scholasticum Philosophico-Theologicum*. Edited by Mariani Fernandez García. Quaracchi: College of St Bonaventure, 1910

Valla, Lorenzo. *Opera omnia*. Edited by Eugenio Garin. MPPR, V–VI. 2 vols. Basel: Henricus Petrus, 1540. Reprinted, Turin: Bottega d'Erasmo, 1962

Varro, Marcus Terentius. *De lingua latina*. Translated by Roland G. Kent. 2 vols. London: William Heinemann; Cambridge: Harvard University Press, 1951

William of Sherwood. *Introductiones in logicam*. Edited by Martin Grabmann. Munich: Bayerischen Akademie der Wissenschaften, 1937

Zeno Veronensis. *Opera*. Edited by B. Löfstedt. CCSL, XXII. Turnholt: Brepols, 1971

✃ Index ✃

This lists historical persons, excluding biblical characters.

❦ Erasmus Studies ❦

A Series of Studies Concerned with Erasmus and Related Subjects